AF540417

CONTEMPORARY INDIAN POLITICS

CONTEMPORARY INDIAN POLITICS

S. K. Khanna

DISCOVERY PUBLISHING HOUSE
New Delhi-110002

First Published – 1999

Reprinted – 2025

ISBN: 978-81-7141-445-1

Contemporary Indian Politics

Published by:

DISCOVERY PUBLISHING HOUSE

4383/4B, Ansari Road, Darya Ganj
New Delhi-110 002 (India)
Phone: +91-11-23279245; 23253475; 43596065
Mobile: +91 9811179893 / +91 9871656464
E-mail: discoverybooksindia@gmail.com
orderdphbooks@gmail.com
namitwasan9@gmail.com
web: www.discoverypublishinggroup.com

Printed at:
Infinity Imaging Systems
Delhi

Preface

The progress that India has made in the fifty years after Independence does not meet India's needs or match its capacity and potential. The massive poverty, illiteracy and backwardness of our people can only be called a massive failure of government. This failure has had an impact on all aspects of our national life, in some cases directly, as in the high crime rate or the huge black economy, and in other cases indirectly, as in the many internal upheavals and secessionist movements. In sectors where the situation is less immediately visible, it is no better; the steady deterioration of national institutions like the bureaucracy, the police, the public utilities, the environment and our permanent natural resources, and arising from all these, the downturn in our defence and international status, and, worst of all, the people's loss of faith in our institutions, our government, and probably in democracy itself. The policies of the government have not been geared to achieving results to meet our requirements or to realising the high potential of this country. If the policies have been inadequate or misconceived, the people who made them, viz. those who have held power, have to be held responsible. Either they were incapable of the vision and action required, or they were under pressures that prevented them from functioning as they should have done, or both.

We cannot drift along in the hope that a great leader like Gandhiji might arise and lead this country out of its travails, as there is no guarantee that such a leader will arise. Equally, we cannot wait for a revolution to happen. It might not happen, and even if it does, it will destroy a great deal, and might turn out to be a remedy worse than the disease; or alternatively, we might just go on in a downward spiral until the country disintegrates without a revolution.

It is necessary that the intelligentsia alerts itself to come up with solutions to arrest the general decline and turn the country around. In this age, we have a larger body of educated, self-aware and articulate people than ever before, and in this country, they are still free to speak and act without undue constraints. The Country's objectives are stated in the Constitution freedom and equality of all citizens, universal literacy, abolition of untouchability and much else, None of this has been achieved. Obviously the instrumentalities have been deficient. Our political systemn is such that it favours anti-national functioning and for that reason favours the rise to power of people who function in anti-national ways.

With the alternative system, we can hope of a generally peaceful, harmonious, orderly and progressive national life, under the aegis of representative and accountable institutions with the full participation of the people at all levels.

Editor

Contents

1

Political Malignancy

The social mobilisation that took place as an integral part of India's freedom struggle was unique in several ways. It was rooted in the Indian civilization, represented a renaissance of the eternal values of freedom, equality, justice and humanism, reinforced by a unique war without violence. It was a movement, with its gravity firmly rooted in the society; the mass of people identified themselves with the objectives of the mobilisation and participated in it. The freedom movement helped India as a country to develop its national spirit. The political process was. inspired by the vision of shaping India's destiny with harmony and development on an evolutionary mode of continuity and change without any trauma and turmoil. Such mobilisation was spurred by the values of liberal democracy. The national vision was best articulated by Aurobindo while reflecting on the question of India's destiny within the framework of eternity, spanning "from Ancient Dawns to the Noons of the Future". Aurobindo envisioned that : "India can best develop herself and save humanity of being herself and following the law of her own nature.... It means simply to keep our centre, our essential way of being, our inborn nature and assimilate to it all we receive, and evolve out of it all we do and create. India has the key to the knowledge and conscious application of the ideal.... she can if she will, give a new and decisive turn to the problems over which all mankind is laboring and stumbling, for the clue to their solutions is there in her ancient knowledge. Whether she will rise or not to the height of her opportunity in the renaissance which is coming upon her, is the question of her destiny". Thus, the vision of India encompassed the entire mankind within the framework of values, 'eternal' and the 'universal'.

The abiding sustenance of the 'power' of political process was morality'; power and morality represented two sides of the coin, the only currency of leadership. Humanist values constituted their ideology during the intense phase of the struggle for political freedom. Alleviation of poverty, elimination of illiteracy and diseases, and promotion of social reform and justice constituted the mission of the leadership. Political freedom, economic growth and social development constituted an integral manifesto of the freedom movement.

The leadership of India's freedom movement comprised of ardent nationalists, statesmen, reformists, and democrats with a profound respect for dissent, even as they strived for democratic consensus. Their style was transparent, they transcended but never transgressed region, religion, caste or language. The leadership represented a case of 'sacrifice', like princes becoming paupers, they gave their all for the cause of the national freedom and resurgence.

Transformation of a movement into structures of power

While Gandhi desired that the Indian National Congress (INC) that spearheaded the freedom movement, should be converted into a social reform movement and a service organisation facilitating the emergence of political structures and processes, there was the other argument that the INC should stay on in order to address itself to the mission and the agenda of social transforination.

Power does not operate in a vacuum; it never allows a vacuum to be created. As the British were preparing to leave, the omnibus Indian National Congress quickly channeled into diverse streams and political structures, variously influenced by the dominant global and national factors such as (a) the socialist/communist revolution, (b) the free market capitalism, (c) the trauma of partition, and (d) the emergence of subnational movements based on linguistic, ethnic and cultural identities. Thus, the postindependence scenario was marked by the evolution of a range of political parties, even as the INC remained an omnibus political chameleon. Like the Hindu pantheon, it became and remained an organisation providing coexistence of several diverse and conflicting ideological strands and thought processes.

When India became a democratic constitutional Republic, the political parties became the operators of the constitutional democracy without themselves being brought under the purview of the Constitution. They were not infused with the democratic constitutional ethos within the framework of even a statute. The founding fathers were all liberal statesmen; the Constitution that they framed was based on a fundamental premise that the quality of leadership in India would remain of the same order as it was during the freedom movement.

With the fulfillment of the mission of freedom movement, political process in India has gradually but clearly and conclusively shifted its focus from 'social agenda' to the capturing of power, reducing the political parties to mere corporate organisations with an almost exclusive concern for power, in all its manifestations, to be secured by all means, and retained at all costs. If the urge for acquisition of power turned them towards gradual 'criminalisation' of politics, the methods adopted to retain power evolved into 'marginalisation' of the Constitution, its institutions and processes vitiating the constitutional culture and traditions of liberal democracy.

If the INC proved the proverbial banyan tree during Nehru's time, it became strident under Indira Gandhi's 'second mobilisation'. The process of power blunted the constitutional ideals as well as the processes. Rajiv Gandhi attempted to bring about radical reform in the political as well as administrative culture, but got devoured by the malignancy that had already set in. Narasimha Rao initiated a process of consensus, but where the political parties and processes were driven value system (ideology), mass-base, and a manifesto, political parties derived sustenance from 'personality-cult' leading to proliferation and fragmentation, authoritarianism, exercise of power without mandate, creation of votebanks, and generation of discord between different sections of the people. Disintegration of political parties due to their exclusive pursuit of power had its inevitable consequence of social fragmentation. Morality parted ways with power; parties defected from people; leadership abused the trust reposed in them by the people. Power ceased to be the means, it became an end in itself.

Yet another manifestation of the distortions in the process of power has been the centralisation of authority and decision-making within the political parties as well as in the process of governance. Causing the emergence of regional structures first within the INC and gradually in the form of regional parties. That power was the prime motive rather than regional issues of development has been brought out by the leaders of the regional parties and factions themselves through their assertions that they were more nationalist than the leadership of the 'national' parties. They went one step further and asserted that the leadership and the political culture of national level parties are seeped in regionalism and other sectarian characteristics such as communalism, casteism, parochialism, and factionalism. The dominant stream of the fragmented Congress party claims that it is an all India party but in almost all the States. There is a State level breakaway party operating as the dissident, or even sharing power with other regional parties. It is not a case of double but multiple standards when its policies in regard to national issues such as prohibition and riverwaters are distorted at the level of States in order to attain their partisan pursuit or power.

The parties that emerged in almost all regions of the country on the basis of local agenda proclaimed that they were more nationalist than the parties operating at the national level. They went one step farther in accusing the national-level parties as more regional. Some of them even coalesced to become a federal front, but have not been able to play any positive role in resolving any of their bilateral or multilateral problems, or even in cooperating with each other on matters of common concern.

Whenever they have failed to resolve inter-State issues of governance, all the parties national or regional have rakedup popular emotions, and converted such problems into hostilities and conflict among the people.

The enervation of political structures was also influenced by two related factors; the nonpursuit of Directive Principles, aimed at promotion of socioeconomic justice as a part of nation-building, and hasty incorporation of two illdefined pivotal expressions viz., "secular" and "socialist" into the preamble of the Constitution. Suffice it to say that on both the counts, an ever increasing damage has been caused to the Republic. The preamble instead of sustaining the vision, and reinforcing the liberal democratic ethos, itself has become the malignant force in the fragmentation of Indian polity into majorities and minorities, generating an ever more strident and competitive populism among the political parties. Citizens are reduced to numbers; as vote banks.

Malignancy in the political process

Indian political organisations have acquired a 'corporate culture' going beyond the system of 'spoils' to the point of 'investments' and 'returns'. Advertisement of 'achievements' at huge public expense, and the style of political campaigns illustrate that they have surpassed corporate organisations. Antidefection law has been converted into the harbinger of 'liberalised' political process in India. The splits and mergers of political groups and parties are affected with greater finesse than the joint ventures/mergers and takeovers in the corporate sector, with single minded dedication to power and pelf. The differentiation between the state, the government, and the party (in power) is diluted, to say the least, they now constitute a continuum of political power. The shortcuts to capturing power through the deployment of moneypower, and lateral entry straight into the Parliament are in sharp contrast to the earlier mode of 'schooling for democracy' at panchayat level and graduation to State and then on to the national level.

If the 'princes' became paupers during the freedom movement, today's leadership represents a case of 'rags to riches' coupled with vulgar display of illgotten wealth and authoritarian exercise of power. The distortions of political process have contributed to black money, parallel economy and financial scams leading to the attraction of 'con-men,' 'god-men' and criminal talent into politics. The known Gross Financial Scams (GFS) alone are estimated, as of 1997, to be of the order i of Rs. 1.5 billion; the value of parallel economy is officially estimated to have crossed Rupees one lakh crores, long ago.

The great debate of yester-years on the ends and means of social transformation is reduced to isolated crafting of manifestos, never related to action much less to any measurement of performance. On the contrary, dramatic constitutional amendments and programs such as nationalisation or quotas were initiated without a democratic debate or mandate. Even as they have failed the Constitution and the nation, some of our political elite have initiated a campaign against the Constitution, stating that the Constitution has failed the people. 'Criminalisation of politics' has become so proverbial that no one raises an eyebrow on hearing the adage. Criminals do have, and meticulously follow, their own 'codes of conduct, but the politicians in India consistently resisted code of conduct for themselves.

There is yet another area of 'consensus', transcending the otherwise bitter party divide, in favour of perks and benefits of office, projected as privileges. While there is an indifference towards the privileges related to their legislative performance such as (a) freedom of expression free of whip and 'anti-defection' controls and (b) democratic debate and dissent within the party for, there is an occasional, but unmet demand for 'conscience vote' as if on all other occasions, conscience can be hung on to the coat-hanger. This indifference to the quintessential democratic ethos is more than matched by their deliberate application of an ever expanding 'privilege' jurisdiction, manifest, in the form of explicitly defined quotas for telephones, cooking gas, petrol distributorship/agencies etc. These privileges are converted into precise amounts of unearned black-income', used and abused in pursuit of power.

Political leaders are 'conscious' and agree that these privileges result in the cumulative loss of their own, that of their party and thus the credibility of the political system. They also recognise and admit that where the political system and process are vitiated, the damage cannot be confined to the political system, but permeates the adjunct institutions as well as the body politic, the Republic.

No use blaming the politicians and parties along. The other elite, the intellectuals, the professions and others have degenerated to equal depths-establishing the fact that political degeneration cannot be contained within the political structures. The political leaders as well as the elite groups tend to rationalise by arguing that : "after all, our leaders and organisations are a part of the society, and thus suffer from its several ills." Such an argument is clearly untenable, and nonavailable to the leaders whose role is to shape the society. They have a mission to fulfil. Certainly they cannot contribute to, and aggravate the ills and evils of the society.

The legislators, the party leaders and the political parties are conscious as indeed the citizens and the society, of the threat to the polity. Individually, like all the citizens, they do want to bring about a change, a reform. They are also aware that, in the process, they have to forego their existing extra-legislative privileges. In the short run their insecurity gets acute; in the long-term they like the quintessential democratic ethic to be resorted; the gravity of the Republic to be protected and sustained. After all, our leaders also have a stake in the Republic.

Dividends of political malignancy

The consequences of the malignancy that afflicted the political process could be even more intense and dangerous to the process of democracy and governance, as is being witnessed and experienced in India. Where the political process turns malignant, it spreads rapidly and shows up, as the first symptom, in terms of decay in the institutions of governance all the instrumentalities even if to varying degrees, for none of them can operate in isolation, and all of them are interrelated and interdependent in achieving their common constitutional objectives, while performing complementary tasks. Institutional decay has taken several forms in terms of collusion, as Vohra Committee authenticates, or in terms of role conflict as is being witnessed between the legislative and the judicial institutions. The debate about the role and place of public interest litigation (PIL) is yet another symptom of political malignancy and inter-institutional conflict.

The adverse consequences of political malignancy to the polity are even more acute; malignancy spreads faster in a pluralist polity. Democratic process has degenerated to anarchic proportions with an upsurge of rights (every one for one self) in place of the democratic ethos, social obligations and consensual mode (one for all, for one); this disposition puts the polity on the track of conflict as nearly the exclusive mode of social change in place of common weal and consensus, the Gandhian tenets of *'sarvasammati' and 'sarvahita'.*

In such a social scenario, citizens can only get marginalised and thus alienated from the state, and ultimately from the society itself. A community that is fragmented, and alienated from the state can only experience the trauma of multidimensional social strife, as we in India witness, nay, are experiencing. When political process finds it too hot for management of strife and thus passes on the problem to the law and order machinery, we have seeds of state terrorism sown from within; a situation congenital for terrorist groups and states from outside to fish in troubled and turbulent waters.

Social turbulence, violence and conflict bring the wheels of development and progress to a grinding halt.

This is best (or worst) illustrated by the fact that we in India have destroyed our own life and property due to internal strife the magnitude of which is many times more than the destruction caused by armed conflict and warfare across the borders.

Political process cannot insulate itself from the social strife and institutional decay that it has created. The over-all apathy among the citizens towards the political process has contributed to the 'negative vote or rejection of the party in power, consistently in successive elections. Even worse, the price that all the political parties are paying at the hands of institutions like the Central Bureau of Investigation, should remind our political elite of the Frankenstein or its Indian version of the *Bhasmasura* phenomenon.

The present generation of leadership transcending their party divide recognised that centralised planning has failed and that people's participation through decentralised democratic structures is a vital prerequisite for democracy to survive and development to take place. So they brought about, unanimously, the 73rd and 74th amendments to the Constitution. But, that the centralised bureaucracy has negated democratic decentralisation has been vividly brought out recently by the otherwise dynamic Chief Minister of Andhra Pradesh when he lamented that: "What is the point of the Chief Ministers coming all the way to Delhi and making proposals if they are summarily brushed aside by bureaucrats? We are wasting our time." Such laments have been heard from many a Chief Minister, many a time.

Democracy cannot become sick; it has the greatest resilience. It is the only process that has built in self-correcting mechanism, as long as it maintains its gravity firmly in the society. The conduct of individuals 'momentarily' manning the institutions can be sickening, debilitating the institutions.

Good governance is a *sine qua non* for the restoration of democracy where the rules of the game are as important, if not more, as the game itself. In the contemporary context of India, good governance has to start with re-engineering the political institutions and processes. Such a reengineering has to be built up on a restoration of the equations between individuals and the I institutions, with primacy to the institutions as the more enduring stabilisers of democratic political power.

Reengineering the political a parties as the prime movers of democratic social transformation is an agenda that calls for a constructive and creative debate. Certain broader premises can b identified, for reengineering the political parties and processes.

1. As the prime movers of a poll with a constitutionally set out vision political parties cannot function as extra constitutional institutions; they have to be brought into the framework of the Constitution. Constitutional culture an democratic ethos are even mor important than mere constitutional status.

The Constitution provides a wide latitude for polity; there is a wide amplitude to formulate, fight, an translate their alternative strategies and programs, without having to change the Constitution the rules, while the game is on. The rules of the game of India democracy are not immutable, there are appropriate and adequate provisions to bring about constitutional reforms.

2. We need to restore the Gandhian ethos to politics as the prime mover of social transformation. Politics sans humanism is the sure highway to all the social evils we witness all over the world.

3. Electoral reform cannot be seen merely as an issue of methods of elections (first-past-the-post;

proportional list system etc.), but much more as the sanctity of the process; (a) the sovereignty of people, as the ultimate arbiters, and (b) accountability of parties to performance measured within the framework of manifesto and mandate. Electoral process should be able to shape the process of power, with its gravity firmly retained in the society.

4. In the Indian multi-party democracy there is an urgent need to check the confrontationist culture of 'Ruling' versus 'Opposition'—all the parties have been in power, and also out of power, some time and some where.

The accusations leveled by all the parties while in opposition against those momentarily in power clearly establish the double standards of all the parties. Prasar Bharati legislation is one of the many glaring examples; inaction while in power inspite of unanimity clearly reflects deformities in the political culture. All the parties while in opposition accused all the parties in power of misusing and abusing the police but no party thought of implementing the vital recommendations of the National Police Commission aimed at reducing the political abuse of police. There is a great need to identify areas such as basic human needs as of national consensus and constitutionally mandated, and lift them up from partisan politics.

5. The ship of Indian democracy is in good shape but the political process in India has turned turbulent assuming proportions of a cyclone. The Indian Constitution has created an infrastructure of umpiring to guide the ship especially in times of turbulence, but unfortunately even the light houses are flickering. The passengers have started wondering whether the crew has turned out to be hijackers.

6. The founding fathers had the wisdom of providing for universal adult franchise as the comer-stone of our democratic Republic. We need to promote the capabilities (knowledge and skills) of our elected representatives and motivate them (through shaping appropriate values and attitudes) within the framework of the vision of democratic Constitutional Republic in order to enable them to play their rightful and legitimate roles as the *Vidhayaks*.
7. As democracy in India as well as the institutions of global governance such as the United Nations turn 50, and the global society is at the threshold of 21 st century, Indian renaissance has the potential not only to promote its national resurgence, but also the capacity to influence and shape the vision of the global society.

Corruption and Prevention

At numerous seminars and group discussions organised to celebrate the 50th anniversary of our independence many eminent participants from different walks of life voiced their anguish and anger at the widespread prevalence of corruption among the politicians and in the public services causing incalculable moral and material damages. The low achievements of the country in economic growth and social upliftment despite massive investments are in no small measure due to corruption, criminal waste and misappropriation of public money by many holders of high public offices. The seriousness of this problem was also highlighted by the new President K.R Narayanan immediately after he took oath of office on 25 July 1997. Corruption, he said, had become "widespread" and earnestly pleaded for a much cleaner public life to improve the climate of integrity and the moral tone of the nation.

The Prime Minister, I.K Gujral too has been expressing his own concerns over the near fatal stage the country has reached due to rampant corruption. At some public function he had observed that "corruption has seeped into the veins of our country"; that "the country appeared to be sinking in corruption". At the recent national conference of Indian Industry he painfully said "I hang my head in shame to know that our country ranks as the eighth most corrupt nation in the World."

While expressing the gravity of the problem of corruption the Prime Minister however did not sound confident or determined to deal with it effectively. He, on the other hand, said that he had "no magic wand" to end corruption. He also pleaded that the people in general should organise "social movement" and noncooperation movement" against corruption.

For the Prime Minister of the country to give such advice amounts to passing the buck to the people. What kind of "social movement would people start against corruption? Are they to beat up any one whom they considered to be corrupt as once advised by the late Biju Patnaik? Will that be safe and rational? The PM also advised the people to take oath to neither take nor give bribes even if they have to suffer inconveniences for this. Sri Prakash, an eminent public figure of great integrity had responded to such an advice decades back that while he would gladly and readily take oath "not to take bribe" he would not be bold enough to take an oath "not to give bribe" under any circumstances. Since bribery had become so common in every official dealing in all departments of the Government and local bodies many would have to go without telephones, electricity, water-supply, health care, driving licenses, birth and death certificates, income-tax and sales-tax clearance certificates, passports etc. and fail to visit sick friends or relatives living in other towns and cities involving rail journeys if oath-bound not to pay brıbes which are almost compulsory and inevitable for all such services and facilities. We have long passed the stage of individual oath taking against bribing some odd public officials for day to day existence. Now corruption is all pervasive and citizens have little choice but to yield to illegitimate demands at most points of dealings with public officials. Such advice is therefore no longer of any practical use to the common citizens already over-burdened by pressing problems of daily life. When the Prime Minister himself could not take action to remove a Chief Minister of a State charge-sheeted for corruption by the CBI for his own or his party's political interests, would it be possible by the multitude of common people to bind themselves by oath not to give bribes'? Are they not more helpless than the Prime Minister?

The higher ones must set examples before advising others in fighting corruption. Moreover, those who preside over the destiny of a country owe it to the nation to devise rational, legal, political and administrative measures to curb corruption. Merely expressing sorrow, shame and anger and to give impractical advice to curb corruption is hardly a solution. The problem infact is that while corruption" as such is condemned and decried profusely the "corrupt persons" are being shielded and spared, particularly those holding high offices. Many recent scams and scandals have revealed the cover up attempts made to hide these for years. This kind of hypocrisy has indeed aggravated the problem of high level political corruption. Though brave words like "to wage war on corruption', "no compromise on corruption"; "the corrupt ministers, chief ministers have to go to jail" have been voiced time and again, no effective institutional arrangements have been made to deal with the high level corrupt individuals.

A number of times in the past, the problem has been studied in depth and sound remedial recommendations also made by some committees headed by eminent persons but little has been done to curb and prevent high level corruption. Only verbal onslaughts are being made which no longer cause any ripples or frighten the corrupt. They take it as harmless fireworks for mass display only.

It is time to recall a few worthwhile recommendations made by a committee of eminent public men and administrators headed by K. Santhanam to prevent corruption particularly at higher levels. This committee was appointed by Lal Bahadur Sastri, the then Home Minister, in 1962 and submitted its comprehensive report in 1964. The committee found and candidly stated: "There is a wide spread impression... that some Ministers who have held office during the last 16 years have enriched themselves illegitimately, obtained good jobs for their sons and relations through nepotism, and have reaped other advantages inconsistent with any notion of purity in public life."

To curb corruption among ministers, the Committee recommended that specific allegations against any of them should be promptly investigated by "an agency whose findings would command respect". For this purpose it suggested the constitution of a "National Panel" of eminent persons by the President of India. Allegations of wrong doing and corruption against any minister could then be referred to an *ad-hoc* committee of three persons out of the larger National Panel. This *ad-hoc* committee should thereafter enquire if there was any prima-facie truth in the allegations to justify initiation of further formal legal action under the Prevention of Corruption Act 1947. The suspect minister as a matter of convention was also expected to resign after a prima-facie case was established against him. The Committee felt that "absolute integrity on the part of Ministers at the Centre and the States is an indispensable condition for establishment of a tradition of purity in public services". The Committee thus gave priority to prevention of political corruption over prevention of administrative corruption. The top had to be made clean to expect cleanliness at other lower official levels. The elected ministers and legislators had to set the tone of integrity for others to follow, No action was however taken on the above recommendation.

The recommendations of the Administrative Reforms Commission of 1966 to set up the institution of Lokpal to investigate alleged cases of political corruption against ministers at the centre was also not implemented. Five times in the past (i.e. in 1968, 1971, 1977, 1989 and 1985) some kind of halfhearted Lokpal Bills were introduced in Parliament but even these were cleverly allowed to lapse. The sixth and the latest Lokpal Bill of 1996 is still pending in Parliament. This new Bill is no better than the earlier ones and provides for a very weak Lokpal. This watchdog body has been disallowed to "bark" at corruption or "bite" the corrupt. This Lokpal can act only on the basis of a complaint and not on his own. He would have no independent investigating or prosecution agencies of his own but would depend on Government controlled CBI. He can only make recommendations but cannot himself lodge prosecution when considered justified. He would indeed be a toothless Lokpal more decorative than effective.

To deal with high level administrative corruption among public officials, the Santhanam Committee had recommended the setting up of an independent Central Vigilance Commission keeping ministers out of its purview but bringing all public servants of the central Government and its PSUs within its jurisdiction, This Commission was to be headed by a high level Central

Vigilance Commissioner (CVC) with the same measure of autonomy, independence and status as a Comptroller and Auditor-General of India, (CAG) and the Election Commissioner. The Commissioner was to be made a statutory body by a suitable Parliamentary law. The Commission was also to be vested with powers to investigate complaints "that a public servant (i) has exercised his powers for improper or corrupt purposes or (ii) has unjustifiably or corruptly refrained from exercising his powers". For discharging this function effectively the Commission was to be legally empowered "to initiate, conduct, and complete such action as may be considered appropriate including prosecution against a public servant found guilty" after preliminary investigations. Powers to initiate disciplinary action or prosecution was to be vested in the Commission itself by withdrawing these powers from Government. In addition, it was recommended that the Central Vigilance Commissioner should be given the powers of a Commission of Inquiry appointed under the Commission of Inquiry Act 1952 so that he may undertake "any inquiry relating to transactions in which public servants are suspected or alleged to have acted improperly or in a corrupt manner."

Unfortunately, the Central Vigilance Commission scheme accepted and notified by Government by a Resolution of 1964 fell far short of the Committee's recommendations. The basic weakness of this scheme, which is still in force, is that the Central Vigilance Commission has no statutory basis yet. It continues to be the creature of the 1964 Government Resolution which is liable to frequent changes at Government's sweet will. This has in fact been happening affecting adversely both the nominal independence of the Commission as also its jurisdiction. For example, the tenure of the Vigilance Commissioner initially, as notified in the 1964

Resolution, was for a period of six years like that of the CAG, the Election Commissioner and the Chairman of UPSC, All these are independent constitutional bodies. In 1977 the tenure of the CVC was reduced to three years, extendable by another two years by Government. This virtually demolished, whatever independence the Commission was intended to have for it was upto the Government to extend the tenure of the CVC or not. The tenure was again raised to five years in 1990. Such changes of tenure of the CVC at the pleasure of Government make him vulnerable to Government's wishes and pressures.

Further, by a mere circular letter of Bureau of Public Enterprises (BPE) in October 1986, the Jurisdiction of the Central Vigilance Commission over the officers of the PSUs, save Board level appointees, was withdrawn without the Commission's consent. This also showed the lack of importance accorded to the Commission in its corruption prevention role.

The Commission has also not been given the recommended power to decide on initiation of disciplinary action or prosecution of any corruption accused public servant. This power continues to rest as before in Government but is now exercised after obtaining the Commission's "advice". Cases of disagreement with the Commission in its "advisory" role may be included by it in the Commission's Annual Report to Parliament. Such Annual Reports are however not to be sent directly to Parliament by the Commission but through the Ministry of Personnel & Training, the designated administrative ministry. In practice, these Reports are often placed before Parliament after much delay and are rarely discussed Thus, cases of non-acceptance of the Commission's advice by Government even in important matters hardly cause any worry or embarrassment to Government The Vigilance

Commissioner has also not been given the recommended power of the Commission of Inquiry, under the Commission of Inquiry Act, 1952.

For purposes of investigation of any complaints made to the Commission, still it has no investigating agency of its own but has to depend on the Government controlled CBI or the Departmental Vigilance Units. The overall position is that the Central Vigilance Commission suffers from a variety of handicaps to be able to effectively prevent and punish cases of administrative corruption. The Commission is not what it was recommended to be by the Santhanam Committee. It can hardly set the law into motion and deal with a suspect culprit.

Thus, presently neither for prevention of political nor administrative corruption are there any independent statutory bodies whose investigation and probe of corruption cases would command public respect.

The Prevention of Corruption Act was first passed as early as 1947 and later replaced by a slightly improved version in 1988. But without effective enforcement agencies, such laws alone cannot prevent corruption particularly at higher levels. A special anti-corruption police force was created in 1941 to deal with war time corruption of central Government employees generally confined to lower levels of administration. This force known as "The Delhi Special Police Establishment" (SPE) was given statutory basis by enacting the Delhi Special Police Establishment Act 1946.

Later, it become a division of the CBI on its creation in April, 1963. But the CBI itself has no other legal basis yet and derives its powers from the Delhi Special Police Establishment Act 1946 which had limited jurisdiction. Accordingly the CBI has no power to investigate cases in any State without their prior consent extending the provisions of the SPE Act 1946 to the consenting States. The States can also withdraw such consent any time. There is therefore need to have a separate and comprehensive CBI Act to vest it with legal powers to investigate corruption cases of higher level politicians and officials throughout the country without the requirment of prior consent of the State Government.

2

Parliamentary Democracy in India

The Parliamentary form of government occupies a pivotal position in the Indian political system. It was not by sheer accident that the framers of the Constitution adopted parliamentary form of government for the country. Their decision was influenced both by historical considerations and practical necessities. For a long time India bad known institutions like 'sabhas' and' 'samitis' which worked as units of self-government.! These institutions possessed the basic ingredients of a Parliamentary democracy even though they differed a great deal from the modern Parliamentary institutioning of the western style. Parliamentary institutions in the western sense were introduced in India by the British. The earliest seeds of these institutions in India were sown under the Charter Act of 183:3 which separated the legislature and the executive and deprived the ~Governor General of the exclusive power of legislation. Thereafter the Parliamentary democracy continued to grow in India under various Council Acts like the Act of 1861, 1892 and the Government of India Act 1919 and 1935 which granted greater powers to the Legislative Councillors. Slowly the nominated element in the Legislature was also replaced by the elective elements even though the electorates continued to be very restricted till India gained independence. In the preindependence period the electorate was seriously restricted and right to vote was given on the basis Of property, educational and tax qualifications. It was only with the universal adult franchise under the new Constitution at the base of the Parliamentary democracy was widened in India.

The practical considerations also greatly influenced the decision of the framers of the Constitution to opt for Parliamentary Democracy. Realising that a vast country like India could be best governed only through democratic principles they decided to introduce institutions at various levels from village Panchayat at bottom to Parliament at the apex and endowed them with adequate powers so that they may be able to work as units of self-government.

It may be noted that the decision regarding the adoption of Parliamentary Democracy in India was not all smooth and there were members like Kazi Syed Karimuddin and K.T. Shah who strongly pleaded for the adoption of non parliamentary government in India. Some members pleaded for the adoption of the system prevailing in United States of America which they considered as more democratic and based on better and sounder principles. But the preponderance of the opinion of the members which included Jawaharlal Nehru, B.R. Ambedkar, K.M. Munshi etc. was in favour Parliamentary system. Dr. Ambedkar, the Chairman of the Drafting Committee while pleading that the choice between Parliamentary and Presidential systems was not easy to make, pleaded adoption of Parliamentary Government. He said:

> "Looking at it from the point of view of responsibility, a non-parliamentary executive, being independent of Parliament tends to be less responsible to the legislature, while a Parliamentary executive, being more independent upon a majority in Parliament becomes more responsible. The Parliamentary system differs from a non-parliamentary system in as much as the former is more

> responsible than the latter but they also differ as to the time and agency for assessment of responsibility. Under the non-parliamentary system, such as the one that exists in the United States of America, the assessment of the responsibility is periodic... It is done by the electorate. In England where the Parliamentary system prevails, the assessment Of responsibility of the executive is both daily and periodic. The daily assessment is done by members of Parliament through questions, resolutions, no-confidence motions, adjournment motions and debates on Addresses. Periodic assessment is done by the electorate at the time of the election which may take place every five years or earlier. The daily assessment of responsibility which is not available under the American system is, it is felt, far more effective than the periodic assessment and far more necessary in a country like India. The Draft Constitution in recommending the Parliamentary system of executive has preferred more responsibility to more stability.'

However, while opting for the Parliamentary system of Government the framers of the constitution did not fully copy the British model and made certain modifications in it to meet the requirements of a federal polity and a large population. In place of a hereditary monarch, they provided an elected President, who acts as a constitutional bead and protects the interests of the units of the Indian federation. Even with regard to the method of the election of the President the Constitution of India deviated from the practice followed in other Parliamentary Democracies like France (where the President was elected by two houses of Parliament) and provided. For his election through an electoral college consisting of elected members of both the Houses of Parliament as well as the elected member of the Legislative Assemblies of the states. The Indian Constitution also deviated from the British Parliamentary principle of Sovereignty of Parliament, and provided a limited government with federal set up and a written constitution. All the organs of government at the Centre as well as state level drew their power from the constitution.

Indian parliamentary system and its features

The Constitution of India provided a Parliamentary system of Government both at the Centre as well as in the states. Though the constitution vests all the executive powers of the Centre and the States in the President and the Governors respectively, in reality they act merely as constitutional rulers and the real power is exercised by the Council of Ministers. The basic features of the Parliamentary System of Government as it operates in India are as follows:

1. *A Titular Head.* The President of India, like the British monarch, is vested with all the executive powers of the Union, but exercises these powers only on the advice of the Council of Ministers. The original constitution did not clearly specify whether the advice of the Council of Ministers was binding on the President or not. As a result, doubts were expressed in certain quarters that the President could ignore the advice of the Council of Ministers, and exercise real powers. However, these doubts were set at rest by the Forty-Second Amendment of 1976 which provided that the President would exercise his powers in accordance with the advice of the Council of Ministers. Thus the acceptance of the advice Of the Council of Ministers was made obligatory for the President. By the Forty-Fourth Amendment of 1978 the President was given the power to refer back the decision taken by the Ministry for reconsideration, but has to accept the advice tendered by the Council or Ministers after such reconsideration.

2. *Real Executive Authority with Council of Ministers.* While the nominal executive power of the Union is vested in the President the real executive power is exercised by the Council of Ministers, headed by the Prime Minister. No doubt, formally the Prime Minister is an appointee of the President but in

actual practice the President has very limited choice with regard to the appointment of the Prime Minister. Under normal circumstances he has to invite the leader of the majority party to become the Prime Minister. He can exercise some discretion in the matter of appointment of the Prime Minister only if no single political party enjoys clear-cut majority in the Parliament or there is no recognised leader of the party. The other members of the Council of Ministers are appointed by the President on the recommendation of the Prime Minister. He cannot appoint any person as a member of the Council of Ministers who is not acceptable to the Prime Minister.

3. *Fusion of Powers.* The legislature and the executive work in close cooperation and there is fusion of legislative and executive powers. All the ministers are taken from the Parliament. A person who is not a member of the Parliament can remain minister for a maximum period of six months only unless he acquires the membership of either house in the meanwhile. The Ministers play an important role in the proceedings of the Parliament. They introduce most of the important bills in the Parliament and with the help of be majority support get these enacted into laws without any difficulty.

4. *Collective Responsibility.* Another important feature of Parliamentary government in India is that the Council of Ministers acts as a team. All the decisions are taken by the ministers jointly. While the decisions are being taken the ministers can express their disagreement or dissent, but once the decision is arrived at they have to accept it as their collective decision. As a matter of convention if a minister does not agree with the decision of the Cabinet he must resign from the cabinet. Ministers like Dr. Mathai,

C.D. Deshmukh, M.C. Chagla, resigned from the Cabinet because they did not agree with Cabinet decision on certain issues. Collective responsibility also implies that a vote of no confidence against any minister entails resignation of the entire Cabinet. In other words the ministers swim sink together.

5. Responsibility to Popular House. The Council of Ministers is collectively responsible to the Lok Sabha and has to justify its policies and actions on the floor of the House. If the Lok Sabha is not satisfied with the justification offered by the Council of Ministers, it can pass a vote of no confidence against it and oblige is to tender resignation. When such a vote of no confidence is passed against the Council of Ministers, the Council can recommend to the President to dissolve the Lok Sabha and order fresh elections. The Prime Minister can advice the President to dissolve the Lok Sabha before the expiry of its normal term, even if no vote of confidence has been passed against the Ministry, to seek mandate from the people in favour of its programme. In December 1970 Mrs Gandhi got the Lok Sabha dissolved one year before the expiry of the normal term and sought fresh elections.

The actual operation of the parliamentary government at the time of the introduction of Parliamentary democracy in India doubts, were expressed in certain quarters that the system would not work successfully because majority of the people were illiterate and did not possess the requisite political experience to work out the system. Some even expressed the view that the spiritual and intellectual heritage of the Indian people was diametrically opposed to the democratic thinking. Thus Prof. Roger Berheim argued that the Parliamentary system "had not grown originally in the country's own political and spiritual climate. It had been introduced readymade, by a small elite educated abroad and hardly able to communicate with the population, the larger part of which is mentally walled in by traditions and conception, thousand of years old. In many respects the spiritual and intellectual heritage of the Indian people is diametrically opposed to the democratic thinking'. The other factors which made the critics sceptic about the successful working of Parliamentary democracy in India were the caste-ridden character of the Indian society bound to effect independent decisions of the voters; distance from the seat of power and lack of communication between the rulers and the ruled.

The actual operation of the Parliamentary Democracy in India for over three decades has demonstrated that the system has not worked that successfully. The mere fact that there has been a widespread debate in recent years for the replacement of the Parliamentary system by Presidential system further bears testimony to this fact. In the main two views have been expressed about the working of the Parliamentary Democracy. According to one view expressed by politicians and ruling members the system itself has failed and is not suitable for a vast country like India. 'I he other view, expressed by legal experts, statesmen and impartial observers, holds that it is not the system which has failed but the politicians who have failed to work the system as it should have been worked. Nonetheless, it is admitted at all hands that the Parliamentary system in India has not worked as successfully as was anticipated by the framers of the Constitution.

Reasons for the Unsuccessful Working of Parliamentary System. In the main following reasons have been responsible for not so successful working of the Parliamentary Democracy in India.

1. *Lack of Proper Conventions and Traditions.* The smooth

and successful working of the Parliamentary Democracy depends on the presence of well established conventions and traditions. Unfortunately so far India has not been able to develop necessary parliamentary traditions. The constitutional norms have been frequently flouted by the political leaders and the well established conventions of parliamentary government existing in Britain have been violated. The constitution has been amended for political gains, and state assemblies dissolved even when alternative government could have been possible to further the political interests. Likewise the politicians have tended to even interfere with the independence of judiciary.

2. *General Public Apathy.* The general public apathy towards the working of the Parliamentary Democracy has also greatly contributed to its failure. The people not only lack education and public consciousness but have tended to make a negative use of their right to franchise. They often vote on the basis of caste, religion, regional and other considerations. As a result even corrupt and dishonest persons have been elected as representatives by the people. There are numerous instances when persons found guilty of corruption by various Commissions staged a successful comeback in politics after a short gap.

3. *Personality Cult.* The presence of a 'personality cult' has also jeopardised the smooth working of Parliamentary democracy in India and introduced an element of absolutism in the Indian political structure. It is well known that Jawaharlal Nehru, the first Prime Minister of India decided the matters as he liked. No doubt he sought the approval of the Parliament but generally this approval was accorded

as a matter of routine and he practically worked as a benevolent dictator. Under Shastri, and for a while under Mrs. Indira Gandhi the Indian Parliamentary system worked in a true spirit. But soon Mrs. Gandhi strengthened her hold on the party and emerged so strong that the Parliament ceased to exercise any effective control over her government. It is true that, to occasions the political leaders were forced to make modifications in their policies in keeping with the public opinion, but by and large they received blind support from the masses. The personality cult suffered a temporary setback in the wake of the national emergency when Mrs. Gandhi was defeated at the polls. However soon she succeeded in staging a successful comeback. It was sheerly by the magnetic pull of her leadership that majority of the candidates of her party won victory in the elections of 1960.

At the state level also politics no centres around certain people have tended to support certain personalities and people had tended to support certain parties not so much on the basis of their policy and programme but because of the presence of certain magnetic personalities. It is well known that in Andhra Pradesh the Telugu Desham Party swept the polls only because it was headed by T. Rama Rao who is held in great esteem by the people. Not only elections are won due to the magnetic personality of certain leaders, even in matters of government these leaders are permitted to act as they like and their supporters blindly, endorse their actions. This trend poses a serious threat to the effective working of parliamentary government in India.

4. *Absence of Collective Responsibility.* The principle of 'collective responsibility' of the ministers, which forms the backbone of the Parliamentary Democracy

has also been conspicuously absent in India, There have been cases when the Cabinet after its defeat instead of tendering resignation as a matter of policy tried to make individual ministers the scapegoat. For example in 1962 when India suffered serious reverses in the Sino-Indian Warl the Cabine did not tender resignation and made the then Defence Minister V.K. Krishna Menon tender his resignation. Similarly, in 1963 when Congress suffered a number of election reverses, instead of taking them as a protest against 'the Budget of the Government (which Contained proposals like compulsory deposit, super profit tax etc.) held Morarji Desai, the then Finance Minister responsible for the same and dropped him from the Cabinet. There have been numerous other cases in which the individual ministers were made scapegoats to escape the collective responsibility of the Cabinet. This trend certainly does not go well with the proper working of parliamentary democracy in any country.

5. *Lack of Effective Opposition.* The lack of an effective opposition has also stood in the way of proper working of Parliamentary democracy in India. A Parliamentary Democracy must native party which can replace the government and have an alternative party which can replace the government and thus check its authoritarian tendencies. Unfortunately in. India we not only possess a multi-party system which by its very nature provides a weak and divided opposition, but these parties are so ill-organised and lack proper ideolgoical basis, that they are incapable of presenting any alternative government. This has naturally encouraged authoritarian tendencies within the ranks of the ruling party which is certainly contrary to the principles of parliamentary democracy.

6. *Frequent Use of Ordinance Making Powers.* The frequent use of ordinance making powers by the Executive has also been against the true spirit of Parliamentary democracy. The Constitution has vested the Ordinance making Powers in the President to make when the Parliament is not in session. This power was clearly bestowed by the framers of the constitution on the President only to enable him, to deal with the extraordinary situation during the recess of the Parliament. Unfortunately, this power has not has been used in the true spirit and ordinances have been issued on the eve of Parliament's session or even when the Parliament is in session. For example in 1974 the Government suspended the right of the persons detained under MISA to move the courts for the enforcement of their fundamental rights through issue of an Ordinance on 16 November, when the Parliament was actually in session. Similarly a large number of Ordinances have been issued on the eve of the session of the Lok Sabha. However, unmindful of this criticism the Government continued to issue ordinances. The issue of large number of ordinances every year has also undermined the authority of the Parliament by confronting it with faith accomplished. This certainly contrary to the spirit of true Parliamentary democracy. In this regard the position in the states is still worse. Not only the number of the ordinances issued by the states has been very large, quite often they have repeatedly re-issued the same ordinance for years without getting it approved from the state legislature and thus by-passed the authority of the legislature. For example in Bihar one Sometimes ordinances are also issued to openly flout the authority of the Assembly in 1981 when Chief Minister Gopal Chandra Barbora refused to resign,

the Assembly refused to pass the appropriation the Assembly and issued an ordinance approving a vote on account. All these developments are hardly conducive to the smooth and effective of parliamentary.

7. *Attitude of Centre Towards States.* The growing interference by the central government in the working of state governments is also contrary to the true spirit of the working of Parliamentary government. This interference is made both if the same political' party is in power in the states as well as if a different political party is in power in the state. In the former case the central leadership tends to give directions to the Chief Minister regarding the composition of the Cabinet as well on policy matters. It has been seen that the Chief Ministers of as such states frequently call upon the central and party leaders for directions. Quite often even the appointment of the Chief Minister in such states is made on the directions of the central leadership. For example after the elections of 1980 Vishwanath Pratap Singh (Uttar Pradesh), A.R. Antulay Maharashtra), Arjan Singh (Madhya Pradesh), and so many others were appointed Chief Ministers of various Congress controlled' states at the instance of the Prime Minister and other members of Party High Command. After the Assembly elections in 1985 also the central leadership of Congress (1) played a vital role in the appointment of the Chief Ministers. In many cases the Chic Ministers were picked up from amongst persons who were not members of the state legislature at the time of their appointment. The appointment of S.B. Chavan as the Chief Minister of Maharashtra can be cited as an instance. All this certainly does not go well with the established conventions of the working of Parliamentary democracy.

The position of the states under the control of the opposition parties is still worse. The Central Government tries to create all sorts of hurdles in the way of smooth working of its Ministry and tries to bring about its fall on various pretexts. For example in Kerala the Communist Party government was dismissed on the plea of maladministration. Similarly in 1976 Karunanidhi Ministry was dismissed on the basis of the report of the Governor (which was said to have been prepared by the Union Home Ministry) even though the ministry enjoyed the backing of 167 MLAs out of 235 members of the state Legislature. This game of toppling Assemblies under the control of opposition parties assumed serious dimensions in 1977 and 1980 when the Janata Government and the Congress (1) Government dissolved nine Assemblies each before the expiry of their term. Likewise in 1984 Farooq Abdullah Ministry in Jammu and Kashmir and N.T. Rama Rao Ministry in Andhra Pradesh were dismissed even though they enjoyed majority backing* All the actions have certainly been contrary to the true spirit of the working of Parliamentary democracy.

8. *Growing Resort to Agitational Politics.* The growing resort to methods of agitational politics which has assumed various shapes like violent demonstrations, gherao, destruction of public properties, dislocation of means of communication and transport etc. is also not in tune with the norms of the working of Parliamentary Democracy. The fact that certain sections were able to get their demands conceded from the Central as well as state governments through these methods has given further fillip to these methods and gave a further setback to the democratic norms.

9. *Frequent Dismissal of Popular Ministries in States.* Another practice which has greatly undermined the working of parliamentary system in India, specially in the states, is that the Centre has often dismissed ministries in states even though they enjoyed majority backing, because they were inconvenient to the Centre. Thus Namboodiripad's Ministry in Kerala was dismissed in 1959 on the plea that it had become unpopular with the masses; Karunanidhi Ministry in Tamilnadu was dismissed in 1976 due to allegations of corruption; Devraj Urs government was dismissed in 1977 two days before the commencement of the Assembly session on the plea that it had lost majority. Similarly in 1984 Farooq Abdullah government in Andhra it, Jammu and Kashmir and N.T. Rama Rao government to the fact Pradesh were dismissed without any justification despair addition to that these governments enjoyed majority support. In these instances on at least two occasions a number of state governments were dismissed because they were controlled by parties other than the party in power at the Centre. Thus Janata Government dismissed nine state governments in 1977 after its sweeping victory at the Centre, and sought fresh elections. Likewise in 1986 Congress (1) in the wake of its victory in Parliamentary elections dismissed governments in nine states and ordered fresh elections in these states because these states were being ruled by non-Congress (I) parties. All this has been against the true spirit and normal working of parliamentary government.

10. *Partisan Role of Presiding Officers.* The presiding officers of the two houses of Parliament and state legislatures also play vital role in the working of Parliament government. They have not only to ensure that the proceedings of the house are

conducted in an orderly manner but also see to it that a proper balance is maintained in the debates by permitting the government as well as the opposition fair opportunity to express their views. But the conduct of presiding officers in India specially in the states has been not up to the mark. They have often tended to act in a partisan manner and adopted a progovernment attitude in the hope of being rewarded with ministerial positions. In fact some of the presiding officers were actually given ministerial posts by the government as reward. In this respect examples of Rao Barinder Singh, Banarsi Das Gupta (both in Haryana) and J.N. Hazarika (in Assam) can be cited. At the Centre also Gurdial Singh Dhillon, Speaker of Lok Sabha, was subsequently make a minister. This partisan attitude of the Speaker has led to disorderly scenes in the legislatures and undermined the proper working of Parliamentary system of government.

11. *Partisan Role of Governors.* The partisan role played bv the Governors has also undermined the working of parliamentary government in the states. The Governors have not always acted as neutral constitutional rulers and have adopted partisan attitude. They either tried to pull down the ministries by dismissing them—as in case of West Bengal where Ajoy Mukerjee ministry was dismissed by Governor Dharam Vita; in Uttar Pradesh and Karnataka where Charan Singh and Devraj Urs ministries were dismissed; or in Jammu and Kashmir and Andhra Pradesh where Farooq Abdullah and N.T. Rama Rao were dismissed in 1994 etc. Sometimes the Governors also tried to save and retain ministries which did not enjoy popular support, by proroguing the state assemblies. Thus in 1969 Governor of Madhya Pradesh prorogued the

state Assembly to prevent it from passing a vote of no confidence (D.P. Mishra): in 1970 Governor of against the then Chief Minister Jammu and Kashmir likewise prorogued the session of Assembly to prevent vote of no confidence against G.M. Sadiq Ministry. Even in the appointment of the Chief Ministers the Governors have displayed partisan attitude and ignored the claims of leaders of the largest party in favour of others on account of partisan considerations. All these trends do not auLer well with the spirit of parliamentary system.

12. *Growing use of agitational methods in the Parliament State Legislature.* The growing use of agitational methods in the Parliament and state legislatures has also greatly undermined the parliamentary system of government in India. Instead of arriving at decisions through deliberations and conversions, the members have often tended to resort to satyagraha, strong arm tactics, aliuses, first fights etc to push forth or stall a matter to which they are committed or opposed. Generally the opposition resorts to these methods to highlight their role in the parliament, which they are unable to play due to their limited strength. Even the ruling party members resort to similar tactics to prevent discussion on matters which may be inconvenient to the government. It is highly desirable that the opposition as well as ruling party members should resist from these practices in the interest of smooth working of parliamentary institutions in the country.

13. *Lack of adequate control over Delegated Legislation.* In India like other democratic countries, the Parliament and state legislatures pass only skeleton laws and grant extensive powers to the gulations. This power of executive to frame necessary rules and re the executive is known as delegated legislation. It is a

common practice that all these rules and regulations formulated by the executive are placed before the legislature for its approval. Unfortunately in India these rules are not always submitted before the Parliament for approval and quite often they come into force without its approval. This has certainly undermined the position of the legislative wing and enhanced the power of the executive. It is true that a Committee on Subordinate Legislation has been created to look into these rules and regulations, but this committee does not possess necessary staff and expertise to discharge its duties. This has undermined the parliamentary system in India.

14. *Bid to Undermine the Judiciary.* Even since the inauguration of the Constitution consistent efforts have been made to undermine the authority of the judiciary. A number of amendments were carried out in the constitution to ouercome the obstacles created in the way of the laws passed by the Parliament and orders issued by the executive. It has often been argued that a handful of judges should not be permitted to override the will of the elected legislators. Effort has been made to make the judge, subservient to the Executive by resorting to supersession of judges which are not favourable disposed to the government. This practice has evoked lot of criticism and does not auger well with the principles of true democracy.

Since the middle of the present century the scholars of political science have paid greater attention to the study of political system rather than the political institutions. They have discarded terms like government, state and nation and preferred the use of %'Political system'. This change in use is not merely a change in nomenclature, but also represents a new way of looking at political phenomena. A number of new terms have been used for the old things and a number of new activities and processes have come to be accepted as part of politics. Whereas in the earlier years the political science was primarily concerned with the study of the formal governmental institutions and no attention was paid to the role of extralegal institutions, at present it is generally accepted that the role of the formal governmental institutions is shaped and limited by informal groups, political attitudes and a large number of other impersonal relationships. In short the concept of 'political system' covers the entire scope of the political activities within a society.

The credit for analysing politics in terms of system for the first time goes to David Easton. In his book The Political System published in 1953 he made an attempt to construct a theory to embrace all the social sciences and emphasised the need of theorising" about the whole political process. Thereafter a number of other scholars like G.A. Almond, Karl Deutsch, Mortan Kaplan etc. also adopted this approach.

Meaning of Political System. To understand the meaning, of "Political system", first of all we must understand the meaning of a system. According to Friedrich "When several parts that are distinct and different from each other compose a whole bearing, a defined functional relation to each other which establishes a mutual dependence of these parts upon each other so that the destruction of the one entails the destruction of the whole then such a constellation, shall be called a system." From the analysis of the above definition of system given by Friedrich we can deduce that a system implies the interdependence of parts and a boundary of some kind between, it and its environment. All the actions are interconnected and each part influences as well as is influenced by the other part. In case the various parts of the system do not cooperate with each other the system shall not work properly.

The political system is a sub-system of the social system and is often described as the legitimate order-maintaining or transforming system in the society. Scholars have offered a variety of definitions of Political System. According to David Easton "Political System is that system of interaction in any society through which binding and authoritative allocations of value are made and implemented." He further says that the idea of political system proves to be an appropriate and indeed unavoidable starting point in research. Although there is often uncertainty about the unity of political science as a discipline, most students of political science do feel quite instinctively that research into political aspects of life does differ from enquiry into any other, sufficiently so to constitute a separate intellectual enterprise."

Almond and Powell bold that "the political system includes not only governmental institutions such as legislatures, courts and administrative agencies, but all structures in their political aspects. Among these are traditional structures such as kinship ties and caste-groupings and anomic phenomena such as assassinations, riots and demonstrations ; as well as formal organizations like parties, interest groups and media of communication."'

David M. Wood says that political system is "a set of interrelated variables conceived to be politically relevant and treated as if they could be separated from other variables conceived to be politically relevant and immediately relevant to politics." Almond offers more details about the political system and asserts it is "that system of interaction to be found in all independent societies which performs the functions of interaction and adaption by means of the employment, or threat of employment, Of more or less legitimate physical compulsions. The Political system is the legitimate order maintaining or transforming system in the society. We use the term "more or less" to modify legitimacy because we do not want to exclude from our definition political systems like the totalitarian ones where the degree of legitimacy may be very, legitimacy may be very much in doubt; revolutionary systems, where the use of legitimacy may be in the process of change; or non-Western systems, in which there may be more than one legitimate system in operation."

Though different scholars have laid emphasis on different aspects of the political system in their definitions, they seem to agree on at least one point, viz., they associate the political system with the use of legitimate physical coercion in societies. For example of severe deprivations, and Dahl of power, rule and authority. Max Weber rightly says that the legitimate force is that threat which runs through the action of the political system and imparts it a special quality and importance.

It is true that coercion is a distinctive feature of a political system, but a political system does not operate through force alone. Again it is wrong to assume that the system alone makes the rules and enforces them. The rules and their operation also exercise considerable influence on the working of a system.

Characteristics of political system

After examining the meaning of political system let us study its main characteristics. Almond highlights three important characteristics of a political system, viz., comprehensiveness, interdependence and independent boundaries. By comphrehensiveness he means that it is not concerned only with the legal structures like parliaments, executives, bureaucracies and courts, or even formal Political interests, groups and media of communication. It also includes all the structures in their political aspects including structures like kinship, lineage) status and caste groups as well as anamoic phenomena like riots, street demonstrations and the like. Secondly, the various parts of the systems are interlinked and change in one leads to change in the other. In other words it means that if the properties of one component in a system change, all the components and the system as a whole are affected. Almond and Powell highlight this point thus : "In political systems the emergence, of mass parties or of media of mass communication, changes the performance of all the other structures of the system and affects the general capabilities of the system in its domestic and foreign environments. In other words, when one variable in a system change magnitude or in quality, the other are subjected to trains and a transformed; the system changes its pattern of performance, or the" unruly component is disciplined by regulatory mechanisms.

Thirdly, each political system possesses independent boundaries. However, the boundaries between the society and the polity differ under different political systems. Further, the boundaries of the political system keep on changing. These changes may take place due to inflation, trade union activities, or activities of pressure, groups and lobbies. Almond and Powell bring out this point thus, "The boundaries of political system are subject to relatively large fluctuations. During wartime the boundaries become greatly extended as large numbers of men are recruited into military service, as business firms are subjected to regulations and as internal security", measures are taken. In an election the boundaries again are greatly extended as voters become politicians for a day. With the return to more normal conditions the boundaries of political system contract.

Classification of political system

The classification of political system also poses a serious problem because the various scholars lay emphasis on different aspects of the political system in which they are interested. Highlighting this problem Robert Dhal says "A geographer might distinguish political systems according to the area they occupy, a demographer by the number of persons who are members, lawyer according to their lea codes. A philosopher or theologian interested in distinguishing `the best' political system will use ethical or religious criteria. A social scientist in determining how revolution is related to economic conditions might classify political systems by relative income and frequency of revolutions. Just as there is no one best way of classifying people, so no single way of distinguishing and classifying political systems is superior to the others for all purposes". However, general the political system fall in to three broad categories—Liberal democratic systems, the totalitarian systems an Autocratic systems.

Indian political system

There is a general impression among the scholars that the Indian Political system is largely a replica of the western political system. This impression seems to the be based on superfluous study of the Indian political system. If we delve deep, we will find that the Indian political system is not merely a duplicate copy of the western system and contains many indigenous elements as well Prof. Palmer, who has made a special study of the Indian Political system says "Upon closer view, however this system (Indian Political system) begins to lose some of the stamp of undigested foreign borrowing, and to assume forms which are more closely related to India's peculiar traditions, experiences and needs. Beneath familiar forms are unfamiliar practices and attitudes. The Indian political structure is still not so clear as one might first assume. The Indianization of Indian politics is still going on."

Prof. Morris Jones also shares the views of be detected in that in Indian political system trends and forces can be detected in non-political movements. He cautions the students of Indian Government and Political trends and force in what he will be tempted to set aside as non-political movements. He should be prepared to find the behaviour of those who hold apparently familiar political positions conditioned by considerations which he would not normally associate with such places. No doubt some of the political institutions adopted in India like the Parliament ' the Cabinet System, the political parties pressure groups etc seem to have been borrowed from the western world but their working shows a clear impact of the historical, cultural and religious conditions prevailing in India. The Indian political system contains the finest Indian traditions of assimilation, tolerance and synthesis. Prof. Palmer rightly observes that "the Contemporary Political Thought "stems from many sources, eastern and western, ancient and modern."

Peculiar Features of Indian Political System. The Indian political system Possesses certain distinct features which can be studied under the following heads

Combination of Centralisation and Decentralisation. In the first Place the Indian Political system is based on twin seemingly contradictory principles of centralisation and decentralisation 'On the one hand India possesses a highly centralised federal system of government which can be converted into unitary one during times of emergency. Not only the Union Government has beer allotted more extensive powers as compared to the states but can also legislate on subjects reserved for the states. It can issue directions to the states regarding the manner in which they should exercise their executive powers. The creation of a strong centre was warranted by historical experience as well as the conditions prevailing at the time of the enactment of the constitution. The experience of other federations of world also greatly influenced framers of the constitution to provide for a federal system with a unitary bias. This highly centralised character of Indian federal,' system has made critics challenge its federal character. Along with strong centre, India possesses Panchayat Raj institutions in which the people have been associated at the grass-root level. They are given great amount of latitude in tackling their local problem of course under the overall direction and control of the higher units of administration.

Important Position of the Leaders. In the second place, the Political leaders occupy an important position in the, Indian political system. This is in keeping with the long-standing. Indian tradition. The Indians have given great respect to their: religious and cultural leaders. In the political sphere they blindly followed leaders like Mahatma Gandhi, Nehru, Vallabhbhai Patel, Indira Gandhi, Jai Parkash Narayan etc. In fact in India some of the political parties have been formed around particular leaders. For example the Bhartiya Lok Dal was formed around Charan Singh. Telugu Desam Party of Andhra Pradesh revolves around N.T. Rama Rao. At present even the Congress (I) revolves round Rajiv Gandh' and his directives are faithfully carried out by members of the party, No doubt, in other political systems too political leaders play at; important role, but in Indian political system their role is certain more effective and significant.

Single Party Dominance. The third important feature of Indian Political system is single party domination. For almost two decades after independence the Congress enjoyed monopoly of power at the centre as well as the states. This monopoly of power provided Political stability to the country. After 1967 the Congress monopoly ended and coalition governments were formed in a number of states like Punjab, U.P., Kerala etc. However, this experiment did not prove a success and in the Fifth General Election the Congress regained the position of dominance. Quite often this position of dominance was misused by the Congress. During the years 1975-77, the Congress Party imposed a national emergency and made a bid to eliminate all opposition. However, this was seriously resented by the people and in the elections of March 1977 the people voted the Congress out of power at the Centre as well as most of the northern states. With the assumption of power by the Janata party it appeared that one-party dominance would end and the country may have two major political parties. However, soon dissensions appeared within the ranks of the Janta Party and it lost power at the Centre as well as a number of states. In the elections held in 1980 the Congress (1) emerged as a dominant party at the Centre as well as most of the states. In the elections of 1984 again Congress secured a victory with an unprecedented majority in the Parliament and in most of the states. However, certain regional political parties succeeded in capturing power in states like Andhra Pradesh, Tamil Nadu, Assam, Jammu and Kashmir, Punjab etc, and thus gave a serious setback to the long prevailing monopoly of Congress. In March 1987 Congress suffered yet another setback when the CPI (M) led front ousted the Congress led front from power in Kerala, and retained power in West Bengal. Despite this, Congress continues to be in power in most of the states and enjoys an overwhelming majority in the Parliament.

Political Parties Based on Religion and Linguistic Basis. Another peculiar feature of the Indian political system is that unlike other democratic systems where the political parties are formed on the basis of social, economic and political programme, a large number of political parties in India have been formed on the basis of religion, language etc. Some of the important political parties which have been formed on the basis of these principles include Hindu Mahasabha, Ram Rajya Parishad, Muslim League etc. on the basis of religion. Akali Dal and DMK on the basis of language etc. Truely speaking some of these political parties do not ossess any social or economic ideology and hence cannot be regarded as political parties in the true sense of the term. Again a number of political parties have been formed by disgruntled landlords, dispossessed zamindars and deposed Maharajas and have chalked out their programmes primarily with a view to protect the interests of these groups rather than promote the general interests of the people.

Absence of Effective Opposition. Another feature of The Indian political system which is intimately connected with the foregoing two features is absence of an effective opposition. As already noted during the first three decades the Congress almost '~Exercised monopoly of power. No doubt a number of opposition Parties existed in the country but they were so small and divided That they could hardly play the role of an effective opposition. It Was only in retaliation to the excesses of the emergency that number of small parties joined hands, formed the Janata Party, and succeeded in wresting power from Congress. The Janata Government was quite conscious of the importance of an opposition in a democracy and therefore accorded the status of a Cabinet Minister,' on the leader of the Opposition. But this situation did not last long~ and due to internal bickerings the Janata Party soon disintegrated, This greatly helped the congress (1) to recapture power. The opposition suffered a further setback in the Parliamentary elections of 1984 when its strength was considerably reduced and Congress managed to secure an unprecedented majority.

Thus we can ay that at present the opposition parties are so fragmented and their strength is so small that they can hardly pose any serious challenge to the authority of the ruling Congress party. In short, it can be said that with the exception of the period between 1977 and 1980 when the Janata Party was in power and the Congress (1) played the, role of an effective opposition, the country has been without effective opposition.

Caste in Indian Political System. Another notable feature of the Indian political system is its highly caste-ridden character Despite the best efforts of the government to discourage caste-feeling by banishing it from the Census Schedules, the caste-system_ continues to be a dominant factor of the Indian political system. Prof. Morris Jones rightly observes that in India "politics is more important to castes, and castes are more important to politics than before." He asserts that the top leaders may proclaim the goal of a casteless society but "the newly enfranchised rural masses know only the language of traditional politics which so largely turns about caste., Behind the formal list of party candidates nominated for the contests, there is probably an inside story of careful calculation in terms of the caste appeal. Prof. Roudolphus also emphasises that caste plays a dominant role in the political system. He says that "within the new context of political democracy caste remains a central element of India's society even while adapting itself to the values and methods of democratic politics. Indeed it has become one of the chief means by which the Indian masses have been attached to the process of democratic politics." Prof. M.N. Srinivas, an eminent sociologist, has also observed that "caste is so tacitly and so completely accepted by all, including those who are most vocal in condemning it, that it is everywhere the unit of social action."

Communalism. Communalism is another important

feature of the Indian political system. Though the framers of the constitution provided a secular polity in the country, communalism continues to dominate the Indian politics. Not only there have been~ a number of riots involving different communities, specially the Hindus and the Muslims, full-fledged political parties like Akali Dal, Muslim League, Hindu Mahasabha etc. have also been organised on communal basis. As Prof. Ghouse says, "Communalism now per, vades the country. Persons born and brought up in this atmosphere, develop communal biases at a very early age." The main reason, which have encouraged the growth of communalism in India have d up by Prof. Ghouse thus "the religious revivalism been suspicion, hatred and distrust between the two major communities organizations, transformation of religious and caste groups into pressure groups to collar of the meagre economic gains flowing from national development, and the reliance of political parties on the voter's loyalty to region or caste have rendered the society in India vulnerable to communal tensions and conflicts.

Ever since independence there have been growing number of incidents of communal violence. Further, in the course of years the nature of communal problem has undergone a change. Whereas, before 1970's the communal riots were confined to certain urban centres, since then the communal riots have tended to spread to the countryside and engulf even those areas which were known for communal harmony. Further, as against the earlier communal incidents which involved the Hindus and the Muslims, in recent years communal incidents involving Hindus and Sikhs have also ~,taken place. All this clearly shows that the base of communalism has tended to widen over the years.

Factionalism. Factionalism is another typical feature of the Indian Political system. The Indian society is divided into a number of "vertical structures of power cutting across castes and divisions", which effect the political stability of the government structure at the centre as well as states. At the centre though factionalism existed even during the times of Nehru but due to his magnetic personality and strong hold over the party he succeeded in keeping it under check. After Nehru's death factionalism at centre gained in strength and culminated in the split of Congress in 1969. Even Mrs. Gandhi succeeded in keeping the factions under check. However, under Janata Government' factionalism had a free play as the party was composed of divergent political groups who pulled in different directions and ultimately brought about the fall of the Janata Government. Thereafter Mrs. Indira Gandhi reemerged as the unchallenged leader. Though some sort of factionalist sentiments were expressed but by and large she succeeded in curbing them at the Centre.

At the state level factionalism has been more strong. This is particularly true of the states of northern India, viz., Bihar, Uttar Pradesh, Madhya Pradesh, Haryana, Punjab etc. Quite often a section of the ruling party worked to bring down the government with a view to replace its leadership. The members of the opposition parties were also victims of factional feeling. Even at present in the states factionalism exists in a big way. With the exception of some of the Chief Ministers who have a stable base of popular support the majority of the Chief Ministers are confronted %with factional fight from the dissidents. In many cases the dissidents have also succeeded in getting some of these Chief Ministers ousted too, viz., A.R. Antulay in Maharashtra, Jagannath Pahadia in Rajasthan, Chenna Reddy in Andhra Pradesh etc

Regionalism. Regionalism has been another important feature of the Indian Political System. Regionalism means love of a particular region or area in preference to the country as a whole,. It indicates an agglomeration of all those forces which are generally considered to be centrifugal polarised to centralism and nationalism, It has been defined as a "subsidiary process of political integration in India". It is a "manifestation of those residual elements which do not find expression in the national policy and national culture, and being excluded from the centrality of the new polity, express themselves in political discontent and political exclusionism". It includes forces which "fail to absorb, assimilate and internalize" The feeling of regionalism has been very strong in India and has manifested itself in the shape of demand for separate states, interstate disputes, and sometimes even secession from the Union. This growing feeling of regionalism in India has been partly due to feeling of neglect and discrimination among certain areas or sections and partly due to the growing political awareness of the henceforth backward people. Thus the demand for Dravid Home Land and Khalistan was put forward because the people of these regions feel, that they were being discriminated against. On the other hand in Assam the agitation for the ouster of the foreigners was launched because the people of Assam had a feeling that they were being exploited by the people from other states. In fact in India regionalism has been so strong that often even the national parties have sought support of the regional leaders to solve the problems. In a number of states the regional political parties have grown so powerful that they have succeeded in ousting Congress from power and forming their own governments. The success of Telugu. Desam in Andhra Pradesh, Akali Dal in Punjab, DMK/AIDMK in Tamil Nadu, Janata Party in Karnataka, Assam Gana Prishad in Assam, Mizo National Front in·Mizoram, National Conference in Jammu and Kashmir and Lok Dal (B) in Haryana bear a testimony to this fact.

Political Corruption. Political corruption is yet another important feature of the Indian Political system. Political corruption includes all the acts of commission or omission by a person holding political position for securing pecuniary or other material advantages directly or indirectly for himself or his family or friends. Political corruption in various forms has existed in India since independence. Even during the times of Nehru political corruption formed a feature of Indian political system. He protected Krishna Menon in the Jeep Scandal case despite the findings of the Public Accounts Committee of Parliament. Likewise be also shielded K.D. Nialviya in Serajuddin deal despite lot of hue and cry raised by opposition. At the state level Nehru offered protection to Pratap Singh Kairon, the Chief Minister of Punjab, even though charges of corruption were upheld against him by the judicial enquiry committee. No doubt, the Parliament, the Judiciary as well as the public opinion have expressed concern about the growing political corruption, but the political leaders have by and large tried to shield even corrupt ministers. This is evident from the fact that since the inauguration the constitution in 1950 investigation by quasi-judicial commissions were made against hardly 10 ministers or ex-ministers and none of them was sent to prison. Often the ministers found guilty did. not find it difficult to reclaim their past position of power after a very brief period of oblivion. Further, the government adopted different procedures to deal with different cases of political corruption and failed to evolve any clearly defined principles to deal with the problem of political corruption. Often the personal, group and party considerations influenced the decisions of the government in this regard.

Defections. Finally, political defection or floor-crossing has been an important feature of the Indian political system. Though the problem of political defections made its appearance in a serious shape only after the fourth general elections of 1967, it has been present in India since independence. But the number of cases of defection in the pre-1967 years was so small that they did not make any impact on the political life of the country, and naturally did not attract any public attention. After 1967 political defections took place on such a large scale that they posed a serious threat to the stability of the governments in a number of states. Political Defection in the words of Subhash C. Kashyap "covers the change of party affiliation both from the opposition to the government side or vice versa as also changes as between the parties on the same side of the House, i.e., between the constituent units of the coalition government or between the different parties sitting on the opposition benches."

During the Fourth General Elections (1967) Congress failed to secure clear cut majority in a number of states. The opposition saw in this development a golden opportunity to seize power and a number of political parties unmindful of their ideological differences joined hands on the basis of some minimum common programme to form the government. A number of legislators denounced their allegiance to their parent organisation and" joined hands with other groups for the attainment of certain political gains. It has been estimated that during a period of five years after the fourth general election over 1050 defections took place. In the subsequent elections the game of defection assumed even more serious dimensions and, the members of the state Assemblies defected en-bloc. As a result, there was frequent breakdown of ministries in the states, which, greatly contributed to political instability. Both the Congress as well as the Janata Governments felt gravely concerned about the evils of "defection' and sought to curb it. The Congress Government appointed, a

Committee under Y.B. Chavan, the then Union Home Minister, in 1967 to "consider the problem of legislators, changing their allegiance from one party to another and their frequent crossing of the floor in all its aspects and make recommendations in this regard. Though the recommendations of the Committee were against defections, this view was not universally shared and man, considered defection as a natural phenomenon. Even the Janata Government indicated its seriousness to bring forth an Anti-Defection Bill in Parliament in May 1977. However, it failed to bring about the necessary statutory enactment concerning defections due to its failure to arrive at some understanding with the Congress Party regarding the definition of defection and how to check the same. In fact soon even the Janata Government fell victim to the game of defections and lost power. The return of Congress Government to power under Mrs. Indira Gandhi once again A witnessed large-scale defections. Though occasional efforts were made to check the evil of defection but much success could not achieve due to lack of consensus among the various political part and various political parties continued to encourage defections promote their narrow party interests. A successful attempt to check, defections was made by Rajiv Gandhi's Government through the enactment of 52nd amendment which provided that the members of Parliament and state legislatures were liable to be disqualified from membership of the house if they leave the party on the symbol which they have contested the election. However, group of people 'leaving the party and splitting it are not covered by this provision. After the enactment of the above amendment defection has been constitutionally banned. In April 1987 the Speaker of Punj Legislative Assembly disqualified a number of members of Akali 'Dal who left the party. The Punjab High Court also upheld t validity of antidefection law.

Growing Impact of Regional Political Parties. The presence of a large number of regional political parties, which have exercise tremendous influence on the politics of the country, has been another outstanding feature of Indian political system. The regional political parties emerged because the regional political leaders wanted to assert their importance. The formation of DMK, Shiva Sena, Jharkhand Party, Mizoram National Front etc. can be cited as an example. Regional parties were also formed to protect and promote religious, linguistic and caste interests of certain sections of society. The other factors which contributed to the growth of regional political parties are growing disparity between various parts of country desire of the regional leader to maintain their, importance and as a protest against the ever increasing centralism, tendencies. The presence of large number of regional politician the one hand deprived the country the bene parties in India has and on the other hand seriously jeopard fits of a strong opposgration by encouraging regional and ized the process of national inter sectarian thinking, and posing a serious threat to the unity and integrity of the country.

A careful perusal of the above features of the Indian Political System shows that it would certainly be wrong to say that it is merely a replica of the western political systems. No doubt India has adopted democratic and representative institutions of the West, but at the same time it contains certain institutions like caste, Panchayat Raj, communalism, factionalism, regionalism etc. which clearly bear the impact of the Indian social system. Hence, it can be said that the Indian political system represents a synthesis of the western and Indian elements and possesses a distinct character of its own.

Confucius, the great philosopher, mentions three vital F's, the three essentials for the protection and preservation of the state. According to him, the first vital essential is Food. Unless adequate supply of nutritious and wholesome food is made available to the population, the State cannot survive for long. So availability of food for all sections of the population must be ensured. The next is the Fort which must be protected against all enemies. The last and the most important, according to Confucius, is Faith, People can manage with some shortfall in food requirements for a while. The fort can be further strengthened if found wanting in some respect or to suit the strategic needs of the hour. But it is the faith of the people that cannot be allowed to be compromised under any circumstances. If people's faith is shaken, even the most impregnable fort and the most comfortable food position cannot save the state. What the great philosopher said long ago in respect of the state seems equally valid today also in the context of the present crisis of democracy in India.

Crisis of faith

The present crisis of democracy in India is that of faith. The faith of the people has been shaken in practically every major democratic institution in the country. There has been a steady erosion of values in public life during the last half century of independence.

The parliament and the state legislatures which once used to be the sacred temples of democracy have been defiled by the intrusion of history sheeters and other shady characters. The Election Commissioner G.V.G. Krishnamurthy has gone on record to, say that the situation is threatening to degenerate into a "government of the criminals, for the criminals, by the criminals". It has become quite a formidable task for the best brains in the country to devise ways and means to keep the criminals out. As things stand, today even the most dreaded outlaw can easily get elected to the parliament if he so chooses. There would be no legal bar to his contesting elections. Today no political party can honestly claim that it has no criminal elements within its fold. The criminal elements have not entered the august portals of the parliament and state legislatures by accident. Rather, the political parties have been busy wooing criminals on a competitive basis during the last few elections. Today they hold the key to electòral success and grabbing power. No one seems to have the least compunction about it. A former prime minister and several former chief ministers and many more former ministers are facing trial on criminal charges including charges of buying votes of members of parliament to save a minority government. The same is true of several sitting as well as former members of the parliament and state legislatures. Some of those languishing in jail as under trial prisoners are yet to be suspended by the party to which they belong. No surprise the conduct of the whole breed of politicians ruling the roost today has shaken the faith of the people as a whole.

Corruption in high places

The top functionaries in the executive in practically every area of government activity have betrayed the nation by their collective kleptomania. In the scheme of the government's working, no member of the political executive can become corrupt without a collusive bureaucracy. The two must go hand in hand. During pre-independence days, lower level functionaries in the police and the courts used to make a little money on the side, and the British looked the other way and sometimes even encouraged it indirectly. But corruption in the higher echelons was seldom tolerated, unless the incumbent happened to be an Englishman like Robert Clive or Warren Hastings. Clive came to India as a clerk in the East India Company on an annual salary of just three pounds. He went back to England with 130,000 pounds 27 years later. The foundations of corruption in high places in modem India were laid by the founder of the British raj himself. Surendra Nath Bannerji then a young magistrate in the ICS, lost his job when a committee of judges found him guilty of carelessness in recording a false service report of summons. Far worse malfeasance has since been institutionalised in the judiciary and now justice through courts is available only to those with means and clout.

Had it not been for the fear of, involvement in criminal contempt proceedings in which the concerned judge himself is also the judge, juror and the hangman, undoubtedly one would have heard much more about the sorry state of affairs with the country's judiciary. Nevertheless, more has been heard about the less known side of judiciary during the last 25 years than ever before in the past. The people's faith in judiciary has been shaken, too, particularly the faith of those who are unluckily involved in litigation. The fourth pillar of democracy, the media, seems to be relatively in a better shape although the integrity of the scribe has also been of late compromised to a noticeable extent.

Seeds of the crisis

The Constitution of India enshrines the doctrine of equality and non-interference in certain matters and nondiscrimination on certain narrow grounds. It also holds as sacred the freedom of thought, speech and expression. All that sounds as music and makes an excellent reading. The real catch is that the underlying philosophy has not yet been imbibed by the people of India in whom the sovereignty of the nation rests. The unwritten Constitution of Great Britain reflects the will of the people more truly as it embodies the conventions and enactments over centuries. Our Constitution is basically a scholarly exercise in compilation of whatever was thought worth emulating. The debates in the Constituent

Assembly were of the highest quality and reflected the erudition and debating skills of the best brains and ideologues in the country, except that the intellectual giants in that august body did not represent the people of the country in the same sense as the members of the parliament and state legislatures are expected to do by virtue of their mandate. The democratic form of governance enshrined in our Constitution did not, in fact, represent the political opinion obtaining in the country in the late forties. Almost 90 percent of countrymen belonged to the schools of thought led by Jinnah, Gandhi and Subhash Chandra Bose. For reasons of history neither of the three could be associated with the framing of the Constitution and choosing the Westminster model of democracy. "We, the People" of India were represented by the opinion leaders claiming the following of a mere residuary 10 per cent of Indians. In any case, thc Constituent Assembly whose members were themselves elected on the basis of an extremely limited electorate was anything but a representative body. While electing the central assembly in 1946 the electors did not know that it would be converted into a constituent assembly and so constitution framing was, outside its mandate to begin with.

People vs the Elite

It is thus hardly surprising that the letter and spirit of the Constitution does not reflect the value system and hopes and aspirations of the people as a whole. Yet, it is the people who have to ultimately work the democratic apparatus. Most of the aberrations in our democracy arise from this simple factor. The fact of the matter is that there is very little of democracy in our daily living. We, the people, alone are to blame for the crisis of democracy in the country if it is assumed that the constitution framers were right in rushing headlong to import the latest fashionable models from the western world without any reference to the Indian value system, no matter how "undemocratic" essentially. For example, less than a third of Indians had a bare minimum of education when the jurisprudence is that ignorance of law is no excuse for its noncompliance. Under our own value system, ignorance is a valid defence. To inspire ready compliance, law should ideally be based on an honest appraisal of the national consensus which is seldom achieved through a head count or hand raising of so called representative of the people elected through a patently un-representative electoral system in which even a criminal can win hands down. Democracy presupposes a value system based on equity, fair play, egalitarianism, respect for others' rights and obligation to perform one's own duty towards the state and the society. In practice, Indian society pathetically lacks all these. Failure to recognise this basic contradiction has led us to more and more steps divorced from the ground realities. Empowerment of people is sought to be achieved by giving more financial and executive powers to the panchayats, without realising that panchayats in most parts of the country are actually engines of repression and medieval justice and have served as a mechanism to further a strengthen the stranglehold of feudal a elements. About a decade ago Rajiv Gandhi realised that just about 15 paise out of every rupee meant for rural development was actually reaching the targeted beneficiaries, and in the same breath he also started the ambitious Jawahar Rojgar Yojana in which the funds were to be placed directly in the hands of the mukhiyas. No one pointed out to him that ever since 1952 the mukhiyas have been personally appropriating at least half the development funds for the benefit of their own relatives and castemen. It is these mukhiyas who have firmly entrenched corruption at the grass-roots level. Most often the schemes are tailor made to suit the needs of their own family members. When the Mukhiya is in no position to benefit himself any more, he would still be the executing agent, i.e., the contractor for all the schemes within the area of his influence, in different names if necessary. When the work involved is palpably fraudulent with the possibility of the executing agent going to jail ultimately, he would get the scheme sanctioned in the name of some ignorant villager who can be made to sign on the dotted line for the smallest consideration. A bookish strategy worked out hurriedly in rarefied air conditioned chambers in the national or state capitals cannot defeat the feudalistic institutions and tentacles. It can only strengthen them.

"Democracy" in action

The Constitution was not designed for a "government of the criminals,, by the criminals and for the criminals". Yet, that is what we have today. What the world saw on the television on October 21 during the live telecast of the proceedings in the U.P. Assembly has made every Indian hang his head in shame. Five years ago the BBC coverage of Ayodhya and its hourly telecast took away a great deal of our credibility as democratic nation, and now the recent shameful incidents have only confirmed he earlier impressions on the world community. Loknayak Jayaprakash Narain advocated the people's rights to recall the elected representatives in certain cases and the recent exhibition of an incredible degree of criminality in the U.P. Assembly should make us think about it once again. The demand of the rebel Congress leader Naresh Agrawal that the membership of the erring members should be immediately terminated on the basis of the video clips alone is also worth consideration.

In effect, not democratic norms, but the continuing feudal tendencies have been strengthened by the bureaucracy and politicians who have the primary responsibility to work the democratic apparatus in our day-to-day lives. Ideological differences among the various political formations have been blurred in a mad pursuit of power. Now labels rather than genuine ideological postures mark one party from another. *If Garibi Hatao* proves the winning slogan, every one grabs it without an explanation why they opposed it until recently. If Mandal magic works, all adopt it without reference to their earlier public postures. The temple issue was sought to be hijacked too to puncture the BJP strategy when Rajiv Gandhi government permitted the *shilanyas* at Ayodhya and later on when a dubious Chandraswamy performed a "secularist" *Som Yajna* there to placate the majority community. The half hearted wooing of the pro-temple electorate on both occasions has made the Congress lose the game both ways. Interpretations vary, but today every party claims itself to be secular or at least minority friendly. That is the demand of the vote bank oriented politics in the country. People want free electricity and irrigation facilities and want all government loans to be waived. And all parties accept all, such demands sooner or later for electoral considerations. To legitimise an illegitimate regime distribution of largesse among all who mattered is an old medieval practice, and our present day political outfits have no qualms about taxing the whole population with a view to nursing or cultivating their pocket boroughs and other pressure groups.

Post ideology age

The same is true of economic liberalisation. It is hard to tell the difference between the BJP's swadeshi plank, Mr. Manmohan Singh's or Mr Chidambaram's globalisation and Mr Jyoti Basu's or Mr Laloo Prasad's wooing of FDIs. Differences, if any, are limited to degrees and form and notion substance. The Congress President Sitaram Kesri has serious objections to the BJP even taking the name of Gandhi, although his party was the first to bury all Gandhian thought such as trusteeship of the society, *gram swaraj,* opposition to industrialisation and all machinery. Today it is labels and icons that sell, not ideas and ideologies be it Ambedkar, Gandhi, Mandal, Kanshi Ram or whatever else.

A functioning political party should normally be expected to propagate its ideology, recruit new members and support its organisational and electoral expenses from the subscriptions voluntarily paid by its members. The members should periodically elect the party's office bearers as per the, party's constitution and have their say in all important matters, including policy matters, at all appropriate forums within the party structure and the leaders should act faithfully according to the consensus among the party members. But what is happening today? No party depends on the humble contributions of the primary members. Many parties have only ghost members and so cannot afford to have anything like the party elections. The money comes from the industrial money bags, often extorted as a *quid pro quo,* and also straight from the crime syndicates. Many parties and so called party leaders have their close connections with the criminals and many criminals have successfully promoted themselves as "leaders". Parties are floated and run like private limited companies by the self appointed leaders who make no bones about the party being their own pocket organisation which they can sell, mortgage, wind up or reconstitute at will without any reference to anyone else at all. There is no internal democracy worth the name within any party with the exception of a few left parties. Transient party interests above the national interests, personal ambitions and interests above party interests and an unabashed resolve to amass as much as possible from all sources, whether party, government or underworld, seems to be the order of the day in the functioning of most political parties. There are some whose declared objective is to grab power by all means. We had a taste of it in U.P. recently. Democracy cannot survive by a free for all scramble for power through every kind of patently undemocratic means. Crime, corruption, casteism, communalism, feudalism and a combination of all these employed as a means of gaining power in a democracy is a negation of the very idea of democracy, We can only make a laughing stock of ourselves if we try to fool ourselves into believing that democracy can coexist even with all these.

The task ahead

The daunting task is to make the democratic apparatus in the country more people friendly and more responsive at all levels. The three areas which may be identified for the purpose of making a beginning are (a) involvement of the people, and not their so called agents, in the planning process and execution of the development schemes at the grass-roots level, (b) depoliticising bureaucracy and (c) de-criminalising politics through rational and pragmatic electoral reforms. These are by no means exhaustive, and every alternative strategy that can deliver the desired results is worth a careful consideration before being pronounced as unworkable. Apart from these, there is a great more that would need to be done regarding improving the state of our educational system and judiciary down to the mofussil courts, removal of illiteracy and superstitions, ensuring social justice to the deprived sections and women, reaching a near 100% employment level, promotion of awareness of citizenship rights and duties and eradication of social evils through a multi-pronged strategy. Making democracy an essential part of an average Indian's life style is a formidable task and it is time every Indian is made to realise that unless conscious and persistent efforts are made in that direction on a long term basis the present crisis of democracy in the country has the potentials of rendering the whole idea of democracy an empty dream without substance, Even the elected members today do not really reflect the true will of the people as few of them ever get more than half the votes in any constituency. This is a major issue underlying the crisis today.

Our national ethos

here can be only two ways in which a country's Constitution can work meaningfully, It should reflect, down to the smallest details and as accurately as possible, the commonly shared values of the society as a whole. Whatever is not part of a national consensus is best left out for another time. Alternatively, if certain ideas which are not already strictly consistent with the national ethos and collective subconscious are being imported from outside sources as most desirable or even ideologically fashionable, the fact should be honestly recognised and a viable strategy to educate the entire population about its virtues must be carefully planned and executed. The people must be allowed a chance to imbibe the underlying philosophy behind the sacred constitutional provisions. Naturally, even with the best of efforts what is culturally unacceptable or what is repugnant to the national consensus will be rejected by the people. Law must follow the society, and not seek to lead it. It applies equally to constitutional law. There is no way one can shove down unwilling throats ideas that people do not subscribe to. If sincere efforts are made, and if the ideas are not diametrically opposite to the deeply rooted national ethos, they can be educated. But the enactments will remain on the paper till the people are so educated and till they truly imbibe them in their thoughts, mental reflexes and actions. It will be a sheer waste of time recounting how many enactments and constitutional provisions have remained on paper to this day and are honoured more in violation than in compliance every day and at all levels.

Dichotomy

The specific aberrations in our democracy are interrelated and feed on one another. The roots of each lie in the inherent hypocrisy of the Indian society and the mutual contradictions of our pretenses and practices. The lofty doctrines of liberty, equality, fraternity, social justice, secularism, fairplay and, above all, rule of law enshrined in our Constitution are yet to percolate into our daily lives. All these noble ideas have been imported from the Western democracies and sought to be planted into our system of governance. The interplay of the powerful social forces on these ideas has inevitably led to the aberrations we see today. "Might is right" has been the most important social reality in India over the centuries, and merely incorporating the modern democratic notions into the statute book could not be expected to produce an instant social transformation. Only a sustained social movement can change the national ethos marginally. It was too much to expect that by merely framing a democratic constitution we can have an overnight change in our national psyche which is still predominantly feudal. It is no coincidence that Mahatma Gandhi was totally opposed to the western political thought in general and parliamentary democracy in particular. Subhash Chandra Bose was against charting out a democratic course all of a sudden. He wanted a dictatorship for at least 20 years in free India.

We are never tired of telling ourselves and others valiantly how we drove out the British 50 years ago, although the plain fact of history is that the British withdrew from India exactly when they decided. It was no longer profitable or in their national interest to maintain a colonial regime. They did so in Palestine and other parts of the world about the same time and it was entirely on their own terms. They never used the word "freedom" or "independence" but "Transfer of Power".

"Power" was the operative word for all concerned, Indians and Englishmen, and so hungry were we for power and in such indecent haste that we did not even pause to consider that if the "Transfer of Power" meant also a transfer of population, it had to be in a phased and well planned manner spread over a decade or so. That would have saved the bloodbath and incalculable human suffering which left its scars on large sections of the population in the three countries. Thus the Indian Constitution was framed amidst most traumatic moments of communal frenzy overtaking the whole country. In an atmosphere of total insanity all around us, our best brains had to do a rush job by way of a command performance by a given date. Nothing was referred to the people to ascertain what they thought or were ready to accept. The people of India, in whom the sovereignty of the country rests under the Constitution, had practically no say in the matter.

Causes of crisis

Among the contributing factors leading to the present mess, caste, corruption, communalism and criminalisation have been widely identified. Few would disagree with that, though may be some additional factors may also appear relevant to some people, e.g. hostility and intolerance towards all ideas except our own. That is plainly the worst possible negation of the very idea of democracy. Undoubtedly, a social stratification along caste lines is repugnant to the very concept of democracy and our society needs to outgrow such notions, though it must be said that the caste system has been arguably the most misunderstood institution in Indian society. Its role in the Society has been changing all the time through history, and during the earlier part of the century it had a community service orientation which led to opening of schools and colleges, and also dharamashalas and charitable hospitals by contributions raised by wealthy members of different castes. It gave a tremendous fillip to education. The Banaras Hindu University, the Aligarh Muslim University, the DAV schools and colleges and institutions founded by the Ramakrishna Math are obvious examples. For thousands of years the highly specialised skills in architecture, crafts and industry were handed down. from generation to generation under the caste system which resulted in an almost matchless accumulation of national wealth. Farmily traditions in various trades were perfected and improved upon generation after generation which resulted in production of goods and services of an astonishing quality. Until the British systematically destroyed them, something still remained to be looted even after plunder by hordes after hordes of marauding bandits over the centuries. Our fabulous wealth and prosperity, thanks to the highly developed professional skills under the much maligned caste system, brought them to India again and again right since the days of Alexander the Great.

Caste politics

During the first decades after independence, the trend was unmistakably towards loosening of caste barriers and had the process been allowed to continue, the scenario would have been very different. But the Insecurity and instability in the emerging power equations during the mid sixties made the politicians carefully nurture all kinds of support groups that could get them votes, Caste naturally was one such factor. So progressively every government played upon sentiments and fielded candidates in elections with an eagle eye on the caste equations. As government after government oriented its policies on caste lines, it was found convenient and politically expedient to keep the caste angle in view not only while forming ministries or fielding candidates in an election but also while deciding the placement of individual members of the bureaucracy and police force. Now it has been completely accepted as the governing principle on such matters, at times outweighing all other considerations. Ambedkar has just replaced Gandhi as a vote catching icon and a ticket to grabbing power quickly. The dalit constituency, so far the most pliable big chunk of floating votes, is now being wooed by one and all desperately. During the Karpoori Thakur government of the late seventies one overzealous district magistrate in Bihar went on record to suggest raising the battalions of the Bihar Military Police along well defined caste lines. It seemed outrageous at that time, but now recently the principle has been adopted in some central para military forces without any fuss at least for the "minorities" It is only a beginning, and in coming years we can expect an extension of the logic to the numerous castes as well. The Supreme Court judgement in the Mandal case five years ago has in effect continued the feudal and patently anti-democratic notion of caste in perpetuity. The police having failed to protect the people, now private armies are being raised along caste lines to protect the life and property of castemen. The clashes of these private armies are a frequent occurrence and are usually reported in the press as gang wars. They are also quite useful during election time, and so all of them receive political patronage.

Exploiting caste sentiments and playing off one caste combination against the other with a political axe to grind, perhaps even more than religious bigotry, is the very antithesis of the idea of rationalism, the corner stone of democracy as well as left wing philosophy. Strangely, no left wing intellectual has yet challenged the perpetuation of caste as a political rallying point in Bihar or elsewhere. On the other hand, they have been twisting logic out of shape in their anxiety to explain the apparent absurdity. They now discover all kinds of virtue in what was deemed to be the most abominable evil and a cancerous growth only a couple of decades ago. Breaking the caste barriers occupied the number one place in Dr. Ram Manohar Lohia's five point political agenda, but those swearing by his name now represent the formidable caste oriented Mandal lobby. Now all shades of political opinion from the right wing BJP to the Marxists have quietly adopted it as if it was part of their own political credo. The monster of naked casteism has all of a sudden mysteriously gained wide respectability as empowerment of the sub-altern India! To preserve it they have the least hesitation in condoning the most unpardonable sins, including the century's most infamous fodder scam and umpteen other scams involving astronomical amounts of public money. For, it is argued, after all, corruption predates Laloo raj, and so it is dismissed as elitist, communalist propaganda launched by reactionary, obscurantist forces! This is expected to be swallowed uncritically as the gospel truth. Ironically, removing corruption was at the top of the agenda of the mass movement led by Jaya Narayan which catapulted the likes of Laloo Prasad into politics.

Amoralpursuit of power

Particularly the last three decades have marked the slide down in value based politics in the country with the disappearance of the first generation political leaders from the scene. Politics came to be increasingly dominated by rank opportunists and time servers, and now during the last decade or so a stage has come when power has passed on to the hands of outright political buccaneers to whom governance is no more than a profitable business enterprise, a highly lucrative get-rich formula. In 1947 Nehru expressed a wish to bang those making illicit money by business in food-grains by the nearest lamp post. One of the worthies arrested, prosecuted and paraded as the *khuddichor* (broken rice thief) in 1948 became the Congress president and a prime ministership hopeful. The minority government at the centre supported by the Congress which continued even after dissolution of Lok Sabha protected those who had made tons of money by plain swindling in the "business" of fertilizer to fodder and whatever else they could manage to lay their hands on. The state had simply withered away, making the Marxian dictum stand on its head.

All hell broke loose when anti-Congressism of the mid sixties gave rise to an unabashed opportunistic power politics totally devoid of ideological considerations. Floodgates of corruption were opened to all as horsetrading of legislators became rampant, to an extent that an anti-defection bill had to be passed. But the change in value orientations can never be corrected by simplistic measures like legislation, and this is amply home out by its miserable failure during the~, last few years. It has only served to send the rates of the potential defectors skyrocketing, It is nobody's case that corruption was invented during mid sixties. But prior to that it attracted a social stigma. From 1967 onwards it gradually began attracting admiration, envy and even respect and is now a sure indicator of social and political clout. A sense of shame and guilt that was always there with the corrupt has now vanished altogether.

Role of Bureaucracy

In the scheme of working of the government under our Constitution, the political executive cannot be corrupt unless the bureaucracy openly cooperates. Hence it was only natural for the political leadership to find the right allies and collaborators in the bureaucracy. If bureaucracy does its job without favour and fear and strictly according to rules and prescribed procedure, there is no way, a politician can make money out of his official position. No minister, chief minister or even prime minister can possibly award a contract, pass a bill for payment or issue an order of any kind. All decisions are to be taken and orders are to be passed in the specific file of the concerned department after due processing and examination in the secretariat with reference to specific rules and policy decisions. The political executive can have its final say in policy matters which have to be defended on the floor of the house.

Usually no one would think of bribing a politician for mere policy decisions which run contrary to the established law and are not capable of being translated into awarding largesse in one form or another. If despite strong advice to the contrary the minister reverses the recommendations from the secretariat in light of the rules, the secretariat has to implement the orders. But then the minister alone must face the music before all forums, including a court of law while the bureaucrat cannot be sued for merely implementing the government decision. If the minister does show that much courage and determination to flout the rules, it would be much easier to nail him down.

Any solutions?

So what is the solution ? There are no magic solutions. But one may venture three possible strategies. The first, of course, is to de-criminalise politics and de-politicise bureaucracy. To achieve this objective, administrative reforms designed to break the corrupt bureaucrat criminalised politician nexus and effective measures to plug all the loopholes in the electoral law and practices can be scarcely over-emphasised. Thirdly, the planning process must be made more people oriented and people friendly. By this I mean that the local needs and the local aspirations of the people should be continuously appraised through direct and indirect methods like economic surveys and then incorporated progressively into the district and state plans. No plans or schemes should ever be imposed on the people without a reference to them. The Planning Commission at the national level should at best confine itself to the tasks of periodic monitoring, review and evaluation, general superintendence and specialised support services.

Crucial factor

One crucial factor that has contributed the most to the unhealthy nexus between the corrupt bureaucrat and criminalised politician is the permanent stake a member of All India Services (IAS/IPS) necessarily has careerwise in the politics of the state to which he is allotted immediately after recruitment. In effect, it has worked out to be detrimental to the very objectives of the creation of the All India Services which include ensuring impartiality and political neutrality of bureaucracy, uniformity and harmony in the administration throughout the country and preserving/strengthening the unity and integrity of the country. Instead it has resulted in promotion and propagation of a work culture in which one can get away with impunity with the most heinous offence committed at the behest of the political bosses but is totally defenceless if he incurs their wrath for whatever reason which is quite often precisely the point where his conscience starts bothering him. The casualty is the rule of law in any case.

The sole rationale behind this permanent bondage to a particular state cadre is that there are local variations of language, culture, etc. from state to state. All these can be and, in fact, are coped with very well in no time by fellow recruits who are by sheer chance allotted to a separate cadre called the Union Territories cadre. By any parameters, what is common to widely different places like Pondicherry, Arunachal Pradesh, Chandigarh, Delhi, the Andaman and Nicobar Islands, Dadra and Nagar

Haveli, Mizoram, Lakshadweep, Goa, Daman and Diu? Some have even acquired full statehood in the mean time and are no longer Union Territories, but are still administrated by officers in the IAS/IPS borne on the AGMUT cadre. Officers belonging to this cadre run the administration of this assortment of widely dispersed territories and are transferred right across the country and yet are actually far more effective and impartial in spite of all obvious handicaps of limited knowledge of the local language, culture, economy, geography, traditions, and even the law and customs. The simple reason is that they stay away from local politics in which they have no career stakes since everybody knows that, they are there only for a while, usually a fixed duration of three years, and so they can afford to ignore the local pressures and act without favour or fear. There is a much higher degree of accountability and impartiality since the officer concerned knows only too well that once he leaves the place no political godfather can protect him if he is hauled up for any of his acts of omission or commission and so he must go by the book and see that his actions stand the scrutiny of even his worst detractors years after he has left the place for good. On the other hand, if an officer belonging to that cadre, finds that the state government of Mizoram is treating him or her unfairly, he or she can just put in the papers and catch the next plane to New Delhi. Officers condemned to serve a particular state for the entire career have no such option, and must dance to the tunes of their criminalised political bosses if they do not want to be earmarked for the rest of their career for "drop dead" postings where there is no work, no place to sit, not even the basic minimum facilities, no budget, and hence no provisions for even a regular salary. There are hundreds of such non-posts both in the IAS and the IPS.

Federalism vs statewise cadres

Recruited through the same common examination conducted by the Union Public Service Commission, officers in some forty group "A" central services are required to serve in different states while those in the Foreign Service are required to keep adapting to entirely new socio-cultural-linguistic settings throughout their career. Even IAS/IPS officers do not mind going to other states when greener pastures are in sight, say as advisers to the Governor of a state under the President's rule where they are expected to deftly manage the affairs of an unknown state at the very top at a crucial hour all of a sudden. Rolling stones gather no moss, except perhaps when they inevitably "settle down" in the national capital, but that is a different story altogether. Similarly, even in the IPS, officers from other cadres, when found politically expedient, are quietly sent to other states facing a tough situation.

If the logic behind the watertight state cadres has any basis in reality, how is it that KPS Gill from Assam cadre and before him Julius Ribenro from Maharashtra cadre are expected to be and actually prove themselves more effective than their colleagues who have spent a life time in trouble torn Punjab when asked to take the reins all of a sudden at the top of the police hierarchy there? Or, even in Bihar, how is it that J.M. Qureshi from Madhya Pradesh cadre is suddenly brought in as the Director General of Police even without any such extenuating circumstances? Why does it not offend against the sacred principles and "higher" philosophy of federalism, the sole justification for creation and continuance of watertight, compartmentalised state cadres, in such cases?

Breaking the nexus

Even within the federal structure often cited as the

constitutional compulsion for continuance of inalienable and sacrosanct state cadres in spite of the obvious price tag, it is very much possible to rotate the members of All India Services between the central and state governments for fixed duration, never to the same state again and never, never to the home state or even a neighbouring state where the danger of playing into the hands of local politicians is obviously quite high. When high court judges and members of the central administrative tribunals, usually in the sixty plus age group, can be transferred right across the country in order to ensure independence and impartiality and without compromising on quality of performance, there is no reason why much younger people in these services should get homesick or fail to cope with the change. At least on an experimental basis a beginning can be made.

Except in the rarest of rare cases, there should be no interstate transfer within 5 years. When an officer is due for such transfer, he should be asked to take a short term orientation course to prepare himself for the new state. Ideally, learning more Indian languages should be encouraged throughout the career and supported by pecuniary and career incentives. Apart from reversing the current trend of criminalisation of administration, it would instill a healthy fear of law in the minds of those who now believe themselves to be a law unto themselves thanks to guaranteed protection from unscrupulous political godfathers.

Poll reforms

Just as the umpteen Tughlakish misadventures of the former Chief Election Commissioner T.N. Seshan have not led to any significant qualitative changes in the composition of our legislature and parliament, Krishnamurthy's strategy to keep the criminals out may not really work for the simple reason that practically every criminalised politician of substance, would escape his net, Krishnamurthy is rightly anguished that the current system has made it possible for as many as 700 persons of a criminal background to get elected as "honourable" representatives of the people in the state assemblies and another 40 in the Lok Sabha. His reform package includes barring the entry of convicts with a five year jail term behind them. However, legally barring the entry of such elements, no matter how desirable, is fraught with serious legal difficulties, and would need many amendments in the electoral as well as the constitutional law. It is not going to be easy, and even then all the holes cannot be plugged effectively. Even by his own parameters, a dacoit who was incarcerated for 11 years as an undertrial prisoner, a ruling party MLA undergoing a life term on being convicted of murder and a former MLA who was bobbitised by his rape victim would still be eligiblc as any to contest elections. It would not prevent some of the most well-known criminals from getting elected. Who exactly has Krishnamurthy in mind? All the 740 worthies listed by him would escape his net, For all you know, one can spend a life time dedicated to a wide variety of crime and never be caught, leave alone being convicted. Those convicted were probably unprofessional or foolish enough to get caught in the act or could not afford a smart go-getter lawyer.

Opinions on such issues vary widely. Once there was a proposal to banish wholesale Shiv Sena-BJP from electoral politics through the religion bill. Illiteracy, having too many children, lack of any stakes in the society, income-tax payee status, property qualifications and the like have been mooted as some other criteria for limiting the universal franchise. It would open a Pandora's box. Those who would sell their, own votes as members of the house if the price is right or those who openly indulge in violence on the floor of the house are no better than ordinary pickpockets, highway robbers and other felons big and small. Similarly simple proposal by Tata Sons Electoral Trust to make contributions to political parties/individual contestants "transparent, nondiscriminatory and non-discretionary" is food for thought, but there are obviously practical difficulties. If the said contributions are actually "nondiscri-minatory and non-discretionary" they become taxes by another name. Why should the business houses volunteer to pay such a tax without compulsion or consideration.

Towards 100% polling

Surprisingly, nobody appears to have seriously considered relatively much simpler antidotes of electoral malpractices like door-to-door polling advocated by many, including the former Bihar Chief Minister Mr Laloo Prasad, among others. Earlier, Rajaji had written to President Rajendra Prasad pleading the same. Provisions already exist in the Representation of People Act, 1951 for constitution of mobile polling parties for areas where even makeshift polling stations cannot be constructed. As a matter of fact, in every election since 1952 the district authorities of necessity had to constitute at least a few mobile polling parties. The same can be easily extended to all voters. Polling parties can be constituted immediately, say within a week or fortnight, after announcement of elections. The presiding officer and his team can be assigned a reasonable number of families which can be actually covered during the course of the assigned polling hours. Their task should be to get to know each voter by face and by name during the month long period available till the electors should be asked to stay at home during the polling hours and the police should have the limited task of keeping the streets clear except for genuine emergencies.

Cutting the costs

This will make elaborate police bandobast and multitiered patrolling parties unnecessary resulting in considerable economy in personnel and all other resources. The presiding officers, who had the custody of the ballot papers and statutory forms may be a responsible government employee as per the current practice, but the other three "polling officers" who merely fold the ballot paper or apply the indelible ink, read out the names from the electoral rolls and tick the entries off need not be government employees except in a polling area where even two or three individuals capable of discharging such routine functions cannot be found. Such local and non partisan volunteers should be encouraged, on due verification of antecedents and on furnishing a bond of good conduct to the local authorities, to form part of the polling parties.

Saving time, money, manpower

After the polling is over, the same party can also complete the counting forthwith in the presence of the candidates' representatives in a well chosen public place in the vicinity. The counted ballot papers and the tabulation sheets can then be sealed in a bundle/ packet after due panchnama and submitted to the returning officer who can have them compiled and announce the result expeditiously. Voting rights need not be denied to even jailbirds, those in hospital or transit or on duty. There need not be a public holiday on the day of polling. Since the number of electors to be covered by a polling party under this plan would be much smaller, polling hours can be restricted to normal working hours and even less to facilitate the movement of office-goers. This plan would cut the cost by more than half and infinitely enhance the quality and content of elections with a near total participation of the electorate. There is simply no scope of litigation, disputes or violence.

Banishing crime and criminals

Criminals can be effectively kept out by having the polls in two rounds. The final round should take place after a gap of two weeks in which only the two best achievers of the first round should be permitted to contest. There should be no countermanding of polls in the event of the death of a candidate unless he happens, to be one of the two finalists. That will be the end of bogus, dummy, transparently fraudulent so called "non-serious" candidates and the size of the ballot paper would be never more than a small slip of paper, thus resulting in considerable economy in cost of paper and printing as well as its handling and transport throughout the election process. People know who's who in the constituency best, and no criminal can hope to get more than 50% of votes in a virtual 100% poll, nor hope to win solely on the basis of appeals in the name of caste, religion, etc. The goddess of justice may be blind to technically "non-convicts" such as bandit kings of "Not-Guilty -Till-Hanged-by-the- Highest-Court" variety, people are not.

While there is every reason to revise the ceiling on poll expenditure by candidates and their parties, the right people to finance an election are obviously those who support the candidates or his party. There can be designated accounts in specified banks in all parts of the constituency where the supporters can deposit their contributions, subject to disclosing their full identity, proof of their status as an elector of the constituency and the last income tax return filed by them. Political parties can have the arrangements over an extended area subject to reasonable conditions and could operate such accounts throughout the year whereas the individual candidate's accounts ought to be opened on filing nominations and closed on declaration of results.

The recent trends towards the opening up of the economy have awakened a growing interest among the nonresident Indian community whose members seem to be exploring a greater role for themselves in the country's development. They have been clamouring for a provision for dual citizenship for them so that they could feel more involved and also get somelegal protection. If their demands are met to their satisfaction and the ten million odd community is given even a token representation in the parliament/ State legislatures, according to the noted economist Swaminathan S. Ankalesaria Atyar, a modest registration and annual renewal fee from them could fetch almost a billion U.S. dollars (or roughly Rs 3,600 crores) every year, apart from accelerating the FDIs. It would be much more than enough to meet the cost of elections, and in case of a fractured verdict of the electorate there would be no longer compulsion to carry on impossible political marriage of convenience in the states and the centre in spite of the forbidding costs in terms of loss of credibility, a debilitating lack of decision making and willingness to take responsibility.

Formidable as the crisis gripping our democracy may seem, such teething troubles are actually part of the growing up process. Fifty years in the history of an ageless India are perhaps equivalent to a fleeting moment in a man's life. With a greater involvement of the people in all facets of democracy in action and conscious efforts to improve the quality of our enormous human capital by inculcating the right attitudes and rational values through a sustained social campaign, democracy in India can be made more meaningful, In fact, having regard to the deep rooted values and customs diametrically opposed to all that is democratic, the real surprise is not the aberrations but the degree to which we are already a vibrant democracy. A casual look at our neighbour with a common history and shared value orientations will be enough to see the point.

3

Coalition Politics in India

India has had the experience of coalition governments in the States as well as at the Centre in recent times. As we analyse the coalitions in India we have to keep in mind the background of various experiments of coalitions in different parts of the world. While in countries like France, Italy and Japan there have been unstable coalition governments, Austria, Germany, Netherlands, Switzerland and Sweden have witnessed fairly stable coalitions. Thus, all coalition experiments have not displayed a uniform pattern.

By and large, both at the Centre and in all the States (except Kerala), from 1952 to 1967, India witnessed one dominant party rule of the Congress, with the non-Congress parties remaining in the opposition. In some States, the political picture in the parliamentary form of government was so unbalanced that the opposition parties were pushed almost to the fringe. This was the hangover of the political climate that emerged from the freedom struggle in which the Congress had occupied a pivotal position and had retained its broad political appeal.

There was however a gradual shift from the pattern of one dominant party rule. The growing political, social, economic and regional tensions gave rise to the emergence of different parties which wielded varying influences in States. In course of time an uneven political pattern was evolved. In those States where non-Congress parties mustered enough combined strength to have the working majority in State legislatures, coalition governments were formed in Punjab, Bihar, Uttar Pradesh, West Bengal, Kerala, Orissa and Madhya Pradesh. The year 1967 turned out to be a watershed in Indian politics, Riding on the crest of mounting non-Congressism, non-Congress coalitions in the form of Samyukta Vidhayak Dal governments were formed in several States. They had ideological heterogeneity. The exceptions were coalitions in West Bengal and Kerala. The coalition in West Bengal was an alliance of left parties whereas in Kerala there was a coalition government of Left and Democratic Front.

The Samyukta Vidhayak Dal coalitions in States collapsed in course of time, as a result of their inner contradictions in the realm of ideology and political orientations of the constituents. Because of relative ideological, political and programmatic homogeneity, the coalitions mainly of the left parties in West Bengal and of left and democratic forces in Kerala had a greater degree of stability and as such they could survive and revive.

The central government continued to be under the dominant Congress Party rule. Many political analysts had persistently pleaded that though the non-Congress coalition governments ruled in several States, it was not so easy to change the political scenario at the Centre. However, one single event that brought about a cataclysmic change in the political scenario at the Centre was the declaration of National Emergency in India in 1975 and detention of many political leaders and activists including Members of Parliament. Trough this action opposition to the amendments in the Constitution encroaching upon the citizens civil liberties, freedom of the press and of the judiciary was sought to be throttled. These repressive actions were a desperate response to the agitation against corruption symbolised by the JP movement in Bihar, Gujarat and elsewhere.

These anti-democratic actions initiated by Prime Minister Indira Gandhi caused an unprecedented anti-Congress wave against the Union Government. In the elections to the Lok Sabha held in March 1977, the Congress faced its worst rout. For the first time the Congress lost its power at the Centre giving room to the government of the Janata Party. The Janata Party was apparently a single party, but in reality it was a combination of the Socialist Party, Bharatiya Jan Sangh, Congress (O), BID and the group of dissident Congressmen led by Jagjivan Ram and H.N. Bahugwia. The Janata government, committed to a common progressive election manifesto 'Bread with Freedom' had caught the imagination of the people and had roused their hopes and aspirations. But temperamental incompatibility of some leaders and fierce inner controversy over the dual loyalty of the Jan Sangh activists to the Janata Party as well as the RSS wrecked the Janata Party and its government and paved the way for the break up of the Janata Party's government which in reality was a coalition government. The split up group of the Janata Party headed by Chaudhary Charan Singh formed an alternate government which proved to be still-born since Indira Gandhi who had lent support withdrew it on the day Charan Singh was to seek confidence vote for his coalition government in the Lok Sabha.

There are occasions when a particular issue becomes a focal point of public indignation and agitation. The corruption involved in the alleged payment of commission to secure the contract for guns by the Swedish Company Bofors was exposed in the press and Parliament. V.P. Singh played a crucial role in giving a sharp edge to the fight against this corruption issue and had to resign from the Cabinet headed by Rajiv Gandhi only to mount a fearless attack on corruption in high places.

In 1989 corruption became the central theme of the elections. It touched the innermost chord of the electorate. The government formed under the leadership of V.P. Singh became the symbol of struggle against corruption. In this coalition experiment, history repeated itself and dissidents from the Janata Dal led by Chandrashekhar formed a new government with the support of the Congress. Thus, the National Front's coalition government was destabilised only by the power motivations of dissidents in the Janata Dal. It is a classic example of how disparate elements like the Congress opposing the coalition government's decision to implement the Mandal Commission recommendations, the JP which with its pronounced communal stance wanted to settle its score on the issue of Mandir-Masjid controversy in Ayodhya raised to sidetrack the Mandal issue and Chandrashekhar who wanted to avenge the election of V.P. Singh as the leader of the Janata Dal in Parliament in the wake of his total opposition, had forged an unholy alliance to break up the coalition headed by V.P. Singh. These are the destabilising manipulations about which those who run and sustain the coalition government at the Centre must remain vigilant.

As a sequel to the communal frenzy released by the demolition of the Babri Masjid at Ayodhya by the BJP and its allies, a coalition government consisting of BJP, Shiv Sena and rebel Congressmen who won the elections and supported the BJP-Shiv Sena combination after their election, came into existence in Maharashtra.

Though the secular forces in Maharashtra secured higher percentage of votes than the BJP-Shiv Sena combine, the rebel Congressmen made the formation of BJP-Shiv Sena coalition in Maharashtra possible.

After the 1996 Lok Sabha poll, Atal Behari Vajpayee, the leader of the single largest party BJP, was invited by the President to form the government at the Centre, and was directed to seek vote of confidence in the Lok Sabha. Many were surprised as to how there was not a single defection from the 13 party United Front formed under the leadership of Deve Gowda to support the BJP government. It must be realised that the national as well as the regional parties that were the constituents of the 13 party United Front had a firm commitment to secularism, federalism, social justice and economic equity. The solidarity of the UF could not be destroyed. Vajpayee therefore did not press for a confidence vote and submitted his resignation to the Rashtrapati.

The UF had no working majority in the Lok Sabha. The choice before the Congress was between forces of secularism and of communalism. Opting for a secular government, Congress extended support to the United Front government headed by Deve Gowda who was unanimously chosen as the leader of the UF in Parliament by its constituents. Despite periodical threats to the stability and survival of the UF government, it has sustained its stability. By the political compulsions of secular politics, altogether a different pattern of coalition government at the Centre supported by CPI(M) and Congress from outside has evolved.

Alarmed by the experiment of coalitions which became inevitable in certain conditions, some political analysts attribute their failure to attain stability, to the Parliamentary system. They, suggest adoption of the Presidential system. In this context, it is well to remember that in the Parliamentary system there might be less stability but it offers more accountability, whereas in the Presidential system, there may be more stability but less of accountability. Let us not forget that the founding fathers of our Constitution, who trained !he constitution in the most unstable conditions of communal violence and bloodshed, in the post-partition period, did not give primacy to stability, but to accountability to make our democracy more meaningful.

Thus, what is needed is not the dismantling of the system of Parliamentary democracy, but introducing electoral reforms to lend more stability to the coalition governments in India. To reduce the gap between the votes polled by the parties and the seats secured by them, a German system based on a combination of the present electoral system as in India and a 'list system' putting premium on votes polled in favour of parties must be encouraged. The evil influence of muscle and money power on the elections must be curbed and a State funding to parties linked up with the percentage of votes secured by them in the previous election should be introduced to reduce the large multiplicity of parties responsible for division of votes and consequent instability. With such a State funding to parties based on the votes polled, small splinter parties with extremely low percentage of votes will have the tendency to merge in large parties which are closest to them ideologically.

Under such dispensation, the stability of coalitions in India can be ensured through appropriate electoral reforms. Of course, for such electoral reforms, what is needed the most is a strong political will.

The Cliche that India has acquired a new and distinguishing feature of coalition politics is only partially true.

In fact, coalitions began with the first general elections in 1952 itself in the then Madras Presidency, a broad non-Congress united front with T. Prakasam as the leader and undivided CPI as the main component won a majority in the Assembly elections. C. Rajagopalachari on the instruction of Pt. Nehru was sent to break up the united front and restore the Congress monopoly of power.

Non-Congress coalition governments were formed aft the 1967 general elections in Punjab, Uttar Pradesh, Bihar, West Bengal, Orissa, Tamilnadu and Kerala, with CPI and Jana Sangh coming together 'in Samyukta Vidhayak Dals or SVDs in many States. P.N. Haksar once caustically referred to these coalitions as Samyukta VD formations. These did not last long.

The Kerala experience was somewhat different. In 1957, the CPI led a non-Congress coalition government Chief Minister E.M.S. Namboodiripad, declared that though his party had won against the Congress, it would implement the Congress programme. The government was dismissed in 1959 but Congress itself could not keep power for long. Alternately, the Congress and the non-Congress parties won and lost elections. In 1969, however, a stable coalition government was formed with Congress-CPI alliance at the core. With C. Achutha Menon providing exceptional and exemplary leadership, this coalition lasted for two decades, carrying out radical agrarian socioeconomic transformations famous as "Kerala Model". Since then UDF and LDF coalitions have won and lost elections by thin margins but both have been guided by the 1969 Model. The Kerala Model has been somewhat narrowly interpreted as only appropriate for economic development in a relatively backward State. In reality, it shows the way for political stability and social advance for the country as a whole. The Congress programme is nothing but the programme of freedom struggle modified in the present altered circumstances. The essence of the Kerala Model and the experience is that the Congress programme has to be implemented by a coalition of parties in which the Congress is the main but not the exclusive force.

Kerala Model is needed by the whole of India because the Indian revolution proceeds even after the 1947 as a national revolution both requiring and reinforcing national unity, with obviously Congress as the central and chief force. But with the greater degree of differentiation in the country classwise, such unity cannot be contained within and by the Congress as it used to be during the freedom struggle. Other parties have to be included, and they have to include themselves in this unity to make it effective.

The long unbroken spell of the CPI(M)'s governance of West Bengal does not disprove the conclusion drawn above. Stability in West Bengal has come only after the CPI(M) gave up the attempted alternative model in that State. Ashok Mitra's exit meant an end to meaningless and costly experiments as also to the strategy of confrontation with the Centre. The Left Front is now implementing what the Congress had promised but failed to implement. Its relations with the Centre, whether Congress or non-Congress, have been those of cooperation. As Jyoti Basu put it, he is not the Prime Minister of the independent republic of West Bengal but the Chief Minister of the State of West Bengal within the Union of India.

West Bengal is not a model because of the obssessive, harmful and self-destructive anti-Congressism of the CPI (M) and its lack of respect for democratic norms. The all India Congress leadership has also made no efforts to draw the CPI(M) into dialogue on national issues.

The present coalition is the continuation of attempts to eliminate the Congress from the Centre. This has failed as was only to be expected. But the Congress response since 1978 to restore its governance at the Centre or to seek only those allies who are opposed to the anti-

Congress and non-Congress parties, too, has not succeeded.

The result is increase in political or, rather, state instability which the nation simply cannot afford. One has to attempt to give political shape to the dialectical unity of opposites. We cannot achieve stability, much less advance, without national unity and such unity cannot be achieved on an anti-Congress or non-Congress basis. Also, it cannot be achieved by the Congress alone. What is needed is not polarisation but reinforcement of unity and this not by anti-Congressism or non-Congressism. Polarisation is to be eschewed but not differentiation. India is not characterised by unity and diversity but by unity expressed in diversity. Each needs the other though the interaction is within the parameters of the nation.

What is needed is not any kind of coalition but a nation reinforcing coalition, whatever be the exact political form in which it is expressed.

With the United Front on the way out and the Congress on the way back, all nationalist leaders and thinkers, wherever they are positioned, have to reflect on all this and act appropriately.

The Fourth General Elections of February 1967 marked a turning, point in the Indian politics in so far as they greatly weakened the monolithic character of the Congress rule. While at the Centre the Congress Government was greatly weakened, in six out of the then seventeen states it had to make way for the coalition governments. Before we examine the nature of coalition politics in India it shall be desirable to understand its meaning.

The term coalition has been derived from the Latin word 'coalition' meaning to go or to grow together. Thus **interpreted** the term coalition means an act of coalescing or uniting into one body or alliance. It indicates the combination of a number of bodies or parts into one body or whole. In the political sense the term coalition is used for an alliance or temporary union between various political groups for the exercise or control of political power. Prof. Ogg defines coalitions in the *Encyclopedia of Social Sciences*, as "a cooperative arrangement under which distinct political parties, or at all events members of such parties unite to form a government or Ministry."[1] Generally such cooperative arrangement is made by the groups to make some gains and rewards of material and psychic nature under certain circumstances and they part company as soon as those circumstances cease to exist. While entering into coalition the partners are expected to give up their rigid stand and make compromises in the spirit of mutual give and take. The parties to the coalition however do not lose their identity and can withdraw from the coalition as and when they find it difficult to continue as partners. As a result of such a withdrawal the coalition may break up or some other group may the coalition or lend support to it. But if the member groups of a coalition decide to merge themselves and form a new party, it ceases to be a coalition. For example when in January 1973 Jan Sangh, Congress (0), Bharatiya Lok Dal and Socialists decided to merge themselves and form the Janata Party they lost their individual identity. This combination of the various political groups was not a coalition but a new political party.

Reasons for formation of coalitions

Generally the coalitions are formed on account of one of the following three reasons:

1. No single political party is able to secure a working majority in the popular house on account of the presence of multi-party system. Under the circumstances a number of like-minded political

parties form the coalition to provide a workable majority and run the government. France provides a typical example of this type of coalitions.

2. Secondly, in a bi-party system a deadlock may be created due of even balance between two political parties. This may lead 'to one of the two parties allying itself with a minor group such as neutrals or defectors to till the majority in its favour.

3. Thirdly, a coalition may be necessitated by a national crisis when the various political groups may suspend their political strife and collaborate in the general cause of protecting and promoting their national interests. In Britain coalition government was formed to deal with the abnormal conditions during the First World War. The various political parties sunk their differences to give a united fight to the enemies of Britain.

In India the coalition governments have mainly been the result of multi-party system. As sometimes no single political party was able to muster clear-cut majority in the Legislative Assembly the parties were obliged to seek support and cooperation of other groups to form the government. Sometimes coalitions are also formed before the elections and a number of political parties chalk out an agreed programme and contest elections on the basis of the programme from a common platform. This type of arrangement "has an obvious advantage in so far as it smoothens the radicalism the parties joining the coalition without in any way effecting the existing image.

Coalitions in the states

As already pointed out the coalition politics in the states made its beginning in a big way in the states only in the wake of the Fourth General Elections of 1967 when the Congress party, which had enjoyed monopoly of political power both at the centre as well as the states, was voted out of power in seven out of the seventeen states. Except in Tamil Nadu, where the DMK obtained a clear-cut majority, in the other six states no single political party was able to obtain a clear-cut majority. This compelled the various political parties to join hands to keep the Congress Government out of power. Thus started the experiment of coalition governments in a big way, which however did not last long. Soon partners of these coalition governments fell apart and brought about the decline of coalition governments, thereby contributing to the political instability in these states. A brief study of the coalition politics in various states at this states is called for.

Kerala

The history of coalition politics in Kerala started even before the Fourth General Elections. The first Coalition Ministry in Kerala was formed in 1960 as in the mid-term elections of 1960, no single party was able to get clear-cut majority. The Ministry was headed by Shri A. Thanu Pillai, who was subsequently replaced,, by R. Shankar. This experiment continued till 1964 when the ministry was voted out of power by the dissident group of Kerala Legislative Congress party. After a brief spell of President's Rule the state once again went to polls but no single party was able to secure a majority in the Legislature. In view of the bitter past experience of coalition government in the state, the Centre dissolved the newly elected legislature and placed the state under President's rule. This arrangement persisted till the state went to the polls in February 1967.

As a result of elections the United Front consisting of CPM, CPI, SSP, RSP, KTP and KPS won an overwhelming victor while the Congress was completely mauled.

Kerala legislative assembly:

On 5 March 1967 a coalition ministry with E.M.S. Namboodiri-pad, as Chief Minister, was formed. However, the ministry soon ran into difficulties due to its failure to fully implement the electoral promises, specially with regard to food and general administration. "The various partners of the coalition levelled charges of corruption against each other and pulled in different directions. The internal cleavage among the partners reached its climax when on 24 October 1969 the CPI members got a resolution passed from the State Assembly which called for a probe into the alleged charges of corruption against certain ministers. Thereupon the Chief Minister tendered resignation of his Ministry.

On I November a new Coalition Ministry under C. Achuta Menon (CPI) supported by CPI, SSP, RSP, the Kerala Congress and the Congress Party, was formed. However, with a view to sabotage the CPI-led coalition ministry, the CPM started fomenting violence and chaos in different parts of the state. They made bid to grab both private as well as government land. In the Assembly also they created noisy scenes during the address of the Governor. They even raised objection to the presence of Chief Minister Menon In the Assembly on the ground that he was a member of Rajya Sabha and heading a minority government. However, the Ministry was able to resist all these onslaughts and get the motion of thanks to the Governor's address adopted despite stiff opposition of the CPM and its allies. In the subsequent months the Marxist MLAs stepped up their unrully activities in the State Legislative Assembly, and succeeded in forcing a resignation from Achutha Menon. Thereupon the Governor dissolved the Assembly and placed the state under Presidential rule.

The state again went to the polls on 17 September 1970. In all twenty-one parties and groups, broadly organised into three fronts contested the election. These three fronts were (1) CPM and its allies viz. SSP, PSP and KTP; (2) CPI and its allies viz. RSP, the SP, the Muslim League and the Congress Party; (3) Congress (0) and its allies, viz., Kerala Congress, Jana Sangh, Swatanta Party, MK and ISP.

As a result of the elections the Congress (N) emerged as the largest single party with 32 seats. The position of the other parties as CPM 29; SSP 6; KIP 2; KSP 2; CPI 16; Muslim League 11; SP 6; PSP 3; Kerala Congress 12; ISP 3 and Independents 12. In October 1970 Achuta Menon formed a new nine-member Ministry king three Ministers from CPI, two from RSP, two from the Muslim ague and one from the PSP. The Congress agreed to support the Ministry from outside.

The term of the Kerala Assembly which expired in September 75 was extended by six months at a time thrice and the state went the polls in March 1977 along with the Lok Sabha.

In the new elections the experiment of coalition politics was carried further. In the contest the various political parties and groups divided themselves into two fronts (1) Ruling Front consisting of Congress, CPI, Kerala Congress, Muslim League, Revolutionary Socialist Party and Praja Socialist Party; and (2) Opposition Front consisting of CPM, Janata Party, Muslim League, Opposition Kerala Congress (0). The results indicated a victory for the ruling from which succeeded in capturing 111 seats. The position of the various political parties in the Assembly was as follows:

A coalition Ministry headed by K. Karunakaran (Congress) was formed but it barely survived three weeks because the Chief Minister tendered his resignation over the Rajan case. Thereafter

> the Front elected A.K. Anthony as the leader and be was duly sworn in as Chief Minister on 27 April 1977.

The state witnessed yet another elections in 1980 which resulted in a resounding Victory for the CPM and its allies, who captured over two thirds majority in the Assembly. The number of seats captured by the various parties was as follows : Congress (U) 21; CPM 35; CP1 17; Kerala (M) 8; RSP 6; AIML 5; Kerala Congress (P) I, Congress (1) 17; IUML 14; Kerala Congress (J) 6; NDP 3 ; PSO I; Janata Party 5; and Independents 1. A new Ministry headed by E.K. Nayanar was formed on 25 January 1980 which remained in office till December 1981 when a new coalition ministry was formed under Chief Ministership of K. Karunakaran. However, the Ministry could not stay in office and internal bickerings brought its downfall. As a result the state once again passed, under President's rule. In May 1982 the state wont to polls along with three other State Assemblies. As a result the Congress (1) led United Democratic Front was voted to power with 77 seats in a house with 140 members. The Left Democratic Front led by CPM could capture only 63 seats. The position of the components of the two Fronts was as follows: United Democratic Front : Congress (1) 20; Dissident Congress (S) 15; Indian Union Muslim League 4; Kerala Congress (Mani Group) 6; NDP 4; Congress (Joseph Group) 8; Dissident Janata 4; RSP 2; PSP I; Rebel RSP I; Independents 2. The Left Democratic Front parties secured seats as follows : CPM 26; CPI 12; Congress (S) 7; the RSP 4; All India Muslim League 4; Janata Party 4; Democratic Socialist Party I Kerala Congress (Socialists) I; and Pro-CPM Independents 4.

A United Democratic Front Ministry under K. Karunakaran was formed. The Ministry contained 4 representatives of Congress; 3 each from Congress (Antony), the Congress (Joseph) and Kerala Congress (Mani) and one each from Janata Party, Socialist,

Republican Party, Revolutionary Socialist Party (Shreekantan) and Praja Socialist Party (Shreekantan).

In the Assembly elections held in March 1987 the CPI led Left Democratic Front ousted Congress (1) led United Democratic Front from power in Kerala. It secured 76 of the 138 seats for which elections were held. On the other hand the Congress (1) led United Democratic Front could capture only 60 seats. Two seats were bagged by the independents. The position of the various political parties in the two fronts was as follows:

Communist Marxist Party and Independents secured one seat each. The Left Democratic Front elected E.K. Nayanar as their leader and he was conducted the oath of office as Chief Minister on 26 March 1987. Thus once again Kerala came to have a coalition government.

West Bengal

The coalition politics in West Bengal also started with the Fourth General Election. In the earlier years, specially after the second general elections the leftist parties started getting closer with a view to replace the Congress Government and formed United Front but they could not achieve much success. The emergence of Bangla Congress, a party of dissident Congressmen, under Ajoy Mukerjee in 1965 gave a further impetus to the efforts for unity among the leftist parties. It was hoped that coalition of these parties would overthrow the Congress government, but due to differences between the two wings of the Communist Party on the question of electoral adjustments completely dampened these hopes.

As a result of the general elections of 1967 the Congress lost majority in the West Bengal Legislative Assembly, while no other party or combination of parties was able to obtain clear cut majority. This shall be borne out by the strength of the various parties in the West Bengal Assembly.

Congress 127; Communist Party (M) 44; Revolutionary Socialist Party 6; Samyukta Socialist Party 7; Socialist Unity Centre 4; Workers Party 2 ; Forward Block (M) I; Bangla Congress 34'; Communist Party (R) 16 Forward Block 13; Praja Socialist Party 7; Lok Sevak Sangh 5 Jan Sangh I; Swatantra I Gorkha League, Independents and others 12.

In view of the above party position neither the Congress nor the Communists were able to form the government. But as all the parties were keen to see that Congress should not form the government they proceeded to form a United Front with a 18 point programme. Ajov Mukherjee was unanimously elected as the leader of the United Front and was sworn as Chief Minister on 2 March 1967. However this coalition experiment did not prove success and shortly differences cropped up among the partners of the United Front on the question of handling of industrial and agrarian disputes, food policies. The common programme announced by them earlier was put into cold storage. The Communists tried to capture all the key positions and started condemning the rightist constituents of the United Front. On the other hand Ajoy Mukherjee also started negotiations with the Central Congress leaders for forming a new Ministry with the support of Congress. The things took a serious turn on 2 November 1967 when Dr P.C. Ghosh, an independent minister tendered his resignation from the United Front Government and informed the Governor that he and seventeen other members of the Assembly had decided to withdraw their support from the United Front Ministry of Ajoy Mukerjee.

On 6 November the West Bengal Governor (Dharam Vira' wrote to Ajoy Mukerjee to convene a session of the Assembly as soon as possible to demonstrate the majority support to his ministry. Ajoy Mukerjee agreed to convene the meeting of the Assembly on 18 December 1967 but the Governor insisted on a session of the Assembly on 23 November which was turned down by the Chief Minister. Ultimately on 21 November 1967 the Governor enquired from the Chief Minister whether he would be willing to advance the date of Assembly's session by few days and when an evasive reply was sent to the Governor, he dismissed the Ajoy Mukerjee Government and appointed P.C. Ghosh as the Chief Minister. The dismissal of Mukerjee ministry was greeted with strong protests and violent demonstrations in the state. On the recommendations of new Chief Minister the meeting of the Assembly was convened on 29 November. However, the Speaker of the Assembly (Bijoy Kumar Banerjee) gave a ruling that the dismissal of Mukerjee's ministry was unconstitutional, and The convening of the session of Assembly by Dr. Ghosh was irregular. He therefore adjourned the Assembly *sine die* and left the Chamber. This was followed by scenes of confusion and uproar in the Assembly. Outside also violent demonstrations were organised against this decision. On the other hand the Legislative Council of West Bengal, with Congress majority, took the stand that Ghosh Ministry was lawfully constituted. In the Lok Sabha also Y.B. Chavan, the Union Home Minister, justified Governor Dharam Vira's action and asserted that Ghosh Ministry was lawfully constituted.

In view of the Union Government's stand on the issue of Ghosh Ministry, Ajoy Mukerjee threatened to launch a civil disobedience movement unless the Ghosh Ministry was removed and United Front Ministry was restored. As this demand was not complied with Ajoy Mukerjee launched a civil disobedience movement. The movement soon assumed serious dimensions and culminated in burning of buses, trams, attacks on police with bombs, destruction of private property. The government was forced to resort to large scale arrests in view of fast deteriorating law and order condition. In view of the serious situation in the state and on the insistence of Dr. Ghosh, the Congress Parliamentary Board permitted six of the Congress members to join as Ministers in the Ghosh Ministry. However, on the same day the Congress members led by Ashutosh Ghosh, withdrew their support from the Ministry on the ground that full justice had not been done to them in the formation of the Ministry. They proceeded to form the Indian National Democratic Front (INDF). The United Front immediately decided to extend support to the INDF and the leader of the INDF put up his claims to form the Ministry.

On 14 February when Governor Dharam Vira came to address the session of the Assembly the United Front members blocked the, door *of* the Assembly. However, the Governor was taken to the Assembly from the side-door. Thercupoon the UF members entered the house and occupied the Governor's Chair. The Governor was not permitted to read his address and forced to leave the house. In view of all these developments Governor Dharam, Vira was convinced that the state government could not be carried on in accordance with the Constitution and recommended the introduction of Presidential rule. As per recommendations *of* the Governor the state was placed under President's rule on 20 February 1968 and the State Assembly was dissolved.

In February 1969 midterm elections were held in West Bengal. These elections also failed to provide a clear-cut majority to any in I arty and the state had to continue with the experiment of coalition politics.

Though in the new Assembly the components of the United Front had a strength of 156, differences cropped up amongst its members on the question of leadership of the Government. Jyoti Basu, the leader of the largest constituent of the UF, wanted the leadership which was not acceptable to other constituents, Ultimately after prolonged negotiations it was decided that Ajoy Mukerjee shall be the Chief Minister and Joyti Basu shall be given the portfolio of Home Minister with charge of police department. The new government assumed office on 25 February 1969. However, soon bickerings started between Ajoy Mukerjee and Jyoti Basu due to failure of the latter to take action against CPM workers who were instigating the labourers to capture surplus land loot property. The Chief Minister protested against this attitude: by undertaking fast along with other workers against the high-handedness of the CPM workers. As the situation did not improve the Chief Minister ultimately tendered his resignation to the Governor on 16 March 1969 and the state was placed under Presidential rule. This marked the end of yet another experiment of coalition government in West Bengal.

The state went to polls in March 1971. Once again no single political party could muster clear cut majority in the Assembly. This is borne out by the position of the various parties in the Assembly which was as follows:

CPM 108; CPI 13; Forward Block 3; SSP 1, Jan Sangh 1; SUC 7; RCPI 3; Independents etc. 13; Congress 105; Congress (0) 2; PSP 3; Bangla Congress 3; RSP 3; Muslim League 7; Forward Block (M) 2; Vacant 6. Both the Congress Party and the CPM led United Left Front put up claims to the formation of Ministry, but the Governor refused to lift the Presidential rule unless he was convinced about the absolute mojority support to any coalition. After prolonged negotiations ultimately a Democratic Front under Ajoy Mukerjee was formed, and he was invited to form the Government. The Congress also agreed to join the ministry. But this coalition also did not survive for long. Due to differences within Bangla

Congress some members left the government rendering its strength at par with the opposition. In the meanwhile the Bangladesh crisis took place resulting in lakhs of refugees from East Pakistan entering West Bengal, greatly straining the administrative machinery. Fearing it would not be possible for him to run the government effectively Ajoy Mukerjee recommended to the Governor to dissolve the Assembly. The Governor obliged Ajoy Mukerjee and the state was placed under President's rule on 28 June 1971.

This state again went to polls in March 1972. This time the Congress Party was able to obtain absolute majority in the state Legislature, while the strength of the other parties was greatly reduced as shall be evident from the following:

A Congress Ministry headed by Sidarth Shankar Ray was formed which stayed in office for a full term of five years. After the lifting of the emergency the state once again went to the polls in June 1977. In these elections the Congress suffered a serious setback. However, the state was spared the uncertainty of a coalition government because the CPM was able to secure an absolute majority. The position of the various parties in the Assembly after the elections of 1977 was as follows: A CPM government was formed under Jyoti Basu, who continued to rule over the state even after the reemergence of the Congress(I) government at the Centre, because the Legislative Assembly of West Bengal was not dissolved and was permitted to continue.

In May 1982 with the end of the term of the Assembly fresh elections were held in West Bengal in which the Left Front secured 238 seats while the Congress (1) and its allies could capture only 56 seats. The BJP and Lok Dal which fought elections on their own without seeking the support of either the Left Front or the Congress (1) were totally eliminated. The Party position in the Assembly was Congress (1) 49; CPM 174; CPI 7; RSP 19; FBL 28; Independents and others 17. In view of the majority of Left Front a ministry under Jyoti Basu was installed in office on 26 May, 1982.

In the elections held in March 1987 the CPI (M) led Left Front once again returned to power by capturing 242 of the 294 seats. The various components of the CPI (M) led Left front secured seats as follows: CPI (M) 187; Forward Bloc 26; RSP 18 and CPI: 11. On the other hand the Congress (1) secured only 40 seats, while other parties secured 9 seats. Left Front once again elected Jyoti Basu as its leader and formed government for third consecutive term.

Punjab

The coalition politics in Punjab also made its appearance with, the Fourth General Election of 1967. Till then the Congress was at the helm of affairs. Even after the general elections of 1967 the Congress emerged as the largest single party with 47 seats in a house of 104, but the opposition parties joined hand and formed a coalition government under the leadership of Gurnam Singh. The main partners in this coalition were Akali Dal (Master Tara Singh Group) 2; Akali Dal (Sant Group) 24; Communists (M) 3: Communists (R) 5; the Jan Sangh 9; Republican Party 3; SSP I and Independents 6; and they succeeded in mustering a strength of 53 members. On the other hand 48 Congress and 3 independent members formed the opposition.

This experiment of a United Front Government coalition did not prove a success because soon cracks began to appear. This was, quite natural in view of the fact that the partners of the United Front Government were drawn from political parties believing in opposite ideologies. Soon certain Akali members defected and extended support to the Congress Party to vote out Gurnam Singh Ministry. The break-away group of the Akalis formed a new party known as Punjab Janata Party and elected Lachman Singh Gill as their leader. The Congress decided to extend support to the government of Gill and accordingly he was sworn in as Chief Minister of Punjab. But soon the members of the Congress got divided on the issue of extending support to Gill Ministry. A sizeable section of the Congress members held the view that the Congress should try to form its own government and pleaded forwithdrawal of support to Gill Ministry. Ultimately on 21 August 1968 the Congress Party decided to withdraw support from the Gill Ministry and obliged him to tender his resignation. Thereafter the-state was placed under Presidential rule.

Mid-term elections were held in February 1969 in Punjab, As a result of these elections Akali Dal (Sant Group) emerged as the largest party in the Assembly. The Partywise position in the Assembly was as follows:

On 17 February 1969 the Akalis with the support of Jan Sangh formed the government under the Chief Ministership of Gurnam Singh. Subsequently some of the Congress and independent members of Legislative Assembly also defected to the ruling party. However, this ministry could not remain in office for long due to differences in the ranks of the Akali Party. The Akali Leadership decided to remove Gurnam. Singh from leadership of the party and elected Parkash Singh Badal as the new leader. Thereupon Gurnam Singh tendered his resignation and Parkash Singh Badal succeeded as Chief Minister. For a while differences in the ranks of the Akali Dal members were patched up and Badal Ministry continued to work smoothly. However, in November 1970 sixteen MLAs decided to withdraw their support from the Badal Government on the issue of the size of the

Ministry. As a result Badal Government was rendered in minority. Ultimately on 13 June 1971 Badal tendered his resignation. Finding it difficult to install a stable government in the state, Governor Pavate recommended that the state be placed under President's rule.

The state went to the polls in March 1972. As a result of these polls the Congress Party was returned to power in absolute majority. The position of the various political parties in the As sembly after the election of 1972 was as follows:

A Congress Government under Giani Zail Singh was formed. With this ended the era of coalition politics in the state. The Congress Ministry remained in power till the next elections in June 1977.

On the eve of elections of June 1977 the various political parties entered into electoral alliances. On the one band the Akalis, Janata and the CPM concluded poll alliance. On the other hand the CPI and the Congress reached an understanding and collaborated with each other.

As a result of 1977 elections the Akali Dal was able to secure an absolute majority in the state Legislative Assembly. The position of the various political parties in the Assembly was:

> Though the Akali Dal could form government by itself, it decided to make the Janata Party its coalition partner. This decision 'was taken in view of the fact that the Akali Dal had agreed to extend full support to the Janata Government at the Centre. A Ministry was formed under the Chief Ministership of Parkarsh Singh Badal.

However, the ministry could not complete its full term of five years because the Congress (1) on return to power at Centre in January 1980 sought the dissolution of Punjab Legislative Assembly. As a result of the fresh elections the Congress (I) succeeded in capturing 63 seats in a house of 117 and formed a government under Darbara Singh. The position of the various political parties in the Punjab Assembly after the elections of 1980 was as follows:

> This marked an end to the coalition politics in Punjab, in view of the law and order situation because of Akali agitation Punjab was put under President's Rule in October 1983.

Punjab next went to the polls in September 1985. The Akalis secured 73 out of 117 Vidhan Sabha seats and their leader Surjit Singh Barnala was sworn in as the Chief Minister on 29 September 1985. In These elections the Congress could capture barely 32 seats. However, the Akali Dal government despite its overwhelming majority could not stay in office for full term because 27 of its members left the party and reduced it into a minority government. But as Congress (1), BJP, CPI and CPI (M) with a combined strength, of 38 members, pledged their support to Surjit Singh Barnala Government, it continued in office. In view of the fast deteriorating law and order condition in the state the state was placed under President's rule on 11 May 1987.

Bihar

In Bihar also the coalition politics made its beginning after-the fourth general elections. As a result of elections of 1967 the Congress secured 128 seats in a House of 318 and naturally refused to form the ministry. As a result Mahamaya Parsad Singh formed government with the support of non-Congress parties. But this, experiment did not last long because B.P. Mandal, a socialist member tendered resignation from the government and formed his own party Soshit Dal. The Congress Party extended him full support. On 25 January 1968 the Mahamaya Parsad Singh Government was defeated in the house and Mandal formed the new government on 1 February 1968. This government survived barely fortyseven days and was defeated in a vote of no confidence on 18 March 1968.

After the resignation of Mandal, Bhola Paswan Shastri formed the government with the support of Binodanand Jha. Subsequently even the Jan Sangh and leftwing parties joined the Shastri Government. However, soon the new government was also confronted with cleavage within its ranks. The trouble started because 18 of the 20 MLAs belonging to The BKD led by Kamakhya Narayan Singh resigned from the party because Bhola Paswan Shastri was not willing to make Mr. Singh the Deputy Chief Minister. Fearing that Mr. Singh may cross the floor and bring forth a no-confidence motion against his government Bhola Paswan Shastri recommended to the Governor the dissolution of the Assembly. After trying to form a government under Mahesh Prasad Singh, the leader of the Congress Legislative Party, the Governor ultimately recommended the dissolution of the State Legislative Assembly and placing of state under Presidential rule.

Midterm elections were held in Bihar on 9 February 1969. As a result no single political party could obtain a clear cut majority. The position of the various parties in the Assembly was as the follows:

As no political party was able to secure a clear cut majority in the Assembly a coalition government was the only solution.' Hari Har Singh, the leader of the Congress Legislative Party, was able to win the support of BKD, Soshit Dal, Hul Jharkhand, the Janata Party, Swatantra Party and six of the independent members and formed the ministry on 26 February 1969. However, the government was not able to give a good account of itself due to internal bickerings of the members belonging to various groups. On 20 June 1969 Hari Har Singh Ministry was defeated on the budget and tendered its resignation.

Thereupon Bhola Paswan Shastri formed ministry with BKD, and Jharkhand Party. Even SSP, PSP, Jan Sangh and the CPI promised to support his government from outside. Subsequently the Jan Sangh group withdrew its" support from the government obliging Shastri to tender his resignation. Finding an alternative government non-feasible the Government recommended Presidential Rule for the state. The Assembly was suspended in the hope that a stable government may be possible through realignment of political forces in the state without holding fresh midterm elections.

In the wake of split in Congress in October-November 1969, Daroga Prasad Rai was elected as the leader of Bihar Congress (1) Legislative Party. Rai soon reached an agreement on a 35-point common programme with CPI, BSP, BKD, Soshit Dal and Jharkhand Party and was able to secure the support of 173 MLAs in a house of 316. On 16 February 1970 the Governor invited Daroga Prasad Rai to form the Ministry. However, the Ministry soon ran into trouble because certain members of Lok Tantrik Congress group led by Bhola Paswan Shastri, were not willing to support the government. Similarly seven of the seventeen PSP members openly declared to vote against the government on 24 June. BKD and Jharkhand Parties were soar over the allotment of portfolios to their members. Even within the ranks of the Congress members serious dissenssions developed and they launched a campaign demanding replacement of Rai by a new leader. Encouraged by the dissensions within the correspondents of the Rai Ministry, the four opposition parties Congress (0), the SSP, the Jan Sangh and Swatanta Party brought forth a no-confidence against the Rai Ministry and defeated the Ministry on 18 December 1970. This entailed resignation of Rai Ministry. Four days later Karpoori Thakur, leader of SVD was invited to form the Government on the basis of his claim that he enjoyed the support of 171 MLAs. However he could stay in office for less than six months, only on account of the constant threat posed by those whom he could not accommodate in the ministry.

Following resignation by Karpoori Thakur, another coalition government was formed by Bhola Paswan Shastri, the leader of Progressive Legislative Front consisting of Congress, the CPI, the PSP, the BKD and Jharkhand and Hul Jharkhand parties: But again the partners of the coalition fell apart and on 27 December, 1971 Shastri was forced to submit his resignation. Two days later the Bihar Assembly was dissolved and the state was placed under Presidential rule.

General elections were held in Bihar in March 1972, result of these elections the Congress (I) won a clearcut majority and formed the government. The position of the various parties the State Legislative was as follows:

> The congress (1) formed government under the leadership of F Kedar Pandey. This put an end to the coalition politics which had plagued the state of Bihar since the fourth general election. No doubt, there were a number of changes in the leadership of the Congress Party but the same party continued to rule the state.

In the elections of 1977 the Janata Party replaced Congress by obtaining a dominant position in the state Legislative. The position of the various parties in the State Assembly after the elections of 1977 was as follows:

> In the elections of 1980 the Congress (1) again succeeded in capturing an overwhelming majority in the state and formed the government. The position of the various political parties in the Bihar Assembly after the elections of 1980 was as follows:

Subsequently Congress consolidated its position by admitting, 20 over members. These included independent members as well as electors from other parties.

In the elections held in March 1985 the Congress (1)

further improved its position and captured 192 seats. On the other hand DMK which bagged 33 seats in 1980 captured 41 seats. The BJP which ad 23 seats in 1980 could manage to capture only 14 seats. Jana. Party captured 11 seats while CPI and CPM managed to get 12 sets and one seat respectively in the 1985 elections. Bindeshwarl Dub(was elected as leader of the Congress (1) and was sworn in as. the Cief Minister. Thus once again the state of Bihar came to have singhparty rule and the era of coalition politics came to an end.

Orissa

Coalition politics in Orissa also had its beginning with the Fourt General Elections of 1967. As a result of the elections of 1967 ie Swatantra Party and the Janata Congress, which fought electios as allies, managed to capture 75 seats in a house of 140. The psition of the various parties in the Orissa Assembly was as follow.

After the election a ministry was formed under the leadership of Swtantra Party leader R.N. Singh Deo wtih the support of Janataongress. For some time the two parties worked with perfect, undersinding and faithfully carried out the agreed policies and progranmes. Even the split in the Congress did not effect the coalition gvernment. The first cracks in the coalition appeared in Januar 1971 when the Janata Congress decided to withdraw its suppor from the government on the ground that the Swatantra membcs were indulging in corruption. Realising that it would not be posible to continue in office Singh Deo tendered his resignation on 9 Inuary 1971. After making a bid to form an alternative Minister the Governor recommended President's rule for the state.

First elections to the Orissa Assembly were held on 5 March, 1971 bit no single political party was able to get a clearcut majority in tte house. The position of the various political parties in the Assemby was as follows:

> In the absence of a clearcut majority for any single party a t of horsetrading followed for the formation of government. Itimately an alliance consisting of Swatantra Party, Utkal Conress, Jharkhand Party and three independent members was formed. he alliance elected Biswanath Das, an independent as their leader. He was sworn in on 3 April 1971. However, following withdrawal of support by the Utkal Congress Das Ministry fell. Thereupon Congress (I) and Utkal Congress collaborated and Mrs. Nandini Satapatbi was installed as Chief Minister of Orissa. Subsequently the Utkal Congress Party adopted a resolution merging itself with the Congress. But this unity was shortlived. Soon defections within the ranks of the Utkal Congress members started and ulti mately culminated in the resignation of Nandini Sathpathi on 28 was placed under Central February 1973. Thereupon the state was placed under Central rule.

In the midterm polls held in February,Congress (1) captured 69 out of the 146 seats. The position of the other parties was : CPI 7 CPM 3; Utkal Congress 35; Swatantra Party 21; Socialist Party 1; Jana Congress I; Independents 9. With the support of the CPI the Congress succeeded in forming a ministry under Mrs.Nandini Sathpathi on 6 March 1974. It may be observed that the CPI did not join the government and merely continued to extend support to the Congress Government. In this sense it was not a coalition government.

In the elections to the state Assembly held in 1978 the Janata Party swept the polls and captured 116 out of the 147 seats. The position of the other parties was Congress 7; Congress (1) 19 ; CPII; CMP 1; Independents 3. As the Janata Party had an absolute majority in the state assembly there was no question of formation of a coalition government. Thus the state got rid of the coalition politics.

In the elections of 1980 once again the Congress (1) staged a comeback and captured absolute majority in the Orissa Legislative Assembly. The position of the various political parties in the Assembly was Congress

(1) 117; Lok Dal 13; CPI 4; Janata 3; Congress 2; Independents 7.

In the elections to state Assembly held in March 1985, the Congress (1) once again swept the polls and captured 117 of the 145 seats. Janata Party with 19 seats emerged the second party in the state Assembly. Bhartiya Janata Party and CPI captured one 1 seat each, while seven seats were bagged by independents and other", parties.

Haryana

The state of Haryana, which came into existence on I November 1966 as a result of linguistic reorgnization of the state of Punjab, witnessed defections and coalition politics from the very beginning. Soon after the formation of the state Bhagwat Dayal Sharma was unanimously elected as the leader of the Congress Legislature Party and became the first Chief Minister of the State. But soon factional differences cropped up among the members of' Congress Party over the selection of candidates for the forthcoming elections. Despite these factional differences the Congress managed to get a clear cut majority in the Assembly in the elections of February 1967. The position of the various political parties in the Haryana Assembly was as follows : Congress 48 ; Jan Sangh 12 ; Swatantra Party 3 ; Republican Party 2 ; Independents 16. As the Congress Party had a clearcut majority in the Assembly its leader Bhagwat Dayal Sharma was appointed Chief Minister on 10 March 1967. However, soon the Congress Party was divided on the question of formation of the Ministry. The opponents of Sharma joined bands with the opposition parties to defeat the official candidate for speakership of the Assembly. The dissident members formed a new party known as Haryana Congress and elected Rao Birendra Singh as their leader. The opposition parties decided to collaborate with the dissident Congressmen and formed United Front. Following resignation by Bhagwat Dayal Sharma, the Governor' invited Rao Birendra Singh to form the ministry. Thus the first United Front Ministry was sworn in office on 24 March 1967.

Rao Birendra Singh Ministry could not stay in office for long because soon differences cropped up between the Chief Minister and Congress leader Devi Lal on the question of growing influence of Jan Sangh. Devi Lal also charged Rao Government of being corrupt. He even stated his claims to form the ministry. On the other hand Rao Birender Singh started the game of securing support of more members by offering them ministerial berths. As a result there were frequent floor crossings by the members. Ultimately on 17 November 1967 following announcement by Devi Lal that he had decided to dissolve his party and merge it with the Congress, the strength of Congress greatly increased. With one Jan Sangh member defecting to Congress on November 1967 the government was rendered in minority. As a result the Governor dismissed Rao ministry on 21 November 1967 and placed the state under Presidential rule.

The state had mid-term polls in May 1968. The position of the various parties as a result of these elections was as follows : Congress, 48 ; Visbal Haryana Party 13; Jan Sangh 7; Swatantra Party 2; Republican Party 1; Bharatiya Kranti Dal 1; Independents 9. As the Congress bad an absolute majority in the Assembly its leader Bansi Lal was sworn in as Chief Minister. On the other hand the opposition parties formed a single United Front and elected Rao Birendra Singh as their leader. Once again the game of defections stared. On 9 September 1968 six opposition MLAS defected to the Government, thus further increasing the support of Bansi Lal Government. But three years later 15 Congress

MLA& led by Bhagwat Dayal Sharma left the ruling party and joined the United Front. In view of the increased strength, the United Front demanded removal of Bansi Lal and put forward their claims to form an alternative ministry. But during the next few days seven of the Congress members who had defected to the United Front rejoined the government. As result of these defections and counter defections the functioning of the Assembly became difficult. Ultimately on the recommendation of the Chief Minister the Governor dissolved tile Assembly on 21 January 1972.

Three months later when elections were held to the Assembly the Congress secured an absolute majority. The party position in the Assembly after the elections of 1972 was as follows : Congress 52; Congress (0) 6; Jan Sangh 2; Visbal Haryana Party 3; Progressive Independents 11; and Independents 7. With the absolute majority at its command the Congress formed ministry under Bansi Lal. During the next few years the state experienced a strong Congress government. Subsequently when some resentment appeared against Bansi Lal, he was provided a berth in the central Cabinet. Even rafter his induction in the Central Government Bansi Lal continued to have a strong hold on state politics and the state continued to have a stable ministry.

In the elections of 1977 the Congress suffered a complete route in the Haryana Assembly and the Janata Party captured 78 out of 90 seats. The position of the other political parties in the Assembly was as follows : Congress (1) 3 ; Congress 1 ; Vishal Haryana Party 57; Independents 2.

With an overwhelming majority at its disposal, the Janata Partv formed government in the state. Despite internal bickerings amongst the various components of the Janata Party the state did not have any coalition government. After the general elections to Lok Sabha in 1980 which resulted in an overwhelming victory for the Congress (1) Bhajan Lal, the Janata Chief Minister, defected to Abe Congress (1) along with a large number of his supporters. As a result the Janata Government was covered into Congress (1) Government and Bhajan Lal was permitted to continue as Chief Minister. Even after this change the government continued to be a Single party government.

In May 1982 the term of the Assembly expired and fresh, elections were held. In the elections none of the political parties was able to get clearcut majority. The position of the various political parties in the Assembly was as follows : Congress (1) 36 : Lok Dal 31; BJP 6; JNP 1. Independents and others 12. Both the Congress (1) and Lok Dal BJP combination put forward their claims to form the governments. But ultimately Governor invited Congress (1) leader Bhajan Lal to form the government. He was able to secure the support of some independent members and also effects some defectors from Lok Dal and Congress (J). The opposition parties raised a lot of hey and cry against the decision of the Governor but could not get the decision reversed, and the, Congress (1) Government continued to rule over the state till June 1987.

In the elections to the State Assembly held on 17 June 1987, the Lok Dal (Bahuguna group) and its electoral ally, the Bhartiya 'Janata Party, made a clean sweep and captured 58 and 15 seats respectively. The Congress (1) could captured only five seats. While CPI and CPM secured one seat each, the independents managed to capture six seats. Devi Lal was unanimously elected as leader of Lok Dal (B) Legislative Party and sworn in as Chief Minister. Although he could form a government of Lok Dal (B) by himself he also included certain ministers of BJP in his ministry. Thus his government can very well be described as a coalition government.

Madhya Pradesh

The state of Madhya Pradesh experienced coalition politic only for a short duration after the fourth general elections. As well as result of the Fourth General Election the Congress was able to secure 167 seats in a house of 296. The position of the political parties was as follows : Jan Sangh 78; Swatantra Party 7; CPIM and SSP 10 ; FSP 9 ; Others and Independents 24. As the leader of majority party in the State Legislature D.P. Misra was appointed as Chief Minister. On the other band the opposition parties formed a United Front and started making efforts to topple the Misra Government. Within the ranks of the Congress Party differences cropped up and charges were levelled against the Chief Minister for promoting casteism and running the state administration in a dictatorial manner. The things assumed serious nature when 30 Congress MLAs defected to the United Front and voted against the government. Following resignation by D.P. Misra as Chief Minister on 29 July 1967, the Governor invited Govind Narain.' Singh, the leader of the United Front to form the Ministry. Thus the state came to have a first coalition ministry on 30 July 1967, its chief constituents being Jan Sangh, SSP, PSP, BKD, Kranti Kair Dal, and Congress defectors.

The coalition government of Govind Narain Singh could not remain united for long and soon dissensions began to appear, amongst its partners. On 22 April 1968 two SSP members of the government tendered their resignation as a protest against the failure of the government to abolish land revenue. Similarly seven Jan Sangh Ministers and one Deputy Minister resigned from the ministry to take part in the agitation against the award on Kutch which went against India. However these members subsequently joined the Govind Narain Ministry and it continued to work till I I March 1969 when the Chief Minister was forced to tender his resignation due to dissensions in the ranks of the United Front.

Govind Narain's Government was followed by Congress ministry under Shyam Charan Shukla, who had succeeded D.P. Mishra as leader of Congress Legislature Party. Subsequently he was replaced by P.C. Sethi as Chief Minister.

In the wake of elections of March 1972 the Congress Party once again secured absolute majority in the Assembly and a stable Congress Ministry was formed under P.C. Sethi. The position of the various political parties in the Assembly was as follows : Congress 217; CPI 5; Jan Sangh 46; Socialists 7; Independents 19.

In the elections of 1977 the state of Madhya Pradesh winessed the emergence of Janata Party with an overwhelming majority and it provided a single party government to the state. The position of the various political parties in the Assembly after the 1977 elections was as follows : Congress (1) 59; Janata 229; Congress 21; Independents 10. The Janata Government could not survive for due to internal bickerings among the various components. After the resounding victory of Congress (1) in the Lok Sabha elections of January 1980 the Congress (1) government sought dissolution of the Madhya Pradesh Assembly. Fresh elections were held in May 1980 which resulted in resounding victory for Congress (I). The position of the various political parties in the Assembly was as follows : Congress (1) 246; BJP 60; Janata 2; CPI 2; Lok 'Dal I; Republican I; Independents 8. Thus once again the state of Madhya Pradesh came to have a stable Congress government.

In the Assembly elections held in March 1985 Congress (1) once again secured absolute majority and captured 250 of the 320 seats. The Bharatiya Janata Party emerged as the second largest party with 58 seats. Janata captured five seats and Congress (S) only one seat. The remaining six seats were claimed by S.S.P. Thus Congress is fully entrenched in the state.

Uttar Pradesh

The state of Uttar Pradesh also had a bit of experience of coalition government. After the Fourth General Election though the Congress emerged as the largest party, it failed to get ark absolute majority. On the other hand the opposition Parties to captured majority of the seats. They elected Ram Chandra Vikal, enformed a United Front and independent as their leader. The Congress, however managed to form the government under C. 13. Gupta with the support of 17 independent and four other MLAs who defected to Congress. But soon dissensions appeared in the ranks of Congress and Charan Singh along with sixteen of his followers defected to the opposition side. He formed his own party known as Jana Congress. Soon four other MLAs also joined this party. At the time of voting on the motion of thanks to the Governor's address Jana Congress voted with the opposition there by defeating the government. As a result C.B. Gupta tendered his resignation.

The United Front thereupon elected Charan Singh as the new leader and he was sworn in as Chief Minister on 3 April 1967. However, the new United Front Government also could not work smoothly and soon dissension July 1967 five MLAs of tons appeared within its ranks* On 17 be UF tendered their resignation and formed Progressive legislature Party to force the government to, pursue policies which were beneficial to the working classes. Similarly four MLAs belonging to

Swatantra Party also withdrew from the government in June 1967. This encouraged Congress to propose a motion of no-confidence against the UF Government but the same could not be carried. The fortunes of the UF Ministry kept on fluctuating for some time due to resignation of SSP and CPI members on different issues. Some components of the UF Ministry criticised the Chief Minister for his failure to implement the Common programme. In view of this criticism ultimately Charan Singh tendered his resignation on 17 February 1968. As the United Front failed to elect an alternative leader, acceptable to all components the Congress leader C.B. Gupta put forward his claims to form the government. Thereupon the United Front elected Harish Chandra Singh as its leader and he also put forward claims to form the government. Under the circumstances the Governor recommended dissolution of the Assembly. In the face of protest, from the SVD the state was placed under Presidential rule.

Fresh elections were held in the state on 9 February 1969 and the Congress secured majority in the Assembly. The position of the various political parties in the state was as follows: Congress 211; BKD 99; Jan Sangh 49: SSP 33; Swatantra 5; CPI 4: PSP 3; Republican Party 1; CPI Marxrist and; Kisan Mazdoor Party 1; Independents and others 1 four inpendent MLAs joined the Congress after elections which further strengthened the position of Congress. C.B. Gupta, the leader of Congress formed Ministry on 26 February 1969.

Following split in the Congress, a section of Congress member& led hands with Karnlapati Tripathi left the ministry and joined leader Charan Singh with a view to provide popular alterative government in the state. But soon differences cropped up between the two groups because Charan Singh insisted on heading Coalition government, which Congress (1) was notwilling-to kept. Taking advantage of these differences C.B. Gupta initiated with Charan Singh. After these talks he submitted his resign-a-on and requested the Governor to invite Charan Singh to form government. The SSP and the Jan Sangh which had in the can while moved closer to C.B. Gupta also assured their support Charan Singh Ministry. But the proposed alliance between the KD, the Organisation Congress, the SSP and Jan Sangh could note forged because Charan Singh refused to accept the economic programme worked out by the Organisational Congress, the SSP and Jan Sangh. Thereupon he entered into negotiations with congress (N) leader Kamlapati Tripathi. Ultimately Charan Singh as invited by the Governor to form the Ministry and assumed office as Chief Minister on 17 February 1970. The opposition parties strongly protested against this decision of the Governor and brought a censure motion against Charan Singh Ministry. However, the same was defeated. But soon differences cropped up between BKD and Congress on the issue of nationalisation of privately owned sugar mills in the state and merger of BKD with Congress. In view of differences with Congress Charan Singh even started a king moves to reach an understanding with Jan Sangh, SSP, and Swatantra to seek their association with the Ministry. The differences between BKD and Congress reached a breaking point hen BKD voted against the abolition of privileges and privy rises of the Princes in the Parliament. Kamlapati Tripathi made open that it was not possible to support Charan Singh Government any more and insisted on an early session of the Assembly to thrash out important policy matters. The situation reached a breaking point with the Chief Minister asking thirteen out of 26 Congress Ministers to resign from the Ministry. When these ministers refused to oblige him he recommended to the Governments to dismiss them. Thereupon Congress immediately withdrew its 'support to Charan Singh Government and demanded dismissal of his ministry on the ground that it bad lost majority. But the leaders of Organizational Congress, SSP, Jan Sangh and Swatantra Party decided to extend support to Charan Singh Ministry. However, the Governor acting on the advice of Attorney General of India asked Charan Singh to tender his resignation. Despite strong protests by Charan Singh the Governor recommended to the President to suspend the Assembly and introduce Presidential rule in the state.

On I October 1970, the Organization Congress, Jan Sangh, and Swatantra Party agreed to form United Legislative Party (Samyukta Vidhayak Dal). Four days later the BKD also joined them. The SVD thus came to have support of 242 members in a house of 425 members on 10 October 1970 the SVD elected T.N. Singh as its leader and requested the Governor to invite him to form the Ministry. On 17 October the Governor invited T.N. Singh to form the Ministry. Thus the President's rule was terminated after fifteen days. As T.N. Singh was not a member of the State Assembly he sought elections from Maniram constituency on 5 January 1971 but he was defeated by the Congress candidate. However, T.N. Singh did not immediately relinquish his office and continued as Chief Minister till 30 March 1971, when the opposition succeeded in carrying out amendment to the official motion of thanks, to the Governor. Thereupon the Chief Minister tendered his resignation.

On 4 April a Congress Ministry under Kamlapati Tripathi was sworn in. However, due to infighting among its members the Congress Ministry could not provide an effective administration to the state. Ultimately on 12 June 1973 Chief Minister Tripathi tendered his resignation. On 12 June 1973 the Governor recommended Presidential rule for the state. The recommendation was forthwith accepted and on 13 June

1971 the President's rule was introduced in Uttar Pradesh. The Assembly was put in suspended animation. On 27 October 1971 Kamlapati Tripathi sought revocate on of Presidential rule in the state. Despite protests from the opposition parties a Congress Ministry under Chief Ministership of H.N. Bahuguna was installed on 6 November 1971.

The state went to polls in February 1974 and the Congress succeeded in securing an absolute majority in the Assembly. The position of various parties in the Assembly was as follows: Congress 215; Organization Congress 10; BKD 106; Socialist Party 5; CPI 16; CPM 2; Muslim League 1; Swatantra 1; Others 2; Independents 5. Congress elected Mr. H.N. Bahuguna as its leader, who formed the ministry with the constructive support offerect by the CPI from outside.

After Bahuguna Congress Ministry under Narain Dutt Tewari continued to function till it was replaced by the Janata Government in June 1977. In the election of 1977 Congress was able to capture only 46 seats, while the Janata Party captured 350 seats. The position of the other parties was as follows: CPI 9; CPM 1; Independents sixteen. Despite internal bickerings amongst the partners of the Janata Government the state continued to have a single party rule and was spared coalition rule.

After the resounding victory of Congress (1) in the Lok Sabha elections of January 1980, it got the Uttar Pradesh Assembly dissolved before the expiry of its normal term and held fresh elections in June 1980. As a result of these elections the Congress (1) captured 306 seats in a house of 425 members. The position of the other political parties was as follows : Lok Dal 59; BJP 11; CPI 7; Janata 4; Janata (S) 4; Independents 17. In view of the absolute majority Congress government was formed and the state enjoyed a single-party government.

In the Assembly elections held in March 1985 the Congress (I) once again secured absolute majority by capturing 266 seats. The DMK Party which was formed on the eve of the election secured 86 seats. The Bharatiya Janata Party managed to capture 16 seats while the Janata Party bagged 19 seats, CPI and CPM captured six and three seats respectively. The independents and other political parties captured 26 seats.

Rajasthan

The state of Rajasthan was also saved the experience of coalition governments despite the fact that after the general election of 1967 no single political party was able to get a clearcut majority in the state Legislature. This shall be clear from the number of seats captured by the various political parties in the state Assembly viz., Congress 89; Swatantra 49; Jan Sangh 23; SSP 8; Communists 1; and Independents 15. The failure of the Congress to get clearcut majority in the state Assembly encouraged the opposition parties like Swatantra, Jan Sangh, Janata Party to form an alliance to stake their claims for forming ministry in the State. However, the Governor refused to invite them. He considered the front or alliance as a combination of persons who had joined hands to acquire power without any ideological base. The Governor on the other hand decided to invite the Congress leader Mohan Lal Sukhadia to form the ministry on the plea that he was the leader of the largest group in the Assembly. This action of Governor was strongly presented by the opposition parties and there were violent protests. In view of violence Sukhadia declined to form the government and on 12 March 1967 the Assembly was suspended and the state placed under Presidential rule.

After weighting the claims of the Congress as well as opposition the Governor ultimately decided to invite

Sukhadia to form the Ministry on 28 April 1967. The Congress Ministry continued to work thereafter first under Mohanlal Sukhadia and then under Barkat Ullah Khan. Thus as a result of the role of the Governor the state of Rajasthan escaped the experience of a coalition government despite the fact that no single political party enjoyed absolute 77, 1 majority in the Assembly.

After the elections of 1971 the position of Congress party was full tiller strengthened in the state Assembly. It succeeded in capturing 144 of the 184 seats. On the other hand the other political parties failed to give a good account of themselves. The position of other parties in the Assembly was as follows: Congress (I) 1; to Swatantra 11; CPI 4; Jan Sangh 8; Socialist Party 4; Independent: 12. Thus the state continued to have a single party government.

In the elections of 1977 the Janata Party was returned in absolute majority capturing 148 out of 200 seats. The position of Congress (1) Assembly was as follows: Congress 20; In-depth the Janata Government remained in office will; fresh independents 11; CPI 1; CPM 1; Progressive Portions to the Assembly were held in June 1980, which once a returned Congress (1) to again were with absolute majority. The Position of the various parties in the Assembly after the elections of 1980 was as follows: Congress (1) 133; BJP 32; Congress 6; Lok Dal 7; Janata 8; CPI 1; CPI (M) 1; Independents 12. The Congress Government remained in office till the next elections.

In the elections to the Assembly held in March 1985 Congress again asserted its superiority and captured 113 of the 198 seats. BJP secured 38 seats and emerged as the second largest party other parties which managed to capture seats in the Assembly included DMKP (27); Janata (10), CPM (1) and independents and others (9).

Thus we find that the state of Rasiasthari never experienced coalition government, even though for a while after the elections of 1967 no single party bad clearcut majority in the Assembly.

Coalition politics at centre

By and large the centre in India has enjoyed a single party government. From the inception of the Constitution till the split of Congress in 1969, the Congress Government continued to rule the country with a comfortable majority. For the first time in 1969, after the split in Congress, some members of Congress Party withdrew their support from the government thereby reducing it into minority. However, the minority Congress Government of Mrs. Indira Gandhi continued to rule with the tacit support of CPI and DMK. It is noteworthy that neither CPI nor DMK was represented in the government. After the elections of 1971 Mrs. Gandhi's party was returned to Power with an overwhelmin "majority and provided a strong, government till 1977, when it was voted out of power and was succeeded by the Janata Government. According to some scholars the Janata Government was a sort of coalition government in so far five political parties with different ideologies constituted this party with a view to provide an alternative to the Congress Party. The coalition character of the Janata Government is further evident from the fact that it welcomed members of Akali Dal and All India A.D.M.K. parties to join the Government. In actual working the five components of the Janata Party always projected the image that they were separate entities and often levelled charges against each other. It was chiefly due to the infighting in the Janata Party that ultimately Morarji government was forced to tender resignation.

The Charan Singh Government which succeeded Morarji Government for a while was a pure coalition government consisting of Janata (S) and Congress (U), while the Congress (1) extended support to this coalition government from outside. However, this government proved shortlived and fell as soon as Congress (1) withdrew its support.

In 1980 when the general elections were held it was widely felt, that no single political party shall be able to get clear cut majority in the Parliament and an era of coalition politics would dawn at the centre. However, these doubts were belied and Congress (1) was returned to the Lok Sabha with an overwhelming majority in the elections of January 1980. This shall be borne out from the position of various political parties in Lok Sabha, which was as follows:

> Congress (1) 351; Janata 31; Janata (S) or Lok Dal 41; CPI (M) 35; Congress (U) 13; CPI 11; AIADMK 2; DMK 16; Akali 1; Others and Independents 24.

With the overwhelming majority at its command the Congress (1) formed a government on its own without the support of other parties. With this ended the temporary era of coalition Politics at centre.

In the Eighth General elections held in December 1984 the Congress (1) secured an unprecedented victory and captured 401 seats, surpassing its earlier record of 371 seats in the Lok Sabha elections held in 1957 under Jawaharlal Nehru. The position of the other political parties was as follows:

Telugu Desham 28; CPI (M) 22; AIADMK 12; Janata 10; CPI 6; Congress (S) 4; National Conference (F) 3; Dalit Mazdoor Kisan Party 3; BJP 2; Congress (J) 1; DMK 1; Independents and others 17.

Thus we find that centre experienced coalition governments only for very brief period.

Evaluation of coalition governments

It is clear from the above survey of the working of coalition governments in various states as well as the centre that the experiment lasted for a limited duration only. In most of the states coalition politics prevailed between the year 1967 and 1971 when the Congress strength in some of the state legislative Assemblies was considerably reduced and the political parties professing faith in different ideology and programme joined hands to capture the power without bothering about a common programme. Once in power the members of the coalition fought for offices and portfolios and did not mind pulling down the credibility of other partners in public estimation to further their own interests. Individual members as well as groups frequently indulged in horse trading and changed their loyalties. This gave rise to the evil of defection. It has been asserted that more defections took place between 1967 and 1971 than during the first fifteen years. This was so because the different political parties welcomed defectors to retain the majority, which was so essential to keep themselves in power.

The coalition governments also failed to follow any clearcut policies. Most of the time these governments continued to make compromises on various principles and failed to take any definite steps or actions because they were more concerned with their existence and survival rather than carrying out set principles or policies. The internal bickerings and political strifes between the members of the coalition contributed to the instability of their government and adversely effected the efficiency of administration. In view of these shortcomings of coalition governments the people reacted sharply and voted back Congress to power in 1971.

However, it would be wrong to say that coalition politics has not left any good impact on the politics of

India. As an Indian scholar who has made a special study of coalition politics in India observes "One of the major effect of coalition politics has been that it has promoted compromise in politics and checked radicalism It also relieved the government of the restraints and responsibilities which are imposed on the ruling party by the opposition benches under the party system" Madhu Limaye has also asserted that the coalition between the Akalis and Jan Sangh in Punjab resulted in welcome reduction in Hindu Sikh tension.

In conclusion it can be said that coalitions in so far as they are based on concrete programmes, and not only on political opportunism and just for power, can greatly contribute to the smooth working of democratic and representative government in India. As Sahni has observed "There should be nothing to deter us from the danger of instability or ineffective or temporary combinations for a stopgap arrangements, since the coalitions are a sound, test of the effectiveness of a political system and of the parties' ability to connive at specific, clear and meaningful policy.

4

Hung Parliament

The British precedent of invitation to the Leader heading the Single Majority Party may be followed provided that the remaining parties do not stake their claim of having a coalition of working majority with an elected leader and a written "Watertight Package" to supply a viable alternative. Appointment of PM on probation is a constitutional depravity. No conditional appointment could be issued by the appointing authority which is incongruous with article 75. As such no probation period could be fixed requiring the PM to obtain confidence of the House by a particular date. The principles of parliamentary democracy do not sanctify the concept of probationary *PM, ad hoc PM,* NMR *PM, i.e..* Nominal Muster Roll PM (Daily Wages Labour) or Contractual PM with string attached to the Appointment Order (Wilson with 301 seats out of 635 in 1974 was not asked to obtain confidence of the Commons. He issued a warning to the Conservatives (297) and Liberals (14) that if they inflict a defeat on the Address, they would face an immediate general election and that was all. The hitherto Indian practice is, to say the least, a gross violation of the letter and spirit of article 75 and the principles of parliamentary democracy. It is also an insult to the people who have implidely voted for a minority government in order to arrest the non-responsive rule of the single party government. It may be treated as an unethical act because the President has no power to direct the PM of the minority Government to commit suicide in the House by asking him to obtain a confidence vote on or before a date fixed by him.

The appointing authority as the umpire is not clothed with the duty to exercise potentially embarrassing discretion of skewing and distorting the peoples' mandate given for a minority Government. Where the sovereign voters have expressed their verdict in the political game against single party rule, his "Royal Interventionism" with eagerness to correct the people's judgment may be tantamount to choosing a "winner" by volunteering himself to be an active player.

Dissolution of the House

According to the British practice, where a minority government holds office, it is for the PM rather than the sovereign to choose the time for an election. When the PM heads a minority/coalition Government after the general election caused by the choice of his predecessor's exercise of the right of dissolution and is defeated on a no-confidence motion in the House, he would then have a choice between resigning or as Mac Donald did in *1924,* seeking a dissolution. This is the right of the PM to seek the first dissolution during his term. When he seeks his first dissolution, it is technically called the "advice" and it "shall" be accepted. In case a PM who had been granted one dissolution and gets a single party majority in the consequent election, he may form a minority government, but on being defeated on No-confidence motion, he could seek a "second dissolution". In that case, his seeking a dissolution shall be technically called a "request" for dissolution and not "advice".

When a PM "requests" for a second dissolution, it could be denied if an alternative leader with watertight package of written agreement made public pledging to provide an alternative government with the existing House is available staking such a claim. Provided that the No-confidence motion or an opposition amendment to the motion of thanks for the address could contain within its wording an humble rider that, if it was carried, the PM should not be granted a dissolution and that another government was available as per the terms in the published watertight package for a majority government in writing.

Nothing less than that would do, if the constitutional head were to feel sufficiently confident to take the novel course of refusing a "second dissolution" of Parliament and of bringing about a new administration. Additionally, the constitutional head shall be obliged to grant the "request" for the second dissolution if the PM having had won a confidence motion earlier now incurs a defeat on a subsequent no-confidence motion under the spell of obstinate politicians.

Role of constitutional head

The constitutional head is not permitted, under the Constitution, to create conditions for destabilising a PM who has obtained a confidence vote in the House After assumption of office. Nor is he empowered to issue any direction/advice (verbal/written) even by a "whisper of throne" to the PM regarding his "term of office" except when he does not demit office without advising for dissolution after the defeat on a no-confidence motion or monetary bill, Indeed, it is to be noted that "pleasure" of the constitutional head is only procedural and limited in "substance" by parliamentary sovereignty. This is the sound "metaphysics of constitutional head".

A parade before the constitutional head or a document of signature showing an anti-PM majority would not be adequate to decommission a PM because it is an opinion expressed by a majority without the "Walls of the House". Loss of the majority through any other method without following the prescribed procedure could not have the effect of a no-confidence motion as it is not accomplished in the legislative capacity of the members though it might be established within the Walls of the House. This doctrine sterlises the propensity of the politicians for enticing the constitutional head of decommission the PM through extramural inveiglement.

Implied Powers of the Minority Government

(a) *Right to vote on account:* The minority Government should enjoy the right to get a Vote on Account passed without division on the basis of the existing budget provisions for a minimum period of three months for the survival of the nation.

(b) *Right to national security legislations by consensus:* Any Money Bill concerning security and defence of the country should be introduced only if it is approved by the all party consensus within the House.

(c) *Right to no-Division on Motion of Thanks:* There should be debate but no amendment or vote on the motion of thanks for the President's Address if its contents conform to the provisions of Part IV of the Constitution.

(d) *Right against arbitary removal:* The minority government could be removed only through a no-confidence motion provided that no such motion should be moved before the adoption of the Vote on Account by the House.

(e) *Right to get the Report of the Standing Committees passed without Division:* All Bills, including Money Bills on introduction shall be referred to the appropriate Standing Committees for discussion, and Report by consensus/compromise. All amendments and cut motions should be discussed at the committee stage with the aid of the movers of the motion concerned and the Minister and the government representatives where compromise and consensus could be adopted in finalising the Report. The Chairman of the Standing Committee shall submit the Report to the House whereupon the House could debate and approve the Report without division and/or refer it back to the same Committee for reconsideration within 14 days. The reconsidered Report submitted by the Standing Committee following the earlier procedure and hearing evidences of members and ministers/ officials/experts shall be passed without division. In short, all bills should be subjected to the test of national consensus and compromise at the committee stage,

Permanent Cure of Hung Parliament

There are two major treatments for permanent cure of the bung Parliament (a) Establishment of a Collegial Cabinet System and (b) Statutory Bi-Party System.

(a) *Establishment of Collegial Cabinet System:* In the event of a hung Parliament the soft but permanent cure requires that the constitutional head shall invite the first three parties in order of their numerical strength in the House which could make a working majority to form a Collegial government with annual rotational headship starting with the leader having single largest party.

The Cabinet shall consist of 10 percent of the members from each participant party. The portfolios shall be distributed by mutual agreement by the three leaders so as to ensure continuity even with rotational change of headship. A party may have the option either to join the government or to accord committed voting support in the House for the full term. Parliament, by law, may provide that refusal to accept the responsibility of governance either by joining or by giving committed voting support when invited under a hung Parliament shall be construed to be an act of (a) disregarding the people's mandate, (b) shirking the national duty, responsibility of governance, and (c) abdicating the right of imposing its will by voting against government measures which do not reverse or radically change the pre-election public policies.

The term of the Collegial Cabinet shall expire on the date of announcement for next election to the Lok Sabha when automatically Lok Sabha shall stand dissolved under the orders of the Constitutional Head.

The parties forming/supporting the Collegial Government shall formulate a Common Minimum Programme (CMP) in conformity with the Directive Principles of State Policy before their oath taking ceremony and it shall be duly reflected 'in the President's Address to the joint session of Parliament. There shall be a CMP Monitoring Committee consisting of leaders of the constituent parties to review and evaluate the working of the CMP every month and their recommendations shall be implemented by the Collegial Government.

The Collegial Cabinet shall not initiate legislation that reverses or makes radical changes in the existing public policies without unanimous decision of the Cabinet and without the previous recommendation of the CMP Monitoring Committee (CMPMC).

Generally, the officials perception of a Minority Government's capability of stability blurs their fear of punishment, as such infertile procastination and procedural parkinsonism become their armours against their perceived enthroned infidels. In order to enforce its writs, the new government shall ensure, if necessary by amending the CCR rule, that the employees/staff, irrespective of their status and position, shall not keep any file/paper with them pending for more than a week without proper disposal and that for each day of delay in proper disposal thereafter, the controlling officer shall make an entry "negligent" ın the appropriate peripheral CCR book. A repetition of three delays, continuous or otherwise, in respect of any employee shall be entered in his CCR as "Inefficient". Approved absence from duties shall be exempted from the operation of the rule.

A new caretaker government shall be established by the Constitutional Head to conduct a free and fair election and it shall continue in office till the successors take oath of the office. The caretaker government shall consist of (a) the retired Chief Justice of the Supreme Court who was the immediate predecessor of the present incumbent and (b) ten of his nominees selected from among the non-partisan and distinguished scientists, intellectuals, jurists, academicians, administrators, generals, media specialists, etc. provided that there shall be atleast one-third women members in the Cabinet. They shall ensure the implementation of the code of conduct issued by the Election Commission,

Establishment of Statutory Bi-Party Mechanism: The Constitution may be amended to provide that there shall be Bi-Party system in the name of the United Front and Composite Front (or Progressive and Liberal Front) to exclusively participate in the elections to the parliamentary and legislative bodies. Each such Front shall be registered with the Election Commission and be regulated by law passed by the Parliament.

It shall be mandatory for the constituents of each Front to adopt a common symbol during the Lok Sabha/ Assembly elections. However, each constituent may have the option to use then own symbol in the Assembly/ Local Government elections if the Constitution of the Front so provides.

An individual member or a group or a constituent party on defection from the Front or on disobeying the whip of the Front shall be disqualified for continuing as members of the concerned House during the remainder of its term. The Election Commission on receipt of the information from the Presiding Officer or otherwise regarding the vacancy arising out of defection etc. shall *suo molu* notify and declare the candidate elected who had secured second position in order of the number of votes in the respective constituency during the election. He shall fill up the vacancy caused by such defection etc. for the remainder of the term of the House. This shall minimise the election expenses and more importantly, respect the voter's second choice. All disputes arising out of such defection or consequential action of the Election Commission shall be decided by Presiding Officer of the concerned House. However, an aggrieved member may appeal to the Supreme Court against the decision of the Presiding Officer.

Something marvellous is happening to our planet but only a tiny fraction of the world population are aware of it. From ancient times and in every known human civilization, people have longed to experience it, some actually have experienced it, albeit to a limited extent. Prophets and seers have foretold its inevitable fulfillment; poets and bards have been singing of it throughout the ages. What is it? The dawning of a new era in human history, India including. This new age will witness the establishment of a just society and the emergence of a united and peaceful world community! In other words, *Vasudhaiva kutumbakam,* or "the Kingdom of God on earth" truly the *Ram Raj,* World history, in its core and in its essence, is the story of spiritual evolution of human society. From this all other activities of human beings proceed and around it all other activities revolve. The spiritual view of evolution is the constant theme of religion or *dharma* (justice and righteousness). Each outpouring of divine guidance refers to the past, looks forward to the future and concentrates upon the immediate need for spiritual regeneration and enlightenment. The crisis India and the world are experiencing is that instead of turning to divine guidance we have been aping the popular culture of rampant materialism that is rapidly penetrating even the remotest corners of our planet. Any attempt to resolve the acute crisis in India must squarely address the issue of religion which is an integral element in the life of all its peoples. Arnold Toynbee, an eminent historian, described religion as a "faculty of human nature". That the perversion of this faculty in man has contributed to much of the confusion in our society and the resultant conflict in and between individuals and communities is the root cause of world crisis. In whichever direction we turn our gaze, no matter how cursory our observation of the doings and sayings of the present generation, we cannot fail to be struck by the evidences of moral decadence which, in their individual lives no less than in their collective capacity, men and women around us exhibit.

Most people see only darkness in both current affairs and recent history; many parts of the world Somalia, Bosnia, Northern Ireland, Afghanistan, parts of northern India, parts of Iraq, Pakistan and, most recently Rwanda are plagued by racial, ethnic and religious conflicts; defenceless peoples, like those of Tibet and East Timor, are oppressed by stronger powers while the United Nations, the single representative of sociopolitical unity, seems powerless.

A broader consideration of history is needed to understand a deeper truth : the human race, like an individual human being, is subject to change, development and evolution, In the history of human relationships, the most primitive stage is that of individual self-interest. This loyalty extends to the family unit, then to the tribe. After the constitutional city states, there is nationhood, whose culmination has been marked by the achievement, in the case of the majority of the world's nations, of independence from the former colonial powers. Now we face the challenge of the last and crowning stage in our collective social development : that of world unity. It is clear, however, that genuine unity must be inspired by more than just political necessity, inasmuch as treaties and resolutions cannot bring about lasting peace. As a UNESCO statement puts it: "Since wars begin in the minds of men, it is in the minds of men that the defence of peace must be constructed."

What is this greater force than politics that can reach our hearts and minds and unite humanity? To many, if not most people, religion is irrelevant. It has become preoccupied with vacant rituals, impoverished by superstitious traditions and thoroughly corrupted by self-serving individuals and groups. Yet these obvious failings lie not in the original, divine teachings of religion, but in the accretions of centuries of human influence. True religion requires personal, independent investigation on the part of each individual. Science, which can produce more tangible progress, may seem more valuable than religion, though the two cannot be opposed: They must operate in harmony, for as Albert Einstein observed : "Religion without science is blind; science without religion is lame."

Religion often denies opportunity and equal rights to women. Until very recently, it was men who tightly held the reins of power in virtually every sphere of human endeavour. This inequality of men and women remains one of the root causes of war, since peace can be built and maintained only upon the foundation of justice. Again, judging from today's world, religion seems the least plausible answer to humanity's manifold and increasingly urgent problems. Inter-religious conflict lies at the heart of almost every war; fundamentalism impels bloodthirsty terrorist groups and spawns dangerous cults.

The greatest obstacle to religion as a source of unity appears to be the differences found among the world's great Faiths. Surely the animosity that has long divided Christian from Jew and Muslim from Hindu can be overcome? For, a closer study of these Faiths shows that the essential message of each is the same.

The foremost challenge to the followers of every religion today, then, is the claim to be the sole possessors of truth, clinging rigidly to their own narrow interpretation of the teachings of their religion. This stubborn refusal to appreciate and accept other Faiths can lead only to bitter antagonism and futile division, as it has in the past. The interfaith declaration entitled "Towards a Global Ethic", which was produced by an assembly of religious and spiritual leaders from virtually every major world religion and spiritual movement at the 1993 centenary of the Parliament of World's Religions in Chicago, suggests that it is indeed possible for the world's religions to find much common ground in this regard. The declaration states: "We affirm that a common set of core values is found in the teachings of the religions, and that these form the basis of a global ethic... There already exist ancient guidelines for human behaviour which are found in the teachings of the religions of the world and which are the condition for a sustainable world order." The Golden Rule, a universal ethic, is part of the spiritual heritage of humankind. It is taught in one form or another in all the world religions and systems of belief and can be found among the traditions of the world's most ancient societies:

Buddhism: "Hart not others in ways that you yourself would find hurtful."

Zoroastrianism: "That nature only is good when it shall not do unto another whatever is riot good for its own self."

Judaism: "What is hateful to you, do not to your fellow men, That is the entire Law, all the rest is the commentary."

Hinduism: "This is the sum of all true righteousness : deal with others as thou wouldst thyself be dealt by. Do nothing to thy neighbour which thou wouldst not have him do to thee after."

Christianity: "As ye would that men should do to you, do ye also to them likewise."

Islam: "No one of you is a believer until he desires for his brother that which he desires for himself."

Taoism: The good man "ought to pity the malignant tendencies of others; to regard their gains as if they were his own, and their losses in the same way."

Confucianism: "Surely it is the maxim of loving-kindness : Do not unto others that you would not have them do unto you."

Jainism: "In happiness and suffering, in joy and grief, we should regard all creatures as we regard our own self,..."

Sikhism: "Be thou not estranged from another. For, in every heart, Bervades the Lord."

Baha'i Faith : "He should not wish for others that which he doth not wish for himself, nor promise that which he doth not fulfill."

Let us, therefore, collectively endeavour to foster an all-embracing approach towards the world's religions; to identify their common denominators, and to map out the shared terrain between them, From the resulting codification of the truths common to all religions, we can begin to work towards evolving a foundation of true justice upon which the lasting and permanent peace on earth would be established. Ultimately we must develop a unified and integrated vision of the nature of the human being and of the world society. Such a vision was supremely achieved by Gandhiji, who sacrificed his all for the salvation of our country and whose favourite bhajan was: *Ishwar Allah tero naam, Sub ko sanmati dey Bhagwan.* The people of India would do well to remember the gospel he preached and practised and live up to his ideals, were too late.

Disunity is a danger that the nations and peoples of the earth can no longer endure; the consequences are too terrible to contemplate, too obvious to require a demonstration. Let us look at the concept of justice in different parts of the globe. In the Chinese tradition Confucianism essentially argued that justice is best achieved through the proper moral education of individuals, who will then act justly in society. The Western approach (as rooted in ancient Greece) essentially believes that justice comes from the establishment and enforcement of good laws, which keep injustice in check. In India the concept of justice is rooted in *Dharma.* In many other societies too, the understanding of justice stems from religious Law. An interface of these ideas would call for acceptance of the individual spiritual development in realising justice, and at the same time the need for establishment of a universal administrative order. Without such an order universal peace, unity and love will be like a beautiful flower which will eventually wilt. Our survival and happiness now depend on our recognition of the oneness and the wholeness of the entire human family and of the essential oneness of religion and the fundamental unity of its founders.

5

Religionalism in Indian Politics

Regionalism has been an important feature of Indian politics since the dawn independence. But in the late sixties and seventies the regional claims verging on parochial demands for separation and autonomy grew so strong that they became a serious threat to the unity of the country. Before making a study of impact of regionalism on Indian politics, it shall be desirable to understand the meaning and dimensions of regionalism. The term 'regionalism' has two conno-tations. In the negative sense it implies excessive attachment to one's region in preference to the country or the state. In the positive sense it is a political attribute associated with people's love in for their region, culture, language etc. with a view to maintain their independent identity. While positive regionalism is a welcome thing in so far as it encourages the people to develop a sense of brotherhood and commonness on the basis of common language religion or historical background, the negative regionalism is a great threat to the unity and integrity of the country. In the Indian context generally the term regionalism has been used in the negative sense and is used to "indicate an agglomeration of all those forces which are generally considered to be centrifugal polarised to cell ism and nationalism. Kousar J. Azam defines regionalism as a process subsidiary of political integration in India. Manifestation of these residual elements, which do not find expression in the national polity and national culture, and being excluded from the centrality of the new polity, express themselves, in political discontent and political exclusionism. It could include forces that, the gravitational or the centripetal forces of a society fail to absorb assimilate and internalize.

The feeling of regionalism may arise either due to the continuous neglect of a particular area or region by the ruling authorities it may spring up as a result of increasing political awareness of forth backward people that have been discriminated against. Quite often the unscrupulous political leaders encourage the feeling of regionalism to maintain their hold over a particular area or group of people. Thus regionalism is a multi-dimensional and composite phenomena which is considered detrimental to the national unity. This phenomena may emerge out of the cumulation of variations pertaining to the sociocultural, economic and political spheres. In fact there are two types of determinants of regionalism, subjective and objective. The subjective components of regionalism are the way of life, customs and traditions, forms of art, language and literature, social heritage, beliefs, attitudes and values related to the group. The objective components of the region are the territorial, regional and the environment complex within which the regional group lives. Taken together these subjective and objective components constitute the determinants of regionalism.

Regionalism is not a new phenomenon in the Indian political system. In the pre-independence days it was promoted by the British imperialists and they deliberately encouraged the people of various regions to think in terms of their region rather than the nation as a whole, with a view to maintain their hold over India. After independence the leaders tried to foster a feeling among the people that they belonged to one nation. The framers of the constitution sought to achieve this by introducing single citizenship for all. With the same objective a unified judiciary, all India Services and a strong central government, as provided. But in view of the vastness of the country and cultures regionalism soon made its appearance in India.

The first vague manifestation of regionalism was the demand, for reorganisation of states on linguistic basis. But the most effective play of regionalism was the victory of the DMK against Congress giants, in Tamil Nadu. Initially the central leadership Felt that regionalism was a peripheral political factor confined to Tamil Nadu and hence did not pose any threat to national unity. However, these hopes were ill-founded. Soon in Punjab the Akali movement gained momentum, while in Jammu and Kashmir Sheikh Abdullah revived the National Conference. During these initial years the all India political parties continued to adjust with these regional forces on the plea that they would ultimately succeed in making inroads into the bases of the regional parties and absorb in their organisations. However, these hopes proved illusory.

The Indian National Congress which enjoyed monopoly, power between 1947-1967 and followed a policy of blowing hot and cold towards the regional forces, also contributed to the growth of regionalism in India. It accommodated the regional forces when was convenient and raised a hue and cry against them when it: was pitted against them. The local Congress leaders also encouraged aged the growth of regionalism and strengthened their hold on local party organisations with a view to increase their bargaining power with the central leaders. In fact a close link developed between central and regional leadership. This close link between the central and regional leadership greatly encouraged the growth of regionalism.

Causes for regionalism

In India a number of factors have contributed to the growth of regionalism. In the first place, regionalism made its appearance as a reaction against the efforts of the national government to impose a particular ideology, language or cultural pattern on all people and groups. Thus the states of South have resisted imposition of Hindi as official language because they feared this would lead to dominance of the north. Similarly, in Assam anti-foreigner movement was launched by the Assamese to preserve their own culture.

Secondly, continuous neglect of an area or region by the ruling, authority and concentration of administrative and political power at one centre has given rise to demand for decentralisation of authority and bifurcation of unilingual states. Even the sons of the soil theory has been put forth to promote the interests of neglected groups or areas of the state.

Thirdly, the desire of the various units of the Indian federal degree of system to maintain their subcultural regions and greater self-government has promoted regionalism and given rise to demand, for greater autonomy.

Fourthly, the desire of certain regional parties to capture, power has also led to rise of regionalism. It is well known that political parties like DMK, AIADMK, Akali Dal, Telugu Desham etc. have encouraged regionalism to capture political power. Finally, the growing awareness among the people of backward areas that they arc being discriminated against has also promoted feeling of regionalism. The local political leaders have fully exploited' this factor and tried to feed the people with the idea that central government was deliberately trying to maintain regional imbalances by neglecting social and development of certain areas. Not only this, at the state level also they have tried to themselves as the champions of the cause of certain regions in order to maintain their position of leadership. This trend has, received encouragement from the tendency of the political basis at centre as well as states to offer berths in Central and State Council Ministers to leaders of various regions.

Forms of regionalism

Regionalism in India has manifested itself in the following forms:

(a) demand for secession from the Indian Union;

(b) demand for separate statehood;

(c) demand for full statehood;

d) inter-state disputes;

(e) demand for State autonomy;

(f) sons of soil theory; and

(g) militant nationalism.

For a fuller understanding of the politics of regionalism in India, it shall be desirable to examine these manifestations of regionalism in some details.

Secession from the union

Secession from the Union is one of the most serious manifestations of regionalism and made its appearance !a number of occasions. The first demand for secession came in the former state of PEPSU (Patiala and East Punjab States Union), a predominantly Sikh region. After the Reorganisation of States in 1956, the bilingual state of Punjab came into existence. This the Akali leaders under Tara Singh put forward a demand separate Punjabi

Speaking state. It may be noted that though outwardly the demand for a separate state was presented on linguistic basis in reality the Sikhs wanted to have a state with a compact Sikh community. This was soon met with a counter demand from the Arya Samaj leader of Punjab for Greater Punjab consisting of Punjab Himachal Pradesh and PEPSU. Both the parties continued to launch various kinds of agitations during the late fifties and 1960s. thin The things took a serious turn when the Alkali Dal leader Sant Fateh A threatened to burn himself alive if the demand for Punjab as not met by 25 Sept. 1966. Mrs. Indira Gandhi who had assumed the reigns of government decided to concede the demand According to Giselher Wirsing, she conceded this demand "not only because of the chaotic condition in the Punjab but also because Indira Gandhi wanted to thus honour the Sikh soldiers and Who formed about 20 per cent of the Indian Army, for their valour in the recent Indo-Pakistan War."

As a result of this decision the state of Punjab was bifurcated About 41 per cent of the area of the state with a population of 11.5 million went to the Punjabi Suba; while 35.8 per cent of area and a population of 7.5 million was given to the Hindi speaking state of Haryana. The rest of the area (22 per cent) with 7.1 million population went to Himachal Pradesh. However, the question of the city of Chandigarh continued to be a borne of contention between the two states. Pending its final transfer to Punjab in return, for surrender of Fazilka and Abohar to Haryana, it was made a Union Territory.

Even after the creation of the Punjabi Suba certain Sikh leaders, Wore not satisfied and continued to plead for the establishment of all independent Socialist Democratic Sikh Home Land. Dr. Jagjit Singh, the General Secretary of the Akali Dal faction led by Sant Fateh Singh even went abroad to mobilise world opinion in favour of creation of a Sikh homeland. However, these activities were not approved by the Akali leadership and Jagjit Singh was expelled from the party.

Realising that an independent Sikh State was not possible the Akalis started insisting on greater decentralisation of political power. They joined hands with other states like Tamil Nadu, West Bengal and Kashmir in demanding greater autonomy for the states. In the Anandpur Sahib Resolution, which was endorsed by the general house of the Dal at Amritsar on 28 August 1977 they demanded that the authority of the Centre should be confined only to defence of the country, foreign relations, communications, railways, and currency. They also insisted on the inclusion in Punjab of certain areas like Dalhousie, Chandigarh, Pinjore, Kalka, Ambala, Una Tehsil, Nalagarh region, Shahbad, six tehsils of Ganganagar district of Rajasthan etc.

During the next few years the demand for Khalistin lay dormant. However with the formation of Congress (1) Government in the state the demand was revived. The demand was supported some of the Akali Dal leaders and factional Congress (1) In March 1981 the Fifty-Fourth Sikh Educational Conference backed the Khalistan resolution. However, the moderate Akali Dal did not support the demand for Khalistan and put forth 45 demands to ratify what they term as 'second class status' for the Sikhs However, the extremist elements continued to insist on separate state of Khalistan. The pro-Khalistan Dal Khalsa hijacked and Indian Airlines plane to Lahore. While the central government clear that it would not tolerate secessionist activities, it 'initiated negotiations with the Akali leaders. But much headway could, be made due to insistence of the Akali Leaders to implement the Anandpur Sahib Resolution without any reservation 'as the implementation of this was bound to effect the other neighbouring states like Haryana, Rajasthan and Himachal Pradesh, the centre could not implement the

Anandpur Sahib Resolution fully. This led to agitation by the Akalis. This provided an opportunity to the extremists to step up their activities. They indulged in killing of innocent people and began misuse of religious places. The situation became so tense that the Central Government had to undertake Blue Star' operation, to evacuate Golden Temple from the extremists.

The operation evoked strong reaction from the extremists and, managed assassination of Mrs. Indira Gandhi, the P.M. of India through her security guards. This led to a serious backlash in several cities like Delhi, Kanpur, Bhokaro etc. Soon after assuming power Rajiv Gandhi made a bid to find a negotiated settlement of the Punjab issue and concluded an accord with the Akali Dal President Sant Harchand Singh Longowal. In terms of this agreement, elections were held and Akali Dal formed government under Surjeet Singh Barnala. Even the Akali Dal government failed 3 keep the terrorists under control and the killings of innocent people continued. Ultimately the central government imposed residential rule in the state. At present also the extremists are engaged in sporadic killings, and demand for Khalistan is echoed. However, majority of the Sikhs are not in favour of secession from the Indian Union. The secessionists are mainly operating from foreign lands.

The second case of demand for cession from the Indian Union was that of Dravid Nad. The demand for secession was put forward by the DMK in 1960 and was followed by agitation. Subsequently the demand was extended to elude areas of Andhra Pradesh, Kerala, Mysore and Madras and carve out an independent Republic of Dravid Nad. However, this demand was not supported by substantial portion of the population these areas, and culminated in cleavage in the party. A sizeable number of members who did not favour secession and merely insisted radical amendments in the Constitution left the DMK and formed the Tamil National Party **under** E.V.K. Sampath. Despite 'is division DMK continued **to** increase its strength and its demand for Secession grew more forceful. However, the demand was firmly, tried down by Pandit Nehru who said "Territorial integrity of India would not be allowed to be violated. Any attempt at Balkanisation of India would be resisted with all the force at our To deal with the secessionist tendencies sixteenth amendment was carried out to the Constitution in October 1963 and the Parliament was authorised to make necessary law to deal with persons questioning the sovereignties and integrity of the Indian Union. In future all the candidates seeking election to the Parliament or State Legislatures were to take an oath of allegiance to the Indian Constitution and swear to uphold the sovereignty and integrity of the country.

In view of the firm stand of the central leadership the DMK abandoned its demand fcr sovereign independent Dravadian federation and carried on necessary changes in the party constitution. However, it reasserted its determination to work for the formation Dravida Union of the states of Madras, Andhra, Mysore and Kerala with as large powers as possible. But this was to be accomplished within the framework of the Constitution and without posing at threat to the integrity of the country. Ever since the abandonment of demand for secession the party has consistently demanded greater autonomy and economic resources for the states. DMK Chief Minister Karunanidhi has been consistently pressing the Central Government to grant greater autonomy to the state. At times he has even, threatened to use other than constitutional methods for the attainment of state autonomy. Thus the party shifted its emphasis on state autonomy rather than insisting on a separate and independent state. Simultaneously in Tamil Nadu regionalism appeared in yet another form. The

Tamilians have been insisting on the reservation of all posts for the Tamilians, to the exclusion of the Malayalis. At times violent demonstrations were organised against the Malayalis. The DMK government even made an open declaration favouring the reservation of 80 per cent of the jobs for the local Tamil people.

The third case of the demand for secession from the Indian Union was that of the people of Mizo hill districts of Assam. The Mizos numbering about 200,000 from demanded secession not only from the state of Assam but also the Union of India. They wanted to form an independent State consisting of Mizo Hill districts of Assam and contiguous areas of East Pakistan and Burma. They formed an organisation known as Mizo National Front to carry out struggle against the government.

As the struggle was of a violent nature, the Government adopted a tough attitude towards the Mizo National Front in 1962. However, the Mizos continued their activities from Cachar Hills and Trip, In view of the policy of repression adopted by the Government of India a section of the Mizo leaders abandoned their demand independent and sovereign states and indicated their willingness to come to terms with the Government. In 1971 the President of Mizo National Front (Chunga) submitted a memorandum to the Government of India highlighting the injustice done to the and demanded a separate state within the Indian Union. Thus they abandoned the demand for secession. The Government also reciprocated well and accorded the status of a Union territory to the Mizo Hills. Huge amounts were spent to improve the lot of Mizoram with a view to bring them into the main stream of India. However, the government could not achieve much stream because a section of Mizos under Laldenga continued to insist on the status of a separate state outside the Indian Union. They continued guerilla activities from China and Burma. The

Government also continued to operate against the rebel Mizos.

Simultaneously the Government of India made bid to arrive at some negotiated settlement with the Mizos during the years 1973 and 1974, However, these negotiations proved a failure. The Mizo rebels also grew more violent and killed the Inspector General of Police and Deputy Inspector General of Police as well as Superintendent of Police of Mizoram. This was too much for the Government to swallow. The Government therefore decided to deploy armed forces and comb the entire area. It also declared its intention not to hold any talks with the underground Mizo leaders unless they abandoned violence.

In view of the tough attitude of the Government of India, Laldenga, the rebel Mizo leader decided to give up arms. He indicated his intention to settle the Mizo problem within the frame-work of the Indian Constitution. After prolonged negotiations an agreement was reached between the Central Government and the Mizos under Laldenga in July 1976. As per this agreement the problem was to be solved peacefully; the Mizos were to abjure violence, and deposit their weapons. However, Laldenga did not abide by this agreement and soon started inciting his followers to scuttle its implementation. He raised volunteers and even arranged for their training in China. During the next one year there was a comparative lull in the activities of the underground Mizos.

In July 1979 the Mizo National Front insurgents again started their activities. They attacked the transmission centre of All India Radio at Aizawl and the police complex of Mizoram. They even prepared a plan to murder the important political leaders as well as civil and police officials. Following the discovery of the plot the Government of India launched massive operations with the help of military. It declared that no talks would be held with the Mizo National Front unless it completely abjured violence. The Centre indicated its willingness to accord status of statehood to the Union Territory of Mizoram, but insisted that the rebels will have to first lay down their arms. For sometime more the Mizo rebels continued violent, activities and posed a serious threat to the law and order of the state. Ultimately in July 1980, the Mizo rebel leaders reached an agreement with Mrs. Indira Gandhi for a permanent political solution of the Mizo problem. The two parties agreed to suspend armed action and find out a solution by mutual consultation within the framework of the Indian Constitution. As a result peace once again returned to the peace-torn state of Mizoram.

Once again this peace proved to be illusory because Laldenga and other underground Mizos continued to secretly re-group the forces, restore their communication link, and impart guerilla training to its men. In March 1981 Laldenga submitted a fire-point plan to the Prime Minister for solving the Mizo problem and sought Government's permission to visit Arakan Hills in Burma *to* consult other leaders of the Mizo National Front. After return from Arakan Hills Laldenga came forward with the demand of a greater Mizoram state containing some parts of Tripura, Manipur and Assam as well. He also insisted on grant of 'some sort of autonomy' through constitutional amendment. This was not acceptable to the Government of India and thus the stalemate continued. In 1982 the centre once again banned the MNF and asked Laldenga to leave the country. He proceeded to London,

A fresh move to come to some sort of understanding with Laldenga was made by Mrs. Indira Gandhi in October 1984 and Laldenga was summoned for talks from London. However, these talks could be held only after about five months in March-April, 1985. As a result of prolonged discussions certain modalities for an accord between the Mizo leader and the Central Government were finalised in December, 1985. However, it took another six months before the accord was finally signed on 30 June 1986. Under the accord the Mizo leader Laldenga arranged the surrender of 600 MNF insurgents and the Centre secured the passage of laws by parliament according Mizoram the status of a state. Parliament provided constitutional safeguards for preserving the identity of the Mizo people with regard to their social system and customs. The Mizo National Front amended its constitution to make it conform to the provisions of the law. On 21 August 1986 a nine-member coalition government of Congress(1) and National Front was installed in Mizoram under Laldenga. The former Chief Minister Lalthanhawala became his deputy Chief Minister. Subsequently elections were held in the state and Mizo National Front Party formed the government. The formation of a government under Laldenga was a great landmark and marked the culmination of the slow process of transformation of the Mizo National Front from an outlawed separatist party into a law-abiding political party operating within the framework of the Indian Constitution.

The fourth case of attempted secession from the Indian Union was that of the Nagas residing in the hills of Assam and Tuengassng division on the Indo-Burmese border. The Naga National Council under Zepo Phizo carried on long drawn out struggle for secession from the Indian Union. The Nagas not only refused to participate irk the elections of 1952 but also threatened to take the issue to the United Nations. They resorted to open violence to pressurise the Government to concede their demand. The Government could not tolerate all this and resorted to severe repression and a large number of

Nagas were put to death. Slowly the section of Nagas who were in favour of remaining within India assumed the leadership. They modified their demands and passed a unanimous resolution demanding the integration of the Naga areas into a single administrative unit to be governed by the Governor of Assam on behalf of the President of India. It also appealed to the rebel Nagas to give up violence. This changed attitude on the part of the Nagas was welcomed by the Government of India.

In 1960 an agreement was reached between the Naga People's Convention and the Government of India regarding grant of statehood to the Nagas. Pending the implementation of this demand a provisional arrangements was made for the administration of Nagaland. Ultimately in 1962 Nagaland was given the status of a full-fledged state, although it was formally inaugurated as a state on 1 December 1963.

However, the trouble with the Nagas did not end and the violent elements led by Phizo continued the policy of violence and arson. The Government of India also took firm steps against the rebels and Phizo was forced to run away from India. He proceeded to London to secure support for the cause of an independent state of Nagaland, but the response was not quite favourable. However, China and Pakistan did extend him some help and he continued the revolutionary activities. After the emergence of Bangladesh as an independent state the Nagas lost their base of operation and their activities were somewhat curtailed. However a section of Nagas under inspiration from Phizo continued violent activities and killed a large number of people with a view to strike awe in the mind of the government. The government also adopted a stiff attitude and took coulter measures. In view of the hardened attitude of the government even some of the hard core rebel Nagas realised that they could not gain anything through violent and underground activities and decided to achieve their ends by extending their co-operation to the Government of India. The Government of India was willing to enter into negotiations with the rebel Nagas for a solution within the framework of the Indian Constitution. Simultaneously the government also continued to take precautionary measures to ensure that the Nagas were not able to procure arms from China or slip to China to get necessary training.

Ultimately in November 1975 an agreement was reached between the. Government of India and the Nagas. The rebel Nagas agreed to give up their violent activities and also to surrender all their arms and ammunition. They agreed to work for solution within the framework of the Constitution. On the other hand the Government of India agreed to release all detained Nagas and withdraw charges of violence and other offences against them. It was also agreed that the other problems would also be resolved on the basis of the proposals to be formulated by the underground Naga. However, the agreement proved short-lived because a number of Nagas started openly violating this agreement and continued to procure arms and ammunition from foreign powers. They also continued to profess open loyalty to the exiled leader Phizo. In 1977 Morarji Desai, the then Prime Minister, met Phizo in London to find a solution of the Nagaland problem, but he could not succeed.

It is true that by now majority of the Nagas have reconciled themselves with the position of a separate state within the Indian Union and given up their demand for an independent state of Nagaland outside the Indian Union but some hard core Nagas still persist with their demand for an independent state outside the Indian Union. The underground Naga leaders like Muivah and Isak. Chishi Swu keep on inciting the Nagas to continue the struggle for the liberation of Nagaland. They issued a manifesto in July 1980 stating, "We rule out the illusion of saving Nagaland through peaceful means. It is arms and arms again that will save our nation and ensure freedom to the people" Muivah and Swu even announced the formation of an Interim Government of People's Republic of Nagaland. Thus there is a section of Naga leaders who still persist with their demand for an independent state. We can only express the hope that with the passage of time these leaders will also realise the futility of their struggle and demand for an independent and sovereign state, and join the mainstream of the Indian political life. .

In the state of Manipur also secessionists groups like People's Liberation Army (PLA), the Red Army, the Peoples Revolutionary Party of Kangleipak (PREPAK), Meitei National United Liberation Front (Meitei Marup) are engaged in secessionist activities. Simultaneously they have been resorting to mass-scale violence to force the non-Manipuri people to leave the state. Some of the sessionist groups have even tried to secure cooperation of Nagas and Mizos to achieve their objectives. In a number of other states like Jammu and Kashmir, and Union Territory of Tripura National Volunteer Organisation (TNV) are operating even though their base is not very wide.

Demand for statehood

Yet another form of regionalism in India has been the demand for separate statehood for a particular area so that the people could develop their culture and language. This form of regionalising is certainly of much less serious nature than the demand for separation from the Indian Union. It simply implies creation of more states out of the existing states within the Union. This type of regionalism gained in strength only after the reorganisation of the states. Let us examine some instances of this type of regionalism.

Though the State, Reorganisation Commission bad favoured bilingual state of Bombay but in the face of the growing demand from Samyukta Mabarashtra Samiti and Maha Gujarat Janata Parishad, which was widely supported by the people, the Government of India was ultimately obliged to divide the state of Bombay into two separate states of Gujarat and Maharashtra. In fact the bifurcation of the state of Bombay (into Gujarat and Maharashtra) was a logical sequel to the creation of the unilingual state of Andhra Pradesh.

The States Reorganisation Commission in its report had favoured the creation of separate state of Vidarbha by taking out certain areas of Madhya Pradesh. However, the Government turned down this recommendation of the Commission. This greatly frustrated the people and they raised demand for a separate state. However, the Government of India stood firm and turned down this demand. After he bifurcation of Bombay into Maharashtra and Gujarat, the demand for separate state of Vidarbha was once again revived. People formed Nag Vidarbha Andolan Samiti which organised violent demonstrations near Nagpur. The government sought to pacify the people by promising special representation and finances for the development of the area. However, it firmly ruled out the demand for separate state of Vidarbha. The movement for separate state of Vidarbha slowly died out.

Demand for Separate State for Punjab. The States Reorganisation Commission also opposed the bifur-cation of the state of Punjab, This recommendation was endorsed by the Government of India, However, the Akalis were not happy with this decision and launched an agitation under their leader Master Tara Singh for the creation of a Punjab State. They alleged that the Sikhs were being discriminated against. The Government of India appointed a commission under S.R. Das to took into these charges. However, the Commission pointed out that there was no discrimination again the Sikhs and hence ruled out the creation of a separate Punjab State. The Akalis did not respond favourably to this decision and once again took to agitational methods. After prolonged agitation, the Government of India appointed a Commission under Justice J.C. Shah, which suggested the reorganisation of the state of Punjab on linguistic basis. On the basis of these recommendations the Parliament passed the Punjab Reorganisation Act 1966. As a result the Punjabi-speaking areas were constituted into a unilingual state of Punjab, while the hill areas were merged with the Union Territory of Himachal Pradesh. The predominantly Hindi-speaking areas were Constituted into a new state of Haryana.

The people of Garo, Khasi, Jaintia were the first to raise demand for a separate state. For the purpose they organised the All Party Hill Leaders Conference and carried out necessary agitation. The Government of India met their demand partially and organised the state of Assam on federal basis. However, this failed to satisfy the people and they revised their demand for a separate Hill State. They tried to pressurise the government to concede their demand by threatening to resign from the Assam Assembly if their demand was not conceded in the Budget Session of 1997. As the Government did not concede to this threat all the nine members of the APHLC from the hilly region tendered their resignation. The Conference organised a hartal and launched a non-violent struggle to get its demand conceded. Ultimately, the Parliament passed the Assam Reorganisation Bill and created the autonomous Hill State of Meghalaya within the state of Assam. According to the new arrangement the State of Meghalaya was provided with its own legislature and Council of Ministers. This arrangement also did not satisfy the hill people and the Meghalaya

Assembly passed a unanimous resolution requesting the Government of India to convert the state into a full-fledged state. This demand was complied with in January 1972 when Meghalaya was given the status of a fully-fledged state.

In Assam the feeling of regionalism appeared in the shape of a demand for the ouster of all the immigrants from other states, who owned most of the industries in Assam. *Lachit Sena Send* was organised by the Assamese and it resorted to, attacks on shops and industrial establishments of the non-Assamese. The Government adopted a firm attitude and suppressed the agitation with firm hand. For some time the demand lay dormant till in 1979 the agitation was revived. A loud demand for detecting, identifying and deporting the foreigners from the state was raised with great force. The agitation soon assumed serious dimensions and the whole administration was paralysed. The agitators resorted to all-round agitation posing a serious threat to the movement of oil as well as law and order situation. in view of the serious nature of agitation the top government leaders like the Prime Minister and the Home Minister made efforts to come to some sort of amicable settlement with the agitation leaders. Despite all the efforts no agreement could be arrived at due to different dates suggested by the two parties as the base year for identification and deportation of foreign nationals in Assam.

In March 1985 negotiations were resumed to find out a negotiated settlement of the issue of foreign nationals in Assam. At these negotiations the AASU, which had been spearheading the agitations adopted more pragmatic approach and agreed to the deportation of foreigners who bad entered Assam after 1971 and disenfranchisement of all the foreigners. The Central Government which was also keen to resolve the issue agreed to the dissolution of the existing State Assembly. Ultimately an accord was signed on 15 August 1985 between R.D. Pradhan, the Secretary in the Ministry of Home Affairs and the Assam agitation leaders. Under the accord it was agreed that (i) the base date for the detection and deletion of foreigners shall be January 1, 1966; (ii) all persons who came to the state prior to that date and whose names were included in the electoral rolls shall be regularised; (iii) The names of persons who came to the state between I January 1966 and 24 March, 1971 shall be detected and deleted from the electoral rolls for ten years, and thereafter these names shall be restored to the electoral rolls; (iv) foreigners who came to Assam on an after 25 March 1971 shall be detected and expelled; (v) constitutional, legislative and admini-strative safeguards shall be provided to protect the social, cultural and linguistic heritage of Assam; (vi) the government shall take speedy measure for the economic development of Assam and for the improvement of the standard of living of the people; (vii) citizenship certificates shall be issued by the central government; and (viii) international borders shall be made more secure to check future infiltration.

In terms of the accord the Assam Assembly was dissolved on 8 August *1995* and fresh elections held in December 1985. In these polls the Asorn Gana Parishad swept the polls and captured 64 seats in 26 member Assembly. On 24 December 1985 the AGP ministry under Profulla Kumar Mohanta was sworn in office.

The demand for a separate state for Telengana was raised by the people of the Telengana region of Andhra Pradesh, because the leaders of Andhra Pradesh failed to comply with the conditions laid down at the time of the creation of the state of Andhra Pradesh in November, 1946. As per this agreement they were expected to (1) from a Regional Committee of all the members representing Telengana in the State Assembly to deal with the matters relating to the region; (2) the entire revenue from the Telengana region, after making some allowance for the common expenditure of the state, was to be spent on the development of the region; (3) recruitment to certain posts in the region was to be made from amongst persons who had lived in the Telengana for at least fifteen years; (4) either the Chief Minister or the Deputy Chief Minister was to be taken from Telengana. The people of Telengana launched a peaceful agitation for a new State of Telengana. However, the agitation soon grew violent. In the light of these serious developments the Chief Minister of Andhra Pradesh (Brahmananda Reddy) announced his intention to faithfully implement the assurances given in 1956 and actually took certain positive steps in this direction. He transferred all the persons from Andhra appointed to its reserved for the people of Telengana. As a result of these 'developments the Telengana agitation was withdrawn.

When the Andhra Civil Servants returned from Telengana, the students of Andhra Pradesh started a counter agitation. This was countered by the people from Telengana region by resuming the agitation. Soon the things assumed serious dimensions and the Government had to call in army for the maintenance of law and order in the state. All the appeals of the Prime Minister to the Telengana leaders failed to have any effect and the agitation continued. During the next few months strikes, demonstrations, destruction of property and police firing became the normal feature. In on the eve of Lok Sabha elections, Mrs. Gandhi submitted leaders of Telengana movement were in no mood to wait fought elections on the basis of separatist programme.

After the election fresh negotiations took place Between the Prime Minister and the TPS (Telengana Praja

Samiti) leader DR. Chenna Reddy, which resulted in an agreement. As a result of this agreement the TPS agreed to merge itself with Congress (N), the Telengana Regional Committee was given a statutory status, separate five year plans for the Telengana region was provided; a person from Telengana was to be the Chief Minister of Andhra Pradesh The Prime Minister was authorised to review the situation after, three years and decide whether a separate state of Telengana should be created or not. This agreement did not find favour with some of the members of TPS and they continued the fight for separate state of Telengana. However, they could not sustain the movement for long and slowly the demand subsided.

The Gorkhas of Nepal living in the Darjeeling district of West Bengal have also been demanding a separate state. This demand, assumed serious dimension in, May 1986 following dumping of trainload of Meghalaya settlers in West Bengal, the Gorkhas under the leadership of Subash Ghising stepped up their demand for Gorkha state either within or without India for 15 lakh Gorkhas who have settled in the hilly districts of West Bengal. In subsequent months the problem grew more acute with a large number of Gorkhas fleeing from the strife torn Assam and settling in Darjeeling and surrounding areas.

For the attainment of its objective the Gorkha National Liberation Front launched violent agitation which resulted in loss of public property and life. However, subsequently Subash Gheising agreed to hold talks with the Union Home Minister to resolve the issue of citizenship of Nepalis and indicated his intention to settle all issues through democratic and peaceful methods. As a step in this direction he suspended the violent agitation and indicated his intention to continue the movement peacefully on a low key. Though the

Centre is willing to give greater autonomy to the regions! It has firmly ruled out the possibility of creation of separate state of Gorkhaland. In addition to the above noted cases where demands for separate states have been put forward, certain other areas or regions have also put forward demands for separate statehood. Some of the areas where such demands were put forward include the areas which formerly constituted the princely State of Mysore, where the people have demanded separation from Karnataka. The hilly regions of Uttar Pradesh, *viz.*, Kumaon, and Tehri Garhwal, have also voiced a demand for a separate state. In the wake of assumption of power by the Janata Party and its profession that it was not averse to small states, a number of regions of Uttar Pradesh put forward' demands for separate states. The people from western parts of Uttar Pradesh insisted on a state of Agra or Meerut containing Dehra Dun. They also insisted on a *Braj* state consisting of certain area of Uttar Pradesh and some parts of Rajasthan. The people middle west demand Rohilkhand. The people from south ern Uttar Pradesh demanded a state of Bundelkhand containing the districts of Madhya Pradesh as well. The people from southeastern Uttar Pradesh demanded trans-Vindhya State. The people eastern Uttar Pradesh insisted on 'Bhojpur' state comprising of eastern parts of Uttar Pradesh and parts of Western Bihar.

The tribal people of Bihar, Orissa, West Bengal and Madhya Pradesh put forward a demand for the creation of state of Jharkhand. April 1975 Jharkhand tribals staged a demonstration in New Delhi, About two hundred of them courted arrest to focus the attention of the government on their demand for a separate state. However, the demand for the creation of these states did not find ready response from the government.

In the third place, regionalism appeared in the shape of demand for full-fledged statehood in certain areas which were accorded the status of union territories under the constitution. Some of the union territories which raised such a demand include Himachal Pradesh, Manipur, Tripura, Pondicherry, Goa, Daman and Diu, Delhi etc. the Government initially did not concede their demand and tried to pacify the people by creating legislatures in some of these territories, viz., Himachal Pradesh, Manipur, Tripura, Pondicherry, and Goa, Daman and Diu. This naturally gave rise to similar demands from other Union Territories. However, in March 1969 the Government of India announced that no new legislative assemblies shall be created in union territories. It further asserted that even in those union territories where these had been created the government favoured either their merger with the adjoining states or their conversion into full-fledged states. The announcement encouraged the people of Himachal Pradesh, to renew their agitation for statehood and ultimately the Government conceded their demand on 31 July 1970. The other union territories also continued their demand for separate statehood but the government resisted the same.

However, in view of the growing popular pressure the Central Government decided to give the status of state to the union territories of Arunachal Pradesh, Mizoram and Goa during the period

Interstate dispute

Finally, regionalism in India has appeared in the shape of numerous disputes over territory, boundary, water etc. among "different units of the Indian Union. Some of the prominent interstate disputes are given below:

1. *Question of Chandigarh.* The dispute over the city of Chandigarh arose as a result of the bifurcation of the state of Punjab. Both Punjab and Haryana were keen to possess this modern city and resorted to

agitations to get the area. Ultimately at the intervention of the Union Government it was agreed that the territory of Chandigarh shall be handed over to Punjab in return for 114 Hindi speaking villages of the Fazilka tehsil as well as the towns of Fazilka and Abohar to be surrendered by Punjab to Haryana. However, both the states were permitted to use the territory of Chandigarh as their capital for the next five years. This settlement did not satisfy either of the two parties and was followed by strong protests and demonstrations. However, with the passage of time the tension slowly died out and the status quo continued

In the eighties the Akalis once again stepped up agitation for transfer of Chandigarh. Pressure was built up on the centre for the implementation of Anandpur Sahib and there were numerous incidents of riots and terrorism. This led to operation Bluestar and subsequent murder of Indira Gandhi which led to further violence. Ultimately on 24 July 1985 an accord was signed by Prime Minister Rajiv Gandhi and Sant Longowal, the Akali Dal President, which inter-alia provided for transfer of Chandigarh to Punjab in return for certain Hindi speaking areas of Punjab to Haryana. However, as no agreement could be reached regarding the Hindi speaking areas to be transferred to Haryana by Punjab the transfer of Chandigarh could not be effected, and it still continues, to be a source of irritation in Haryana Punjab relations.

2. *Mysore-Maharashtra Boundary Dispute.* The dispute over the Marathi speaking territories of Bijapur Belgum, North Kanara and Dharwar, which at present constitute part of Mysore is another manifestation of regionalism. The Government of Maharashtra approached the Union Government for the settlement of dispute over these territories. The

Government appointed a one man commission under former Chief Justice Mehar Chand Mahajan to look into the dispute. But before the Commission could submit its report violent agitation broke out in Maharashtra as well as Madras. Subsequently when the Mahajan Commission submitted its report, the same was firmly turned down by the Sampoorna, Maharashtra Samiti. On the other hand these recommendations were accepted by the state of Mysore. In view of the differences between the two parties the matter was referred to the Parliament for final decision. This evoked strong protests from the people of Mysore and violence broke out in many towns of Mysore. 'The Mysore Legislative Assembly also passed a resolution urging government of India to implement the Mahajan Commission commendations and enact necessary law. Thus the government in a dilemma, but somehow the tension was kept under control. In 1973 the trouble once again brewed and clashes took Place, between the Marathi people and the police at Belgaum. Soon trouble spread to Kolhapur where the hotels of Kannadians were looted and set on fire. Riots also broke out in Poona, Bombay a boundary dispute between Maharashtra and towns. This boundary dispute between Maharashtra and Mysore was ultimately resolved in 1975 with the of Jagjivan Ram.

Regional feeling also found outlet in the various disputes between states over the sharing of river waters. The distribution of water of river Krishna continued to be a source of tension among the states of Maharashtra, Madhya Pradesh, Orissa, Mysore and Andhra Pradesh, before the issue was referred to a tribunal headed by Justice D.M. Bhandari, a retired judge of the High Court of Rajasthan, in 1969. The tribunal submitted its report in 1979 regarding the sharing of the water and the final settlement regarding the sharing of water was arrived at, similarly, for a long time dispute persisted between The utilisation of the waters of, Tamil Nadu, Karnataka and Kerala over Cauvery. This dispute was ultimately resolved through the dedication of Jagjivan Ram. Another dispute arose over the propertilisation of the water of river Ravi between the states of Punjab jammu and Kashmir and Himachal Pradesh. These states also could not arrive at any settlement regarding the ownership of the Thehri Dam Project. The chief point of dispute was that while Punjab insisted on an exclusive right to utilise the water, the other two were not willing to forego their claims. The issue was ultimately decided through the intervention of the Central Government. As a result of the agreement Punjab was made to surrender its sole ownership rights and an inter-state board was set up to look after the proper utilisation of water of river Ravi. This Board contained representatives of all the three states.

Despite the above arrangement a dispute persisted for long between the states of Punjab, Haryana and Rajasthan over the hiring of the water of Ravi and Beas. This was ultimately resolved the intervention of Prime Minister Indira Gandhi in December '81, when the Chief Ministers of the three states signed an agreement at New Delhi. As per this agreement Punjab was given an additional, 0.72 million acre feet of water. Similarly Rajasthan's share was, also increased. However, the share of Haryana and Jammu and Kashmir remained unchanged at 3.50 million acre feet and 0.55 million acre feet respectively. The agreement enjoined upon the Bhakara and Beas Management Boards to take necessary measure to ensure delivery of supplies to the concerned states in accordance with their entitlements. The Board's decision regarding election of control points was made binding on the states. However if a state contested the decision of the Board the Central Government was given the power to decide the matter within three months and its decision was to be final and binding.

In the recent years regionalism has assumed serious dimensions. The rise of a large number of new regional parties in various parts of the country poses a serious threat to the existing political landscape of the country. In the north-east the regional tribal sentiments are very strong on the issue of foreign nationals which has greatly contributed to the popularity of the regional parties in the area. In West Bengal, the CPI(M), though an all India Party, has displayed powerful regional overtones. In Punjab where the militant regionalism, which was so far confined to a small group of extremist Akalis, is in full cry. This has encouraged rise of regionalism in Haryana because the people feel that Haryana is being made to pay the price of keeping Punjab quiescent. In Kashmir the National Conference has passed the resettlement bill which provides for the return to the state of those who had left it after I March 1947 to settle in Pakistan.

It is very clear from the above discussion that regionalism has been an important factor in the Indian politics and has posed a serious threat to that federal structure and unity of the country. Some of the states like Tamil Nadu, Punjab, Andhra Pradesh, Jammu and Kashmir, West Bengal etc. have eagerly supported the demand for greater autonomy for the states. They have come forward with numerous suggestions to drastically cut the power of the Central Government.

It may be observed that the states alone are not to blame for encouraging the feeling of regionalism. The Central Government must also share equal blame for encouraging regional sentiments. In view of the variety of languages, cultures and religions found in India, it would have been proper to create the units on the basis of religion, languages etc. No doubt, this would have resulted in larger number of states with small size, but it, would have satisfied the aspiration of all the sections of Indian society, and contributed to balanced development of all the regions and areas. Given to operate within their respective region, the local leaders would have concentrated on the solution of the problems of their respective regions and thus relived the national politics of evils like factionalism and regionalism.

Certain scholars have Opposed the idea of division of country to too Many states on the basis of language, religion etc. on the ground that it would jeopardise the unity and integrity of the country, However, this fear is ill-founded. It is a matter of common knowledge that the United States of America, which has only one-third of India's population has fifty states. The existence of so many states has in no way posed a threat to the unity of that country. On the same analogy it can be argued that the creation of large number of the states will not in any way effect the unity of Country. The actual working of the small states like Haryana, Himachal Pradesh, Meghalaya etc has demonstrated that the small sized states can make quick and rapid progress. It can therefore safely be suggested that if different linguistic and cultural groups are granted separate states with a firm control of the Central Government over subjects of national importance, this would lead to greater development of the various regions of the country without in any way posing a threat to the unity of the country.

The prevailing regionalism in the country is merely reflective of the diversity of a plural society and the new awakening among the people of India. As Nehru observed the "regional difficulties are not only consequential to the past but also emerge due to the country's progress." Viewed in this context regionalism is a milestone on the road to political development. As the country makes further progress in the direction of industrialisation; urbanisation sophisticated means of transport and communication, and balanced development through planning, regionalism would lose its grip. The process of regionalism can be further checked through reforms in the administrative and economic machinery, revision of centre-state relations, and evolving a system of national education which cuts across parochial caste, linguistic and regional thinking.

6

Religious Role

Religious processions involve the question of reconciling competing claims of religious freedom. One group may claim the right to take out on a highway a religious procession accompanied by music; the other may stake his claim to offer prayers in a place of worship located on the highway 'in a calm and peaceful manner. Such claims have generated a lot of communal tension and have led to considerable violence. The Government India Act, 1935 did not guarantee religious freedom. District Magistrates could, therefore, easily treat the problems of processions as simple matters of law and order. After the promulgation of the Constitution, the right to take out a religious procession attracts three fundamental rights under Articles 19 (l) (b), 19 (l) (d) and 25. Clause (b) of Article 190) guarantees the right to assemble peaceably and without arms. A procession, as Pointed out by Benson J., is an assembly in motion.' Clause (d) of Article 19(l) establishes the right to move freely throughout the territory of India. The right to freedom of speech and expression under Article 19(l) (a) will also be attracted in cases where the procession carries placards and shouts slogans. These rights are subject to the restrictions under Articles 19(3) and 19(5) respectively. The right to assemble peaceably and without, arms is subject to any law imposing reasonable restrictions in the interests of the sovereignty and integrity of India or of public order. The right to move freely throughout India is similarly subject to any law imposing reasonable able restrictions in the interests of the general public or for the protection of interests of any Scheduled Tribe. The right to religious freedom under Article 25 is subject to public order, morality and health and to other fundamental rights under Part III of the Constitution. In Manzur *Hasan v.* Muhammad *Zaman* the Privy Council upheld the right to take out a religious procession, if permitted by the District Magistrate, without interfering with traffic on public highways and the rights of the public. The Supreme Court has repeatedly upheld the law as settled by the Privy Council in *Manzur Hassan's* case. It has held that the State cannot impose unreasonable restrictions.' The, law enabling the authorities to make rules to regulate processions is, in fact, in aid of rights under Article 19(l) (b) and (d). In *Mohammad Sidique v. State of Uttar Pradesh,* the Allahbad High Court observed that difficulties arose when by reason of members of one particular sect or religion doing something in public, the religious susceptibilities of others are hurt and there is a danger of breach of peace. The Court held that the Magistrate could fix the time and the route for a religious procession and even prohibit a procession if he was satisfied that a breach of peace could not otherwise be averted. The Court would not sit in judgement over such a prohibition and perform the functions of a Magistrate. In *Himmatlal v. Police Commissioner Ahmedabad'* however, the Supreme Court held that the po·, er to regulate did not include total prohibitions, but restrictions would involve partial prohibition, as where a procession is asked to take one route and not another. Courts have also held that where two fundamental rights collided.

For example, the right of one group against another, a court will not hold restrictions on the right as unreasonable. In a dispute over playing of music by a procession near a mosque, the Supreme Court held that

Manzur *Hassan's* case had settled the law and the right to take out the procession with the accompaniment of music was subject to the orders of the competent authorities on the maintenance of law and order and regulation of traffic Playing of music cannot also be considered as a part of worship and its suspension even for a few minutes as an intermission of worship. The right has to be reconciled with the right of the other group to offer worship in its own place of worship.

The State assumes an extensive role in regulation of practices associated with religion for the primary object of preservation of public order. There is a vast expanse of regulatory measures. Sections 30 and 30A of the Bombay Police Act provide for licensing and regulation of processions. There are measures to regulate sacrificial slaughter on the days of *Id-ul-adha.* Section 144 of the Code of Criminal Procedure arms the authorities to prohibit processions and meetings during times of communal tension. The Indian Penal Code (IPC) has a full Chapter 15 that deals extensively with offences relating to religion: The various sections in the IPC punish respectively the destruction, damage or defilement of any place of worship or any object held sacred by any class of persons with intent to insult their religion (Section 295); the use of spoken or written words with malicious intent to outrage the religious feelings of any class of persons (Section 295A); the deliberate disturbance of public worship (Section 296); trespass on a sacred place with the intent to wound religious feelings (Section 297); and the utterance of words so to wound religious sentiments (section 298).

The Indian position with respect to freedom of expression stands out in contrast to the American and the English approach to the subject. In view of the delicate communal situation in India, the freedom of expression is strictly subjected, and rightly so, to considerations regarding maintenance of public order. American history, on the contrary, places a greater value on civil liberties. As the United States Supreme Court observed in *Cantwell v. Connecticutt* in 1940:

> In the realm of religious faith and in that of political belief, sharp differences arise. In both fields, the tenets of one man may seem the rankest error to his neighbour. To persuade others to his own point of view, the pleader, as we know, at times resorts to exaggeration, to vilification of men who have been, or are, prominent in church or state, and even false statement. But the people of this nation have ordained in the light of history, that inspite of the probability of excesses and abuses, these liabilities are, in the long view, essential to enlightened opinion and right conduct on the part of citizens of a democracy.

In England, the Church of England is the established church. As such, the law assumes the truth of Christianity; and as highlighted by the current fierce controversy regarding Salman Rushdie's blasphemous book *'Satanic Verms'*, rightly banned in India, the law of blasphemy in England extends protection only to the Christian faith and to no other religion. The law is, indeed, partisan and, in its inadequacy, cannot be called secular in nature. It is also an offence in England to 'attempt to convert anyone from the religion of the country even by most gentle persuasion.

The second Report of the Indian Law Commissioners' on the Indian Penal Code (1847), in its zeal to promote free religious discussions in India, advanced an interesting argument. It argued that as the truth or falsehood of any religion is not assumed by law to be beyond controversy, "a bonafide attempt to convert ought not in this country to be treated as a crime, even though the intention to convert be an intention to do so by wounding the feelings of the persons addressed. Pilgrimages and *melas* also attract governmental regulation. The government may also spend a considerable sum of money for an orderly conduct of these melas and pilgrimages. Such an expenditure cannot be deemed to be an expenditure in aid of or for establishment of any particular religion. A Central Act appoints a Haj Committee for purposes connected with Muslim pilgrimages for *Haj* and *'Ziara'*. An upper ceiling is also imposed upon the total annual number of Haj pilgrims to Holy Makkah. There are now restrictions also as regards allotment of accommodation to pilgrims in the holy city and there is a lot of resentment against these restrictions.

The role of the state as social and religious reformer

The role of the state as a religious reformer is, indeed, incompatible with the concept of a secular state. As we have already seen, the role has been dictated by the exigencies of the Indian situation. Legislative measures were enacted to deal extensively with several Hindu religious practices Eke *sati,* untouchability and temple entry, various practices associated with temple worship as animal sacrifices and *devadasi* dedication, and temple administration. There was also extensive codification with drastic alteration of Hindu Law.

The reform of religious practices by a State calls for a serious consideration of issues involved. Such reforms may endanger religious liberty. They have potential power to strike at the very root of our conception of a secular state. Our Constitution emphasises the basic neutrality of the state towards all religions. Reform of religious practices by the State is in the nature of the State promoting the particular religion. This is in a way 'establishment of religion'. When the Madras Legislative Assembly was discussing in 1950 a Bill to prohibit sacrifice of animals and birds in Hindu temples in the State of Madras, V.I. Muniswamy Pillai said:

> Taking into account how the world views the religion of the Hindus, I think it is high time that these small blemishes that are a blot on the Hindu religion should be removed It will go a longway to show to the world how sacred our religion is and how pure its worship.

Similarly, earlier when in 1936 the proclamation of the Maharaja of Travancore withdrew restrictions on temple entry by the Harijans, Srimati Rarneswari Nehru declared that the opening of the temples to Harijans "will revitalise our religion and put new life and strength into it.

This is not to suggest that a secular state must refrain from intervention even in the extreme case where a particular religious practice puts public interest in serious jeopardy, as in the case of sati, infanticide, untouchability and the like. The State must however, act with great caution and restrain. As A. Fonseca puts it, "it has to enforce only what is minimally acceptable and is socially necessary." Donald E. Smith elaborates:

> Religious reform *per se is* not a valid function of the secular state; it is not the business of the secular state to concern itself with religious matters. Furthermore, any such interference is likely to violate religious liberty, lead to the state promotion of religion, or both. Religious reform should never be the motive behind state legislation. Valid reforms of religion by the secular state are the incidental results of state protection of the public in cases where religious practices clearly tend to injure human beings physically or morally, where religious institutions grossly misuse offerings and endowments made by the public, or where social institutions connected with religion violate basic human rights.

In the West, too, the State had engaged itself with the reform of the Church. The motives varied widely. The reform of the Russian Orthodox Church by Tsarist Russia was undertaken in a spirit of hostility and was in fact, an instrument for establishment of Tsarist authoritarianism. Religio-political considerations moti-vated German princes to side with Martin Luther in the sixteenth century and to impose the Protest Reformation, In the case of Scandinavian countries, the Swedish King coveted the enormous wealth of the Church for its depleted treasury. In England, reforms were ushered in by the royal decree and acts of Parliament to free the church of alleged abuses. However, in all these countries, the state intervention was a sequel to accepted church-state system. The church was the officially established state church and the state had the responsibility of strengthening and promoting the church.

It is strange that contrary to the concept of a secular state which, in Indian context, enjoins minimal intervention in religion, the Supreme Court of India has deemed it fit progressively to widen the area of State intervention. It is respectfully submitted that the Supreme Court has deviated from nationally accepted direction. The Indian concept of a secular state, as distinct from the Marxist concept, is not infested with any hostility towards religion which may necessitate the judiciary to throw its weight against the scope of religion. Any such hostility would be judicial prejudice in favour of those who believe in no religion over those who do believe.

Articles 25 and 26 of the Constitution guarantee religious freedom. But it is not merely these articles that are relevant in the context. The right to liberty of thought, expression, belief, faith and worship find the prime of place in the Preamble to the Constitution itself. The Supreme Court has, adopting the observation of Latham C.J. held that Article 25 guarantees not only the freedom of religious opinion but also acts done in pursuance of religious belief as was clear from the use of the expression 'practice of religion'. Thus rituals, ceremonies and religious practices are 'matters of religion' within the meaning of Article 26(b). The Supreme Court has also ruled that a law providing for social welfare and reform is not to reform religion out of existence or identity However, the Supreme Court has developed a novel technique of classifying religious practices into two categories of essential and nonessential religious practices. Constitutional protection is extended only to the essential practices sanctioned by a religion." Initially, the Court warned that "what constitutes an essential part of the religion is primarily to be ascertained with reference to the doctrines of that religion itself'. The Court went on to reiterate forcefully:

> No outside authority has any right to say that these are not essential parts of religion and it is not open to the secular authority to restrict or prohibit them in any manner they like...

In *Devaru,* the Supreme Court went further to state that matters of religion in Article 26(b) included even practices which are regarded "by the community" as part of its religion, and treated the law as so settled.But soon thereafter, the Court, in another case ignored the law as settled and even disregarded *Ratilal* that 'no outside authority has any right to say that these are essential parts of the religion.' And then in yet another case the court struck a strong discordant note in saying that "in order that the practices in question should be treated as a part of religion they must be regarded by the said religion as its essential and integral part", and that "even practices though religious may have sprung from merely superstitious beliefs and may in that sense be extraneous and unessential accretions to religion itself."

In a severe criticism of the *obiter,* Seervai points out that the judgement substitutes the view of the court for the view of the denomination on what is essentially a matter of religion. He comments:

> The reference to superstitious practices is singularly unfortunate, for what is "superstition"to one section of the public may be a matter of fundamental religious belief to another....... It is submitted that in dealing with the practice of religion protected by provisions like those contained in s.116 Commonwealth of Australia Act or in Art. 26(b) of our Constitution, it is necessary to bear in mind the observations of Latham C.J....... namely, that these provisions must be regarded as operating in relation to all aspects of religion, irrespective of varying opinions in the community as to the truth of a particular religious doctrine or as to the propriety of any particular religious observance.

Nevertheless, the court in *Shri Govindlalji v. State of Rajasthan* reaffirmed that the practices claiming protection must be such as are regarded as essential and as "integral" part of the religion itself and declared that "this question will always have to be decided by the court.

It is strange that in a secular State, the court in its enthusiasm, should 'don the mantle of a Prophet' and sit to cleanse the religion of its unessential elements, superstitious beliefs and extraneous accretions. Such a role as religious reformer is alien to the philosophy on which a secular state is founded. Nor is it borne out of the long course of history. The essential-non-essential dichotomy, which the court has read into the provisions of Articles 25 and 26, is, in fact, alien to these Articles. There is nothing in these Articles to restrict constitutional protection to essential practices alone. The queer judicial innovation serves no useful, secular purpose, too. The people of India have, in the light of their historical experience and exigencies of the Indian situation, given unto themselves a Constitution that secures for them liberty of faith and worship subject only to the inevitable considerations of public order, morality and health and to such few other restrictions specifically incorporated in Articles 25 and 26. It is apparent that these restrictions have a useful, secular purpose to perform in the context of the Indian environment rather than attempt merely to limit the effective scope of benign religious influence.

There is an age-old and widespread practice of endowment for religious purposes. Though the State does not interfere in matters of religion in its doctrinal and ritual aspects, it does exercise control over the administration of properties endowed for religious institutions treating it as a public purpose, if the institutions were themselves dedicated to the public. As the scriptual or customary laws do not envisage any institutional supervision or control over the trustees to ensure utilization of the trust property in furtherance of the objectives of the trust, the state has always stepped into the breach. The Hindu kings exercised general supervision and intervened in cases of mismanagement. Kautiliya's *Arthasastra,* Ashoka's edicts, etch all indicate that from very early times in history, religious and charitable institutions received state protection. The policy of correctional intervention was pursued by the Muslim kings, too The British government was pressurised to abandon the policy but this abstinenance proved short-lived and it entailed disastrous consequences. Article 26 of the Constitution secures to religious denominations the right, subject to public order, morality and health, to manage its own affairs in matters of religion. It also has the right to administer its property in accordance with law. Thus, *in Lakshmindra, the* Supreme Court observed:

> It will be seen that besides the right to manage its own affairs in matters of religion, which is given by cl.(b), the next two clauses of Art. 26 guarantee to a religious denomination the right to acquire and own property in accordance with law. The administration of its property by a religious denomination has thus been placed in a different footing from the right to manage its own affairs in matters of religion. The latter is a fundamental right which no legislature can take away, whereas the former can be regulated by law which the legislatures can validly impose.

A host of judicial pronouncements govern the law. The Supreme Court has held that the administration of the denominational property, though subject to law, cannot be validly taken away altogether by the state. "A law which takes away the right of administration from the hands of religious denomination and vests it in any other authority would amount to violation of the rights guaranteed under clause (d) of Article 26. The scale of expenditure incurred in connection with religious observance could be controlled by a secular authority in accordance with a law, for it could not be the injunction of any religion to destroy the institution and its endowments by incurring wasteful expenditure on rites and ceremonies.

In Ratilal, the Supreme Court ruled:

> A religious sector denomination has the undoubted right guaranteed by the Constitution to manage its own affairs in matters of religion and this includes the right to spend the trust property or its income for the religious purposes and objects indicated by the founder of the trust or established by usage obtaining in a particular institution. To divert the trust property or funds for purposes which the Commission or the Court considers expedient or proper, although the original objects of the founder can still be carried out, is to our minds an

> unwarrantable encroachment on the freedom of religious institutions in regard to the management of their religious affairs... The state can step in only when the trust fails or is incapable of being carried out in whole or in part.

The Supreme Court *in Tilkayat Shri Govindlalji v. State of Rajasthan* upheld the entry of a person into the temple for inspection of property and seizure of hidden documents related to an inquiry into the affairs of the institution. In *Durgah Committee case,* the Court upheld the constitution of the Durgah Committtee under the Act to manage and supervise administration of the endowed property. It held that "if the denomination never had the right to manage the properties endowed in favour of a denominational institution, as for instance by reason of the terms on which the endowment was created, it cannot be heard to say that it has acquired the said rights as a result of Article 26 (c) and (d).

The Indian approach as regards corporate religious freedom strikes a similarity with the American approach. The West has well organised churches with tradition of complete autonomy, while the religious institutions in India are highly un-organised. Yet, however, there is a marked similarity in the approaches. The courts in the two countries have repeatedly emphasised that the religious denomination should be free to manage its religious affairs. Both the courts have also admitted the need for secular intervention to prevent mismanagement. The *Watson case* and the *Presbyterian Church case* permit the secular correctional intervention through 'neutral' principles of law. Taking off from Watson, the American judicial approach, too has progressively enlarged the basis for judicial intervention for preventing maladministration of church property while upholding ecclesiastical freedom... *Watson* required deference of the court to ecclesiastical autonomy. *Hansel* ruled that church-doctrines repugnant to public policy could not claim deference of the court under *Watson.* In *Gonzales* the Court held that "in the absence of fraud, collusion or arbitrariness, the decisions of the proper church tribunals on matters purely ecclesiastical, although affecting civil rights, are accepted in litigations before secular Courts as conclusive because the parties in interest made them so by contract or otherwise. In another case U. S. Supreme Court held that judicial intervention in ecclesiastical matters was unconstitutional under the free exercise clause." In the *Presbyterian Church case* the Court observed:

> It is obvious, however, that not every civil court decision as to property claimed by a religious organisation jeopardizes values protected by the First Amendment. Civil courts do not inhibit free exercise of religion merely by opening the doors to disputes involving church-property. And there are neutral principles of law, developed for use in all property disputes, which can be applied without 'establishing' churches to which the property is awarded.

When in *Lakshmindra,* Mukerjea, J., emphatically declared that the right of religious denomination to manage its own affairs in matters of religion was a fundamental right which no legislation can take away whereas the right to, administration of property could be regulated by a legislative enactment and then proceeded to examine the validity of the impunged Madras Act, he echoed the letter and the spirit of the Indian Constitution and the judicial approach compared favourably with the American approach. Justice Douglas observes that "the Indian cases have the flavour of American decisions" dealing with church property.

Recent Indian cases tend more to uphold the power of secular authority to supervise management of trusts. These may be due to the strictures contained in the *Report of the Hindu Religious Endowments Commission* (Government of India, 1962). The Report of the *Durgah KhaWaja Sahib (Ajmer) Committee of Enquiry* (Government of India, 1949), too, exposed glaring malpractices. However, one may here strike a note of caution to avoid the danger of civil authorities implicating themselves in the affairs of the religion contrary to our concept of the secular state. Donald E. Smith points out:

> The state certainly has a valid negative function to prevent the misappropriation of endowment funds by establishing procedures for effective supervision. The question is how deeply involved the state should become in the positive function of furthering the objects of religious endowment

In the field of administration of trust property, the assumption of powers by the state dis-proportionately greater than the need to avoid maladministration, would invariably implicate the state directly in establishment and promotion of religion. The function of the secular authority in relation to religious endowments should, therefore, be kept at the minimal social level necessary to prevent misappropriation of funds. This would ensure religious autonomy and mark an advancement towards the required separation of religion and politics in India. Several states in India have passed laws for administration of Hindu endowments. A mention may here be made of the battle of Madras Legislature with the judiciary to maintain effective control over the temples. Several provisions of the Madras Hindu Religious and Charitable Endowments Act, 1951, were struck down by the courts. The Act was then amended by the legislature in 1954. A number of provisions were again struck down by the Madras High Court in 1956. The legislature then enacted the Madras Hindu Religious and Charitable Endowments Act, 1959, despite fierce criticism. The debate on the Bill in the legislature pointed out the incompatibility of the claim to be a secular state with drastic powers over the internal affairs of religious institutions. Some alleged it to be a stealthy move towards nationalisation of temples. Nevertheless, the state emerged from public criticism and legal battles with a full-fledged department of Hindu religious endowments under a Minister exercising detailed regulation of the Hindu institutions through the commissioner. It is criticised that the commissioner for Hindu religious endowments holds powers 'greater than those of the Archbishop of Canterbury over the church'. He exercises power even to make additions and alterations in the budgets of the religious institutions. Even a cursory reading of the annual reports of the department, with all its claims for a drive towards renovation and repairs of temples, another drive for improvement of religious atmosphere of temples, etc., creates a picture of an official ecclesiastical structure with the commissioner as the new Archbishop of the state. As pointed out by Smith", the entire distinction between the regulation and the promotion of Hindu religious institutions is blurred and the status of the secular state is seriously compromised.

There is also a Central Wakf Act, 1954 and the Bombay Public Trust Act, 1950. The schemes of such Acts, too, should reflect the same approach to the question of religious endowments. This is more so when regulatory powers affect the affairs of minorities. The Central Wakf (Amendment) Bill passed by the parliament has not been brought into force. There are serious objections to various provisions of the Bill. Another amendment Bill is said to be on the anvil. It is sometimes argued that the Bombay Public Trusts Act, 1950 represents a more secular approach than the practice of separate enactments for different religious denominations. It deals equally with religious and charitable trusts belonging to all the denominations. However, separate enactments can effectively deal with and take cognizance of the peculiar situations facing each denomination. In so far as they conform to constitutional requirements they cannot be said to suffer from any infirmity in their approach.

The right of a religious denomination to own, acquire and administer property may also come into conflict with the right of the state to acquire or requisition the said property for public purpose. The Supreme Court in *Bihar v. Kameshwar Singh* rejected the contention that property already dedicated to a public purpose could not be acquired for another public purpose. It has been held that Article 26 (c) and (d) do not take away the right of the State to acquire property. There is an oft repeated demand that property belonging to religious denominations be exempted from the state's power of acquisition. The government has not responded to the demand. However, the government has replied to this author in the Lok Sabha that instructions had been issued to the concerned authorities to avoid acquisition of trust property. Serve suggests two possible solutions for resolving the conflicts of rights:

(1) The Courts should hold that a law which takes away property of a religious denomination without compensation or on payment of grossly inadequate compensation would be void against all religious denominations for violating Article 26; and

(2) When any complaint is made before a court that an impunged law for the acquisition of property deprives a religious denomination of its fundamental rights under Article 26 (a) to (c), or gravely abridges that right, the courts could restrain the enforcement of the law against the particular

denomination whose right under Article 26 are so affected, e.g., where the acquisition is for such an illusory or inadequate compensation that the place of worship would have to close down, the religious denomination having no money to put up another place of worship.

The conflict of rights is a serious threat and needs to be taken cognizance of lest the exercise of the right by the state should completely destroy the rights of individual denominations. Moreover, the question of wakf properties and places of worship raise serious issues.

Restriction, or provisions which have the effect of restrictions on creations of valid religious endowments is another area that needs attention, Obviously, a religious endowment is an endowment for a religious purpose. The court's jurisdiction and approach in determining what is a religious purpose is again a sensitive issue that saddles the judiciary with the same delicate responsibility of tender concern for religious freedom. The proposition that what is religious is to be determined according to the beliefs and practices of the community itself is, as we have seen, again begging the question. Further, that a practice is superstitious can be no bar against its being religious. In *Saraswathi Animal v. Rajagopal Amnial,* the Supreme Court had to decide on the question *of* building *of samadhis* (commemorative structures) for deceased Hindus other than *sanyasis* and ruled that the practice was not countenanced by Hinduism.

Certain provisions *of* the Indian Income Tax Act, 1961 also have the effect *of* placing restrictions on creation *of* trusts. Clause (b) of subsection (1) of section 13 provides that a charitable trust or institution that is created on or after April 1962 for the benefit of any particular religious community or caste shall not be entitled to enjoy tax exemption. As per Section 13(l) (a) income from property held under a trust for private religious purposes also does not qualify for exemption. Similarly, no exemption is available where the income of a religious or charitable trust established on or after I April, 1962 ensures directly or indirectly for the benefit of the founder, his relative or other specified persons [section 13(l)(c)(1)]. Further, these tax exemptions, it is provided, would be available only to such trusts as would conform to a specified pattern of investment of trust funds. The Taxation Laws (Amendment) Act, 1975 inserted a new subsection (5) in section 13 of the Income Tax Act laying down a pattern of investment of funds of charitable or religious trust if they were to continue to enjoy the tax exemption. In order to enable the trust to change over to the new pattern of investment in a gradual and a smooth manner, the law provided that the new pattern may be adopted before 1 April, 1978. This date was subsequently extended to 1 April, 198 1. The Finance Minister while presenting the budget for the year 1980-81 (Final) put the trusts on notice that this time limit would not be extended. As, however, all the modes *of* investment prescribed by the Act yielded income by way *of* interest, which is prohibited in Islam, this writer pointed out in the Lok Sabha that the modes of investment discriminated against Muslim trusts and *Wakfs* and pleaded that investment in immovable property be also permitted to qualify for tax exemptions. A deputation also waited upon the then Prime Minister Smt. Indira Gandhi. Accordingly, the then Minister *of* Finance R. Venkataraman made a statement in Lok Sabha on 31 March, 1981 which said:

> It has been represented that the modes *of* investment prescribed by section 13(5) yield income by way *of* interest, acceptance of which is contrary to tenets of Islam. The Government have, therefore, decided to modify the patterns *of* investment prescribed under section 13(5) *of* the Income Tax Act so as to permit

> charitable or religious trusts or institutions to invest their trust funds in immovable property as well. Suitable amendment to the Income Tax Act will be sponsored at an early date and shall be made effective from 1 April, 1981.

The statement and the consequent amendments are the crowning glory of secularism in India. They reflect due consideration to both the questions of religious freedom (Articles 25 & 26) and equality before laws (Article 14) in the regulation of trusts by the State.

Political involvement of religious functionaries

None of the major religions in India has an organised ecclesiastical form in the Western sense. The clergy in Hinduism comprises a wide variety of functionaries. These include temple priests, *sadhus, gurus, tantriks,* astrologers, family priests, *sanyasis,* and others. Islam has no priesthood. The *ulema* and the faqihs are generally those who have studied in any one of the traditional schools *(Darul-uloom).* Anyone can become an Vim, even through private study. The learned Maulana Abul Kalam Azad, for example, did not go through any recognised *Darul-uloom;* he was a class by himself. Those familiar with the institution and the history of the organised churches in the West may consider the Indian situation in this respect readily amenable to the separation of the church and the state. Indeed "the western phenomenon of sustained power struggle between church and state, each armed with its own weapons" may not have its counterpart in South Asia. Nevertheless, religious functionaries in India command a great political influence.

The question of clerical involvement in politics engaged judicial attention in 1955. In *Mathai Mathew Manjuran v. K.C.Abraham"* the Election Tribunal at Ernakulam, presided over by K. Sankaranarayana Iyer, referred to and quoted approvingly from Parker's *Election Agent and Returning Officer.*

> All clerical and spiritual influence is not, however, undue. In the proper exercise of their legitimate influence, priests and clergy may lecture the people, and address these congregations upon the conflicting claims of the different candidates, even in their chapels, for a priest is a citizen and entitled to have his political opinions, and to exercise his legitimate influence legitimately. So also, if priests believe that a spirit of antogonism to their church, religion or clergy has arisen, and recognise in a particular party elements of danger to religion, they may use their influence to assert and maintain due respect to religion, and may express their opinions, in suitable language, that issues of great importance to religion are involved in a pending political contest. But a priest must not pass the bounds of legitimate influence; he must exercise his just influence without denunciation, and he has no privilege to violate or abuse the law, or to interfere with the rights and privileges of other subjects.

The Tribunal held:

> Perhaps the locus classicus of the law on the subject is to be found in the judgement of Fitzgerald, J. in *Longford* The Catholic priest has, and ought to have, great influence. His position, his sacred character, etc. ensure it to him. In the proper exercise of that influence on elections, the priest may counsel, advise, recommend, entreat and point out the true times of moral duty, and explain why one candidate, should be preferred to another, and may, if he thinks fit, throw the whole weight of his character in the scale; but he may not appeal to the fears, or terrors or superstition of those he addressed. He must not hold outhopes ofreward here or hereafter, and he must not use threats of temporal injury or of disadvantage, or of punishment hereafter. He must not threaten to excommunicate or withdraw sacraments.

The Tribunal examined the question of 'undue influence' with reference to the role of the priests. 'Undue influence' is deemed to be a corrupt practice under section 123 of the Representation of the People Act, 1951.

It was alleged that during the Andhra Pradesh election, the Bishop of Nellore issued a circular dated 20 January, 1955 to the churches in his diocese which said, *inter alia:*

> As the Andhra State Elections are coming nearer, I request you to instruct our people that it is their duty to vote, a conscientious duty, to be fulfilled according to the laws of God and of the Church....... I further request you to warn our people against joining or supporting the Communist Party in any way, either by voting or by spreading its literature or by becoming members of the Communist Party......... We solemnly exhort pastors of souls to warm those committed to their cause, in season and out of season......... that a Catholic who, even though he does not admit these false doctrines, knowingly and freely joins or supports a Communist Party, may not be admitted to the Sacraments and that he endangers his eternal salvation.

Another circular dated 23 September, 1959 was allegedly issued by the Bishop of Mangalore at the time of Kerala elections. The circular said:

> While giving one's votes, a Catholic should clearly bear in mind that he is forbidden under pain of ex-communication to vote for the communist candidate. It does not matter what enticing promises he makes or what beneficial undertakings he gives, the very fact that he is a communist he is unworthy, unsuitable and a dangerous candidate for us Catholics.

The circular, however, permitted a Catholic candidate at the PODS to receive or canvas for communist votes provided that by doing so he did not play into their hands nor sacrificed Christian principles. The circular enjoined that it be read in all churches and public chapels of the Diocese on any Sunday in October and that it be explained in the appropriate vernaculars.

Moving the Bill in the Lok Sabha on 1 April, 1960, the Communist member from Andhra Pradesh, T. Nagi Reddy declared that religious incursions in politics had to be put to an end if the secular democracy in the country was to be strengthened. The Bill was moved by Nagi Reddy in the absence of another member T.B.Vittal Rao who had introduced the Bill earlier. He took strong exception to threats of excommunication and regarded them as dangerous interference in the political life of a nation. He pointed out that Article 25(2)(a) of the Indian Constitution permitted restrictions on political activities associated with religious practice. He clarified that the Bill did not seek to put on the Catholic Church any religious restrictions; it only sought to restrict the political activity of an organised Church. Elaborating, he referred to an answer given by Rev. Maria Doss in the court during a cross-examination that should there be a Papal Edict directing Catholics in India not to vote for the Prime Minister Pandit Nehru, the Church in India would demand laymen of the community strict compliance with the directive of His Holiness.

The Bill, entitled the Catholic Church Premises and Ecclesiastical Order (Restriction of Political Activity) Bill, 1959, provided that no Catholic Church and/or church premises or resources be used for any Political activity. The expression 'political activity' was defined to mean any activity in favour of or against Government or any political party or group or propagation of political groups. Clause 4 of the Bill laid down that:

(i) any person who used any Catholic Church or the Church premises or resources for any political activity and

(ii) any Cardinal, or Archbishop, Bishop, Vicar, dignitary, functionary, or officer of the Catholic Church who took part in or encouraged political activity,...would be liable to be warned by the appropriate Government and his name together with the warning would be published in the official gazette.

In a strong rebuttal of the allegations against the Church and in an elucidation of the role of the Church, an Honourable Member Maniyangandam" quoted from the instructions issued by the Holy Sea to its Ministers as early as 1659:

> Keep entirely aloof from political interests and matters of State so that you never meddle with the administration of civil matters even though requested and even importuned by many prayers to do so.

The Honourable Member maintained that the policy was consistently followed by the Church and pointed out that the policy was even incorporated into the Regulations promulgated by the Plenary Session of the Catholic Archbishops and Bishops of India held at Bangalore in 1950. Rule 75 promulgated at the session forbade the clerics to employ authority of their ecclesiastical state in order to promote the cause of political or popular parties. But, argued Maniy-angadan, that did not mean the authorities of the Church were denied their citizens' right. A Bishop or a priest, in exercise of his right as a citizen, could take part in politics. Accordingly, Rule 175 said:

> Priests and religious men who are citizens of this country shall exercise their political rights and as citizens they may rightly have their political opinions and manifest them as private opinions. But the exercise of this right must never be an impediment to the efficacious exercise of their ministry. Since, however, as priests and as shepherds of the people, they have a state in the Church and represent her before the people, they must abstain from giving their name to any political faction.

In addition to the right of the clergy to participate in the political process of the country as ordinary citizens, an important duty, too, devolved upon them. So, Rule 161 says:

> All should remember that it is up to the Bishops to declare to the faithful whether the intention or the activity of any political party offends against God's law or that of the Church, to warn the faithful, who are their subjects, against the dangers of faith and morals or harm that might result from their adherence to any such party and for this reason even to forbid their membership.

A guiding principle was acordingly enunciated to say that among many associations to which, according to the above norms, one may not belong are associations or parties which are imbued with the principles of communism or which follow Marxian principles such as materialism, the use of violence in political matters and other similar things which are opposed to the 'Divine Law' and the doctrines of the Church.

In the opinion of Maniyangadon, nobody could object to an organisation, whether political or religious, to frame rules which prohibited its adherents to join organisations which were against its basic objectives. Similarly, there could be no objection to the organization framing rules to exclude from it such persons who worked against its objectives or against the fundamental and basic principles on which the organisation was founded. Lok Sabha member Ignance Beck also advanced similar arguments."

Bhupesh Gupta from West Bengal moved the Bill for consideration in the Rajya Sabha on 22 April, 1960. Arguments ran on almost similar lines as those made in the Lok Sabha. Bhupesh Gupta, during the course of his speech in the Rajya Sabha, referred to and quoted from a letter which he said he had received about his Bill from the Kerala Catholic League General Council, Ernakulam. The letter stated, *inter alia:*

> As citizens, Catholic priests too have all rights of citizenships including the right to take part in political activity...... We shall not feel called upon to protest in the event a Catholic priest or for that matter any priest were to address a public meeting and to include party politics in his speech. If, however, the priest were to include party politics in his sermon inside the church to a religious congregation, we shall regard this as a breach of Secular State that India is.

An objection against the Bill was that it discriminated against the Catholic Church as against all places of worship and violated Article 14 of the Constitution which guarantees equal treatment before law. The Minister of State in the Ministry of Home Affairs, Shri Datar, in his intervention during the debates in both the Houses of Parliament, felt that the existing law was sufficient to take care of the situation. He said that unless a very strong case could be made out by which any religious Organisation could be legitimately held responsible for what could be called subversive activities, it would not be proper to take away this important right they had." He raised a question whether "certain dignitaries of a particular denomination or of a religion should or should not teach correct religion in so far as even what are properly called political question are concerned. As, however, the subject was in the Concurrent List of the Constitution, the Minister wanted the State Governments to consider the entire issue in the light of the situation in their respective states.

The question of ousting the presence of clergy from the vast expanse of the vaguely defined territory of political activity, or even from its restricted area of electrol process, involves, apart from its doubtful validity, substantial questions of law and its implementation. Both the dominant religions of India, Hinduism and Islam, do not conceive of any organised ecclesiastical structure. The 'clergy' in India is therefore composed of a wide and a diverse variety of religious functionaries and the term, consequently, is not susceptible to any precise limitations of a definition. The religious functionaries have their fundamental rights as citizens of the country, too. Though the right to vote or stand as a candidate for election is not a fundamental right but is a creature of, and is subject to, the statute, the right to freedom of speech and expression, etc. are fundamental rights. These rights cannot be circumscribed or abrogated without impairing seriously the basic democratic character of the Constitution. Khushwant Singh rightly wonders: But how are we to prevent people enjoying religious status from pronouncing on matters which are not strictly concerned with religious ritual but have bearing on problems concerning respective communities. Article 19 of the International Covenant on Civil and Political rights, 1966 declares that everyone shall have the right to hold opinions without interference. Paragraph 2 of the Article states that every one shall have the right to freedom of expression, including the right to seek, receive and impart information and ideas of all kind.

Accordingly, the Parliament has enacted the Representation of the People Act, 1951. Chapter III of Part II of the Act lays down certain disqualifications for membership of Parliament and State Legislatures. These disqualifications are on grounds of conviction of certain offences (section 8), corrupt practice (section 8A), dismissal for corruption or disloyalty (section 9), subsistence of government contracts (section 9A), office under Government company (section 10), and failure to lodge account of election expenses. Chapter IV lays down disqualification for voting arising out of convictions for certain offences punishable under the Indian Penal Code or for corrupt practice under the Act (section 1 1A). It is sometimes suggested that another provision be introduced to Chapter III of Part II of the Act to disqualify 'religious heads' from contesting elections. A similar suggestion was even made at the seminar conducted by the Supreme Court Bar Association in Delhi on 17 October, 1987. But, notwithstanding the practical difficulties of such a law, it may be noted that though film-stars of late have entered electrol battles as candidates, the entry of 'religious heads or persons holding religious offices' has not assumed any significant proportions in India.

No law in any democratic country in the world (except in Mexico where the clergy, that had supported the colonial masters and opposed the revolution, is stripped of voting right) prohibits religious functionaries or institutions from participating in politics. As cited in a judicial pronouncement examined earlier, the clergy can freely participate, address the congregations, counsel on the merits and demerits of issues involved and even serve as election agents for candidates. The Supreme Court in India has conceded that religious leaders have right freely to express the, opinion on the comparative merits of the contesting candidates and to canvas for such of them as they considered worthy of the confidence of the electorate." Certain Churchmen are, however disqualified from being elected to the House of Commons. According to the House of Common, (Clergy Disqualification) Act, 1801, 'no person having been ordained to the office of priest or deacon or being a minister of the Church of Scotland. is or shall be capable of being elected to serve in Parliament as a member of House of Commons. The Act is also applicable to Northern Irelanc Similarly, Section 9 of the Roman Catholic Relief Act, 1829, so disqualified, the Roman Catholic priests. It says that

> no person in holy orders in the Church of Rome shall be capable of being elected to serve in Parliament as a member of the House of Commons; and if any such

> person shall be elected to serve in Parliament as aforesaid such election shall be void.

On the dis-establishment of the Welsh Church, the holders of ecclesiastical office in the Church of Wales were exempted from disqualification. Section 2(4) of the Welsh Church Act, 1914, says that

> on and after the date of dis-establishment no person shall be disqualified or liable to any penalty for sitting or voting in the House of Commons by reason of having being ordained to the office of priest or deacon if the ecclesiastical office he holds is an ecclesiastical office in the Church of Wales.

The date of disestablishment was fixed at 31 March, 1920 by section 2 of the Welsh Church (Temporalities) Act, 1919. Ministers of the Nonconformist Churches are also not disqualified. Thus, Church of England clergymen and Scottish Ministers and Roman Catholic priests are disqualified by the statute. The dis-establishment of the Church of Ireland in 1869 by the Irish Church Act 1869 has not removed the disqualification imposed upon clergymen of that Church by the Act of 1801.

The grounds on which certain clergymen in England are disqualified from being elected to the House of Commons need attention. According to the Journals of the House of Commons (C.J.), Prebendary Nowell was excluded in 1553 as the clergymen of the Church of England were taxed by Convocation and represented in the Convocation.63 That was, however, the old constitutional position. The House of Commons (Clergy Disqualification) Act, 1801 was justified on the ground that as the benefices of a great number of clergy were in the direct gift of the Crown, or of nobility, the admission of clergymen would diminish the purity and impair the independence of the House of Commons.' The Clerical Disabilities Act of 1870 rendered it possible for any clergyman of the Church of England legally to relinquish the rights and privileges of his office and so become eligible for election to Parliament. Suffice it to say, that the ground, namely, holding of office of profit under Crown, for disqualification of certain clergymen to contest elections to the House of Commons, has no relevance to the Indian situation. In the United States, no law prevents the Church or any religious order from participating in any political activities. Nothing in the Constitution warrants their exclusion. On the contrary, James Madison, the Primary architect of the First Amendment wrote to Thomas Jefferson:

> Does not the exclusion of Ministers of the Gospel as such violate a fundamental principle of liberty by punishing a religious profession with the privation of a civil right ?

Restrictions on the exercise of the ordinary rights of citizenship by clergymen are neither regarded as any integral part in the legal or constitutional arrangement for separation of state and religion nor as conducive to liberal democratic traditions. The so-called 'secular' political parties in India have not hesitated to draft religious personalities, Imams (those who lead prayers in mosques) and such others in their election campaigns. Even artists who have played the roles of *Ram* and *Hanuman* on the television serials have been inducted into election tours to cash on their 'reflected reverence'. In the United States, Nixon wanted to utilise the Church but had to beat a retreat in the face of strong, adverse press and public opinion. In fact, an effective check to unwholesome practice in political activities lies in educated public opinion rather than in the realm of mere legal or constitutional regulations.

Appeal to religion during elections

Another important aspect of Religio-political interaction during elections is the appeal to the electorate on ground of religion. An appeal to religion during an electoral process has a vast potentiality to generate such powerful emotions of divisive nature as to be destructive of the country's integration and the concept of secular democracy. Religious influence may enter the electoral field through (a) an appeal made to vote or refrain from voting any person on the ground of his religion, caste or community or (b) the abuse of religion, caste, etc. to promote feelings of enmity or hatred between different classes of citizens. The law in India in order to prevent the exploitation of religion for unfair electoral gains is contained, 'with its obvious limitations in the Representation of the People Act, 1951. The election of a returned candidate is liable to be set aside as void where any corrupt practice is committed by a returned candidate or his election agent or by any other person with the consent of the returned candidate or his election agent. Where a corrupt practise is committed by a third person without the consent of the candidate or his election agent the election is liable to be set aside where, among other conditions, the third person was an agent of the candidate. The corrupt practices, as we have seen, include appeal on grounds of religion and undue influence. The appeal by a Candidate or his agent or by any other person with the consent of the candidate or his election agent to vote or refrain from voting for any person on the ground of his religion or use of, or appeal to religious symbols for furtherance of the prospects of election of that candidate or for prejudicially affecting the election of any candidate, is corrupt practice under section 123(3). The paramount and basic purpose underlying this section, as pointed out by the Supreme Court, is the concept of secular democracy. The Court has clarified that the section was enacted so as to eliminate from the electoral process appeals to divisive factors such as religion, race, caste, community or language which give vent to irrational passions. Court has observed that powerful emotions generated by religion should not be permitted to be exhibited during election and that decision choice of the people are not coloured in any way. The section seek curb communal and separatist tendencies in the country. Even a sin appeal on ground of religion, etc. would be corrupt practice. An allegation of corrupt practice would, however, have to be proved beyond reason doubt. A corrupt practice in this section can be committed by appeal to the voters to vote for the candidate on the ground of his religion, even though his rival candidate were to belong to the same religion. Similarly the promotion or attempt to promote, feelings of enmity or hatred between classes of the citizens of India on ground of religion, is a corrupt practice under section 123(3A). Undue influence by the candidate or by his age or by any other person with the consent of the candidate or his elect agent also vitiates the election. These provisions of law are applicable to all and make no distinction between ordinary people and the clergy of divine displeasure is 'undue influence' irrespective of whether the is invoked by the religious head or by any other person provided that religious head or that other person is an agent of the candidate or does threaten with the consent of the candidate or his election agent. A that voters who vote for rival candidates would go to hell was held to invoking divine displeasure and amounted to exercising undue influence Reading out communal articles and declaring *Jehad* in public meeting was held to be a corrupt practice by exercise of 'undue influence Printing of the word *'hukam'* (an injunction) in very bold type in a circular issued by a religious leader to vote for a certain candidate was held exercise of 'undue influence'. Where it was represented to the electorate that certain candidate was a nominee of Akal Takht by no less a person than the former Chief Minister of the State in the presence of the candidate m also made the same statement, and where all the consequences of *Hukamnama of* Akal Takht was highlighted before the electorate, it held that appeal was made in the name *of* religion and that the returned candidate was guilty *of* corrupt practice. The candidates at election co not also be allowed to tell the electors that their rivals were unfit to act their representatives on grounds *of* their religious professions or practice. To Permit such propaganda would be to allow assaults on what sustains basic structure *of* our democratic state!' It would not be an appeal religion if a candidate is put up by saying 'vote for him' because he is good Muslim, but it would be an appeal to religion if it is publicised that not to vote for him would be against Sikh religion or against Christian religion or against Hindu religion or to vote for the other candidate would be an act against a particular religion. It would be an appeal on the ground of religion if an impression is created that it would be irreligious not to vote for a particular party or person. Where one of the contestants was a Jain and the other a Sanatan Dharmi Hindu, the cry that the *Sanatan Dharma* was in danger at the hands of the Jains, that a *Sanatan Dharmi* had therefore been set up against a Jain and that votes should be cast in his favour to save the *Sanatan Dharma,* was held to be an appeal made on the grounds of religion and community

An election petition of sweeping importance came up before Justice S.P. Bharucha of the Bombay High Court. Thee Court closely examined,, the validity of the election contested on the planks of Hinduism. *Hindutva* and *Hindu Raj.* The Court even served notice on the Shiv Sena Chief *Bal Thackeray* (who was not a party to the petition) in connection with the allegation of corrupt practices 19 and the Shiv Sena Chief filed his affidavit in pursuance thereof. It was deposed before the Court that Shiv Sena stood for the protection of Hinduism and that it was on that stand that it proposed to step into the Legislative Assembly. The Court was told that the stances of protecting Hinduism had been adopted by the Shiv

Sena in 1985. The Court found that the general refrain of the speeches of the Shiv Sena Chief was that India belonged to the Hindu; that the government followed a policy of appeasement of Muslims; that Hindus were subjected to all sorts of injustices; that the Shiv Sena candidate was a candidate of Hindus and Hindus should vote for him alone; that if Shiv Sena came to power then everybody would be converted to Hinduism; that if every mosque was dugup, beneath it would be found a temple; that Muslims had multiplied considerably in numbers and were threatening to edge 'Ram' out of his house; that most or many of the Muslims were anti-nationalist; that the victory of the Shiv Sena candidate would be a victory for the protection of Hinduism, otherwise the Hindu was finished, etc. On the question of the fundamental right of free speech under article 19(l) (a) of the Constitution, the Court noted that the point would seem to be covered by the decision of the Supreme Court in *Jamna Prasad Mukhariya v. Lachhi Ram*. The provisions regarding corrupt practice, it was held, did not stop a man from speaking; they merely prescribed conditions which had to be observed if he wanted to enter parliament. Justice Bharucha also observed that freedom of religion did not imply that one may traduce the community or religion of another.

He ruled.

> Those who participate in the process of elections which are held under the provisions of the Constitution, must abide by the Constitution's cardinal tenets.... To campaign on the ground that India belongs to the Hindus......... is to flout a cardinal tenet of the constitution. Every citizen of India is equal before the law, irrespective of religion and community. To campaign on the ground that India belongs to the Hindus is to say that all those who are not Hindus are, or ought to be, second class citizens who are not entitled to the same treatment as the Hindus. The statement would create enmity and hatred by fostering resentment among Hindus that Muslim citizens who

> should be getting treatment inferior to that which they are getting were, in fact, getting the same, if not better treatment.

The court held that appeal was made to the voters to vote on grounds of religion and that corrupt practice was also committed on the ground of promotion of feelings of enmity or hatred on grounds of religion and community. Appeal against the decision of the Bombay High Court is in the Supreme Court.

Use of the premises and resources of religious institutions for political purposes

On 17 February, 1961 a non-official resolution ' was moved in the Lok Sabha by Parulekar asking the Government "to bring forward legislation to prevent the use of places of religious worship and pilgrimage for Political propaganda and agitation." Indrajit Gupta pleaded that for election Purposes at least, the government should bring some suitable amendment to the Representation of the People Act to prohibit the use of places of worship for the purposes of election propaganda. The Minister of State in the Ministry of Home Affairs Shri Datar agreed with the principle that there ought not to be any misuse of places of worship, but expressed difficulties in accepting the resolution. He pointed out that the subject, namely Religious institutions and endowments, came under Entry 28 of the Concurrent list, and though the Parliament ' could undertake legislation, a salutary principle was followed to leave the matter for the initiative of the State Governments. He said that it was open for the State Government, to sponsor legislation on their own or, subject to the provisions of the Constitution, request the Central Government to do so, He offered to send a detail summary of the proceedings of the House to state governments. Referring to elections, he said that the political parties did not air merely political views, but had what could be called their own ideology about life. The ideology might not be acceptable to those who followed certain established principles of religion. It might then be a part of their religious dogma to protest against it. He added that the state governments could go into the legal and constitutional questions involved. He, however, observed that the evil was not of such intensity as to warrant a central legislation in this respect.

By 1988, the central government deemed it expedient to move in the matter. In the opinion of the central government, the 'evil' had assumed such an intensity that the govenment could not even wait for the Parliament Session. On 26 May, 1988, the President of India promulgated the Religious Institutions (Prevention of Misuse) Ordinance, 1988 to prevent misuse of religious institutions for political and criminal purposes. The ordinance was necessitated by the situation in Punjab and the events of a fortnight earlier when the Golden Temple at Amritsar was cleared of terrorists. The Statement of Objects and Reasons of the Bill which later replaced the Ordinance admitted that "in the light of certain incidents in the State of Punjab, it had become necessary to immediately bring out legislation to prohibit the carrying on of political and other activities in religious institutions." However, in its reach and scope, the legislation embraced the entire country and applied in equal measure to gurdwaras, temples, mosques and churches. It was explained that the question of misuse of religious institutions for political and other purposes had been engaging the attention of the government for some time and assurances had also been made in Parliament and outside that necessary legislation In this regard would be brought out soon. It was also claimed that the Ordinance was the first step in separating religion from politics and it represented the sentiments expressed by members of the National Integration Council who had called from time to time for such legislation. The Ordinance, it was claimed, would promote the principles of secularisrn enshrined in the Constitution and strengthen the sovereignty, unity and integrity of the country. After the promulgation of the Ordinance, the Centre also wrote to the Chief Minister of all States, seeking their utmost cooperation in implementing the provisions of the Ordinance. The daily Tribune wrote:

> The idea of the Centre drawing attention of all States to the provisions (of the Ordinance) is to remove the impression that they would be applicable only to Punjab.

The Jammu and Kashmir Government was also requested to take necessary steps to adopt the Ordinance for the State. The Ordinance was replaced by the Bill passed by the Lok Sabha on 11 August 1988 and by the Rajya Sabha on 19 August 1988. The Bill received the assent of the President on 1 September 1988 as Act No.41 of 1988.

According to section 1(3) the Act shall be deemed to have come into force on 26 May 1988. Section 3 of the Act is indicative of the seriousness of the situation and the sweep of the Act. It prohibited a religious institution or manager thereof to use or allow use of any premises belonging to, or under the control of, the institution for promotion or propagation of any political activity. It also prohibited the use of any such premises for harbouring any person accused or convicted of an offence under any law for the time being in force, for storing of any arms or ammunition, for keeping any goods or articles in contravention of any law, and for the carrying on of any unlawful or subversive act, or acts which promote or attempt to promote disharmony or feelings of enmity, hatred or ill-will between different religious, racial, language or regional groups or castes or communities. It also prohibited the carrying on of any activity prejudicial to the sovereignty, unity and integrity of India or any act in contravention of the provisions of the Prevention of Insults to National Honour Act, 1971. The erection or putting up of any construction or fortification, including basements, bunkers, towers or walls without a valid license or Permission under any law is also prohibited. Section 4 and 5 respectively make it obligatory for the religious institutions or the manager thereof not to allow the entry of arms and ammunition into a religious institution and the use of funds of religious institutions for the benefit of any political party or for purposes of any political activity, etc. Section 6 prohibited a religious institution to allow any ceremony, festival, congregation, procession or assembly organised or held under its auspices to be used for any political activity.

The Act prescribes an imprisonment for a term which might extend to five years and with fine which might extend to ten thousand rupees for the manager and every person connected with contravention of the provisions of the Act. The offenders under the Act would stand removed from the office held by them in any religious institution and would further stand disqualified for further appointment for a period of six years. It shall also be obligatory for every manager or other employee to give information to the officer in charge of the police station of the locality of any contravention or any impending contravention of the provisions of the Act and any failure to do so would entail punishment under section 176 of the Indian Penal Code.

Several acts of misuse of religious place prohibited under the Religious Institutions (Prevention of Misuse) Act, 1988 are, however, already covered by the provisions of other statutes in force. Section 153A of the Indian Penal Code penalises all attempts to promote enmity between different groups on grounds of religion, race, place of birth, residence, language, caste or community and doing acts prejudicial to maintenance of harmony.

Section 153B penalises a person for making imputations or assertions prejudicial to national integration. Subsections (2) of sections 153A and 153B specifically refer to and enhance the punishment for these offences if committed in a place of worship or in any assembly engaged in performance of religious worship or religious ceremonies. 'Me Unlawful Activities (Prevention) Act, 1967 deals with both the associations and the individuals indulging into unlawful activities. The Act covers activities directed towards bringing about sucession of any part of the territorial integrity of India. It is strange enough that despite all claims for deterrent punishment, a guilty under section 7 of the recent Religious Institutions (Prevention of Misuse) Act, 1988, is punishable with imprisonment of a term which might extend to five years and with fine which might extend to ten thousand rupees whereas the existing section 13 of the Unlawful Activities (Prevention) Act, 1967 provides for similar offences more stringent punishment of a term which might extend to seven years and a fine without any specified maximum limit!

The Religious Institutions (Prevention of Misuse) Act, 1988 has been hailed as a significant step towards separation of religion and politics. Accordingly, the provisions of the Act do not confine themselves to the prevention of misuse of religious institutions for only the criminal and illegal acts. The Act lays down that no religious institutions or manager thereof shall use or allow use:

(1) of any premises belonging to, or under the control of, the institution for promotion or propagation of any political activity [Section 3, clause (a)];

(2) of any funds or properties belonging to or under the control of, the institution for the benefit of any political party or for the purpose of any political activity [Section 5];

(3) of any ceremony, festival, congregation, procession or assembly organised or held under its auspices for any political activity [Section 6]

The expression 'political activity' is defined by section 2(d) to include:

> any activity promoting or propagating the aims or objects of a political party or any cause, issue or question of a political nature by organising meetings, demonstrations, processions, collection or disbursement of funds, or by any other means, and includes such activity by or on behalf of a person seeking election as a candidate for any election to Parliament, any State Legislature or any local authority.

The definition thus casts its net far and wide. The term 'political activity' includes not only activity promoting the objects of a political Party but also 'any cause, issue or question of a political nature'. The expression is extremely vague and breeds confusion. Both religion and Politics deal with the conduct of man. It would be an exercise in futility to Say precisely where the social or religious nature of an issue or question ends and the political nature begins. The ambit of political activity so defined is highly flexible and the rights of citizens are put 'at the mercy of the policemen, magistrate and judges whose notions may vary according to their whims and fancies'. The question of a uniform civil code, for example, is multidimensional social, religious and political. So are many such issues. In Subhas Chandra Bose v. Gordhandas, the court reiterated that the matter must be expressed in sufficiently clear language so that the courts may be able to enforce it. It was accordingly held that the term 'political uplift' was vague and unenforceable.

Further, Article 25(2) of the Constitution allows regulations or restriction of a secular or political activity which may be associated with religious practice. A blanket ban would thus be violative of the fundamental right guaranteed by the Constitution. The term 'religious institution' too carries a very wide definition. Clause 2(f) of the draft Bill had defined it to mean any place or premises used as a place of public religious worship by whatever name or designation known. The, official amendment adopted by the Lok Sabha extended the definition to mean an institution for the promotion of any religion or persuasion and to include any place or premises used as a place of worship by whatever name or designation. Educational institutions imparting religious instruction, institutions interpreting religious injunctions or giving fatwas' on various questions, as also halls and premises belonging to religious institutions and made available by them for public purposes to earn some income may all fall within the purview of, and may be hit by, the mischief of the Act.

Political expressions in pluralistic societies:

Political behaviour of people in pluralistic societies often finds expression in institutional devices which may appear alien to societies marked by a degree of cultural homogeneity. These institutional devices are both a product of multiple societies and an indispensable condition for successful operation of democracy in such societies. According to Arend Lijphart, the success of democracy in pluralistic societies requires, among other conditions, that the various segments of the society enjoy a high degree of autonomy. Yogendra K. Malik, too, observes:

> Besides this segmental autonomy, such institutional devices as a federal system of government and a proportionate system of representation in legislative bodies or the civil services, and coalition government are some other ways wherby such societies can resolve their conflicting claims within democratic system.

The founding fathers of the Indian Constitution were fully conscious of the heterogenous nature of the

Indian society and the claims of its various segments. Accordingly, the various provisions of the Constitution extend segmented autonomy to religious denominations to manage their own affairs in matters of religion, to all sections of citizens to conserve their language, script or culture, to the minorities to establish and administer educational institutions of their choice, and to the Scheduled Castes and Scheduled Tribes in matters of protective reservation. Implicit in these recognition of the rights of minorities and the various segments of the society is the legal or constitutional recognition of communities as distinct entities. The denial of one recognition will be the denial of the other.

In a heterogeneous society, legal recognition of its constituents as distinct entities and their segmental autonomy are pronounced characteristic features of and *sine qua non* for success of democracy. As D. Miller explains:

> Whereas, the action and non-actions of the state are necessarily political: whatever they are, they will have, and must have, political consequences. And the most significant consequence is undeniably differential impact on the different segments of the society. This, of course, is so everywhere; but because of the heterogeneity of Indian society the impact of the state there has to be even more uneven.

Thus, in as much as the policies and actions of the state have different impact on different segments of a pluralistic society, the response patterns of these distinct entities may differ considerably and, lest the response should get muted or suppressed with disastrous consequences, they need distinct institutional devices for their expression. These institutional devices may take the form of politics oriented interest groups or parties, adoption of appropriate elective devices, coalitions, proportionate reservations, etc. These cannot be simply wished away or dubbed as undesirable, reactionary, communal, etc. They may appear anomalous to the Westminster model of democracy. But the Westminster or the British model is not the only model of democracy. In fact, it is a model that is best suited to homogenous societies. In case of pluralistic societies, it is equally rational and logical that the model necessitate an indigenous adaptation. This gives, what contemporary political science calls 'consensus, or 'consociational' model of democracy. Here, in the operation of liberal political institutions transplanted from the West, normative commitments are harmonised with pragmatic contextual considerations. The search for conflict regulating strategies which strike a balance between excessive normative commitment and cynical political opportunism holds the prime place in contemporary studies. Lijphart, Lorwin, Daalder and Steiner all address themselves to the great political question of regulating 'intense but conflicting preferences' within democratic polity.

During the freedom movement, Muslims demanded representation as a community in all cases to which representation applied, from municipalities and district boards to the Imperial Legislative Council. They suggested this as being the only effective means of safeguarding the minorities and as the only possible way of working representative institutions in India. However, more than two decades before this demand was formulated, Lord Dufferin had in 1883 emphasised

> the necessity that in India representation will have to be, not in the way representation is secured in England, but representation by interest.

The Indian Council Act of 1892, while avoiding the use of the word, election', indirectly introduced the principle of election. Some non-official members were nominated while others were appointed on the recommendation of local bodies, universities, chambers of commerce, landlords' associations, and others representing important interests. The Directions were issued to Provincial Governments by the Government of India to provide for certain classes and interests and Muslims were specifically mentioned among them. However, the Act could not secure proportionate representation to Muslims. In August 1906, the Viceroy Lord Minto appointed a committee of his Executive Council to inquire into the working of the Act. As a result of their enquiries, the committee found that:

> the Muslims had not been sufficiently represented on the existing Councils, that the few elected members had not been really representative and that nomination had failed to secure the appointment of the Muslims of the class desired by the community.

Ram Gopal observed:

> Rightly did Muslims begin to entertain the fear that they could not get representation on the Councils even in proportion to the population, for the 1892 Councils gave them under-representation.

But he opined that the search for adequate Muslim representation in the Legislative Council formed from time to time under the Act of 1892 was bound to be in vain. The Act gave representation to landlords, universities, commerce, etc in which Muslims were generally conspicuous by their absence. He, therefore, contests the assumption that Muslims might not be adequately represented by the general electorate and that the representatives of the Muslims need be chosen through a separate electorate.

The next important stage came in 1906. The Secretary of State Lord Morley made it known that the Liberal Government which had assumed office in England was contemplating to introduce further constitutional reforms in India. A deputation of leading Muslims waited upon the Viceroy Lord Minto on 1

October 1906. The deputation is generally assailed as to be a 'command performance' with the principal of Aligarh College, Archibold, playing the main role in organising the deputation and in formulation of its proposals. The deputation, it is alleged, was in furtherance of the British policy to 'Divide and Rule'. Jamiluddin Ahmed, on the other hand, narrates the events as under:

> The lead in the matter of protecting Muslim interests in view of the forthcoming constitutional reforms was taken by Nawab Mohsin-ul-Mulk Secretary of Board of Trustees of the Aligarh College, who, after Syed Ahmed Khan, was generally looked upon as the leader of the Musalmans. He was vacationing in Bombay. On morning in August, 1906, he read in the papers the speech of John Morley, the Liberal Secretary of State for India, regarding constitutional reforms.
>
> Nawab Sahib at once had an idea. He wrote a letter to Mr. Archibold [sic],Principal of Aligarh College, who was holidaying at Simla, asking him to approach Col. Dunlop Smith, Private Secretary to the Viceroy, and tell him that the Muslims of India wished to place their demands regarding political rights before the Viceroy and to ask him for a reply. Meanwhile, Nawab Sahib also received letters from some Muslim leaders like Nawab Viqar-ul-Mulk, Khawja Yusuf Shah and Sahibzada Aftab Ahmed Khan, requesting him to take steps for protection of Muslim interests under the projected constitutional reforms. Mr. Archibold after meeting Col. Dunlop Smith sent a reply which showed that the Viceroy would be willing to receive the deputation of the Muslims.

At the request of Nawab Mohsin-ul-Mulk, Nawab Imdad-ul-Mulk Syed Husein Bilgrami of Hyderabad came from Hyderabad to Bombay to help draft the address that was presented to the Viceroy. A meeting was held at Lucknow under the presidentship of (Sir) Abdur Rahim to consider and finalise the draft address. Archibold had, while replying to Nawab Mohsin-ul-Mulk and informing him that the Viceroy had agreed to receive the deputation suggested that the address to be presented "should represent that the system of nomination and not election, should be adopted as Muslims would benefit only from the system of nomination. The suggestion was summarily rejected by the Muslim leaders. The address clearly asserted that as far as possible appointment by election should be given preference over nomination and represented that for election to Legislative Councils, important Muslim landowners, lawyers, merchants, and representatives of other important interests, the Mohammedan membersof the district boards and municipalities and Mohammedan graduates of Universities of a certain standing, say for five years, should be formed into electrol colleges. Separate electorates, implicit in these proposals, was the best elecive device Muslim leaders could suggest for the protection of Muslim rights and identity consistent with the system of representative institutions. The Viceroy, in his reply, recognised the principle underlying the demand for separate electorates and declared that:

> The Mohamedan community may rest assured that their rights and interests as a community will be safeguarded in any administrative reorganisation with which I am concerned.

Though the demand for a separate electorate had been practically conceded by the Viceroy, it could only be secured from the British government after sustained efforts. There were vociferous protests from the Congress. The Secretary of State Lord Minto, though convinced that Muslims should be adequately represented, was initially not inclined to favour the system of separate electorate. He proposed in November 1908, a system of joint electorate with reservation of seats for the communities The proposal did not succeed. Buchanan, Under Secretary of State for India, observed during his speech in the House of Commons on 1 April, 1909:

> If you start from our theories of representative government, of course, all such special representation is an anomaly, but we have to deal with the practical problem which is before us - the best practical solution which is available.

Finally, Morley-Minto reforms of 1909 established separate electorates. The scheme incorporated in the Indian Council Act of 1909 gave Muslims a separate electorate and also retained their right to vote in the general electorate. The principle of separate electorates was also extended to other Communities.

The concept of separate electorate has come under fierce attack. It is denounced as unleashing communal tendencies and as having nourished the spirit of separation which led to the partitioning of the country. It is alleged that separate electorates served imperial interests. "The minority community," it is argued, 'was favoured and the majority spurned because it was necessary to thwart the purpose of the nationalist movement. It is said that separate electorate was a device of the British with the motive to 'divide and rule'. As Seervai points out:

> There was an element of truth in this; but a legislative provision may be desirable, or necessary, independently of the motive which originally led to its enactment.

From among the Congress leaders, S.P. Sinha (later Lord Sinha) and Gopal Krishna Gokhle, in particular, recognised the genuineness of the Muslim demand. Sinha said:

> I am strongly in favour of provision being made for the separate representation of the Muslmans to an extent which will enable them to be adequately represented on the Legislative Council, regard being had to their numerical proportion, their influence and their position in each province of the country at large.

In the same vein, Gokhale too realised the practical necessity of separate representation apropos the Indian context. His clear perception of the situation led him to concede that:

> Confronted by an overwhelming Hindu majority, the Muslims are naturally afraid that release from the British yoke might in their case mean enslavement to the Hindus. This is not a fear to be ridiculed. Were the Hindus similarly situated in regard to numbers and other things would they not have entertained similar misgivings? We would undoubtedly have felt the same fears and adopted the identical policy which the Muslims are adopting today.

He, indeed, did not favour the idea of two watertight compartments for Hindus and Muslims separately and believed that it would not promote the best interests of the country. He, therefore, suggested a two-tier plan in which the separate electorates would be superimposed on the general electorate. He wanted a substantial number of seats to be selected on a territorial basis in which all qualified to vote would take part without distinction of race or creed; and then supplementary elections could be held for minorities which numerically or otherwise were important enough to need special representation, and these could be confined to members of minorities only.

In fact, within a short time a complete accord was reached between the Indian National Congress and the 1916 between the Congress and the Muslim League confirmed the adoption of separate electorate. The pact provided for election of Muslim members to provincial legislature through separate electorate in the following proportion, namely: Punjab 50%, and Bombay 33.3%. In the central legislature, one-third of the Indian elected members were to be Muslims elected by separate electorate in the same proportion. It was provided that no Muslim shall participate in any of the other election to the Imperial or Provincial Legislative Councils, save and except those by electorates representing special interests. The pact, in order further to protect the interests of communities, laid down that:

No bill, nor any clause thereof, nor a resolution introduced by a non-official member affecting one or the other community, which question is to be determined by the members of that community in the Legislative Council concerned shall be proceeded with, if three-fourths of the members of that community in the particular Council, Imperial or Provincial, oppose the bill or any clause thereof or the resolution.

The Lucknow Pact of 1916, thus, confirmed a political thought'originating from India which proved a landmark in the country's political history. The same principle of separate electorate, which had been characterised as sinisterly divisive, provided the basis to confront the British with a united demand for constitutional reforms. M. A. Jinnah, the main architect of the Pact, was hailed as the 'Ambassador of Hindu Muslim Unity'.

The scheme envisaged in the Pact became the basis, though not in full measure, of the Montague-Chelmsford reforms of 1919.

However, certain irritants were created in the working of the Principle of separate electorates. Hafeez Malik refers to the working of the first Council constituted in Punjab in 1921. To cite an example, when the Chief Minister Mian Fazl-i-Hussain attempted to correct the representation,in municpal bodies, those who had enjoyed greater representation were not prepared to give up their privileged position, and even proposed a censure against the Chief Minister. Forthwith, there was a change of tactics and it was claimed that separate electorates were a vicious prduct of reactionary thinking.

The Nehru Report, prepared by a committee presided over by Pandit Motilal Nehru and appointed by the All Party Conference in May 1928, rejected separate electorates for the Muslims. The report was considered in the All Parties Convention at Calcutta in December 1928. M.A Jinnah presented a compromise formula, well-known as Jinnah's Fourteen Points. All the amendments were rejected one by one and the history recorded the unfortunate "parting of the ways". There were attempts to bridge the gulf. The pact between Bhulabhai and Liaqat Ali, known as the Desai-Liaqat Pact, and the recommendations of the Sapru Committee, presented the concept of parity. Maulana Abul Kalam Azad in his letter dated 2 August, 1945 to Gandhiji, recommended, inter alia,joint electorates with reservation of seats and parity of Hindus and Muslims in the Central Legislature and the Central Executive till such time as communal suspicion disappears. Similar views ware also advanced by some outstanding Muslims interviewed by the Cabinet Mission on 16 April, 1946. The concept of parity was opposed by the Congress as an 'unreal method' opposed to the basic principles of democracy. Commenting on the developments, Seervai returns a severe verdict:

> The Congress stand on parity indicates an approach to the framing of a Constitution, which is fundamentally unsound. The Congress overlooked the fact that although in arithmetic 3 is not equal to 1, purely theoretical considerations have no place in framing a Constitution. The first thing in framing a constitution is to consider the goal which is to be achieved. The undoubted goal of the Congress was to secure independence for a *united* India. That goal must determine the means to be adopted for reaching it. If the grant of parity would enable that goal to be secured, parity should be adopted. As was in fact done by Bhulabhai Desai in the Desai-Liaqat Ali Pact, as was recommended by the Sapru Committee in its Report, as was strongly advocated by Azad in his letter to Gandhi, and as was equally strikingly advocated by nationalist

> Muslims before Cripps and Alexander. Democratic principles do not exist in a vacuum; they have to be adopted to thecircumstances in which a Constitution is to be framed.

The principle of separate electorate continued till independence. Independent India abolished separate electorate. The Supreme Court, too, held that elections based on separate electrorates for members of different communities offended Art. 15(1) of the Constitution. The Article prohibits discrimination on grounds of religion, race, caste, sex or place of birth.

The controversy about separate electorate continued in Pakistan. The Muslim League was insistent on the continuation of separate electorates while Hindu leaders opposed them. The phenomenon was the same, but reasons were diametrically opposite. The Muslim League knew it well that united Hindu votes, particularly in East Bengal could tilt the balance in a system of joint electorate. The *ulema* considered joint electorate incompatible with the concept of Islamic State. Finally, however, the National Assembly voted in April 1957 to establish joint electorate throughout the country.

The draft Indian Constitution, while adopting joint electorate, had a provision for reservation of seats for Muslims. The matter was revived in the Advisory Committee. Ambedkar objected that as the safeguards had already been accepted by the Constituent Assembly, they should not be reconsidered by the Advisory Committee. He suggested that instead the procedure should be to move amendments to the provisions accepted in the Draft Constitution. Sardar Vallabhai Patel, the chairman, ruled that the Advisory Committee could recommend reconsideration of the whole matter; but he did not like to vary any decision already taken unless there was a general agreement among the representatives of the minority communities. The meeting on 30

December, 1948 revealed differences among Muslim representatives on the question of reservation of seats. Sardar Patel adjourned the meeting to give Muslim members time to come to a unanimous decision. K. M. Munshi gives a vivid and illuminating account of the proceedings of the Advisory Committee on 11May, 1949:

> The matter of reservation of seats for Muslims was taken up by the Advisory Committee at its meeting held on 11 May, 1949. It was a critical situation. The representatives of the Nationalist Muslims sat silent. I learnt later that Maulana Azad, to his great credit, had instructed them not to press for reservation.
>
> There was no one to propose that the Muslims did not want reservation, and the fate of the most important issue - joint electorates without reservation hung in the balance. When the item was called out, there were a few anxious moments of silence. Sardar looked at me significantly. I, in my turn, whispered to Begum Rasul, who was sitting next to me, that Sardar expected her to speak.
>
> Ultimately, somehow she summoned courage and walked up to the lectern. She pleaded in a very hesitant manner for abolition of reservations for Muslims left in India; they were an integral part of the nation, she said, and should play their part in the general electorate.
>
> No sooner had she resumed her seat than Sardar, who perhaps was aware of Azad's instructions, said:
>
> I am very glad that the Muslims are unanimous in favour of joint electorates without reservations. We will now adjourn."

The Advisory Committee adopted the resolution that the system of reservation for minorities other than Scheduled Castes in the legislatures be abolished. When Sardar Patel presented the revised report of the Minorities Committee to the Constituent Assembly in May, 1948, he emphasised that the Muslim representatives had favoured abolition of reservation of seats for them in legislatures. Frank Anthony insisted that there were no imposed decisions and that the decisions concerning the minorities were the result of unanimous agreement.

A few studies have been conducted into the operational aspects of joint electorates in India. Donald E. Smith, Sisir K. Gupta and Theodre P. Wright Jr. all hold that numerical representation of Muslims in the legislatures has generally been very poor in comparison to their proportion in the total population. The Muslim representation in the indirectly elected upper houses and the Rajya Sabha have, however, been found to comparefavourably. The poor representation of Muslims in the Lok Sabha and the legislatures may be viewed in the context of the assurances given to the rninorities while abolishing separate electorates. The Congress had then assured all the minorities based on religion, of continuation of more or less the same benefit so long enjoyed by them under the system of separate electorate. Dr. Pattabhai Sitaramyya, the then Congress President, had said

> It is a gentlmen's agreement that we have enered into, a terrible responsibility that we have taken upon our shoulders, when we asked them (Muslims) to give up their reservations and their separate electorates. We have to find as many representatives from the Muslim community through the medium of the joint electorate as would have been their legitimate share, if they had their separate electorates. Even so (was the case) with the Indian Christians and others.

However, despite the assurance having proved ineffective, Anirban Kashyap complains that the change in the system was effected in name but not in practice. In addition to the quantitative aspect of representation, Theodore P. Wright has also looked into the qualitative aspect. After a sociological analysis of 332 Muslim legislators, he discovered that in their career characteristics they were from a typical cross section of their community. The minority elite, hence, faces a greater risk of alienation should a competing counter elite emerged with more radical programmes. Second, Muslim representatives from 'secular parties' have, with few exceptions, maintained a 'mounting silence' on issues concerning their community. The few exceptions far and between have been found to have risked their 'ticket'in the next election or got shifted to less safe constituencies. Third, Congress Muslims generally preferred to take up individual cases of hardships than community or religious grievances. Fourth, representation in legislatures on community or religious issues have come more freely from those belonging to overtly Muslim political parties."' In a Rajya Sabha discussion in 1964 N.M. Anwar, a Congress member from Madras came Out with jolting frankness. He declared:

> if you want to look for the real leadership of the Muslim India, do not go to the show boys and charity boys. They are going to be not assets, but liabilities of the Hindu society. The show boys and charity boys are those who by flattering the powers that be get into good position to betray both the Hindu and Muslim communities instead of bringing their relations closer together.

He went on to add:

> Under the present system of joint electorates., the Hindu society has no opportunity to get to know the real mind of the Muslim community because most of the Muslims whom they have adopted in the secular state have naturally got to be considered as the show boys of the majority community.

It is a matter of common knowledge, confirmed by, comparative electoral research, that a system of joint electorate, too, is not free from the influence of religion, caste or language. Consideration of class, caste or creed are prime determinants of political behaviour. These factors continue to exercise a strong influence on the choice of candidates and parties. This is especially true of pluralistic societies. Socio-economic factors hold the political behaviour in their sway in industrialised democracies that are religiously homogeneous societies. However, when both socio-economic and religious factors compete, the influence of the latter is stronger. Philip E. Converse points out that religious differentiation intrudes on partisan political alignments in unexpectedly powerful degree wherever it conceivable can.

Thus, communal, linguistic, ethnic, and such other loyalties In political behaviour are not a phenomenon exclusive to India. Religion and language are powerful factors in voting behaviour in Belgium, Canada and Switzerland. Arend Lijphard refers to the findings of voting behaviour research that established the general hypothesis that where the socio-economic issues compete with the religious ones, the latter emerges as the more powerful factor.

A basic function of the electoral system, adopted as per the needs of the society, is to ensure that the parliament it creates holds a true mirror to the nation. For a parliament to be truly representative in character there has to be neither over-representation nor under-representation of parties or crosssections of the society. The justification of any electoral system is determined with respect to its capability to yield proportional results while translating votes into seats. The electoral formula, which is referred to in Britain as the "first past the post" formula is the simplest but centuries old system in which the candidate with the majority of votes cast is declared elected; all other votes go unrepresented. United Kingdom, Canada, New Zealand and the United States elect their parliament according to this plurality formula. India, too, follows this system.

The Fifth French Republic and Australia adopt slight variations in attempt to secure "true majority". Most other democratic countries Austria, Belgium, Denmark, Finland, Germany, Israel, Italy, Nether-lands, Norway, Sweden, Switzerland, etc. follow the list system of proportional representation: Parties nominate lists of candidates in multinumber constituencies, voters vote for the partylist and seats are allocated to parties in proportion to votes polled by them. Ireland has the form of proportional representation by single transferable votes. The list system can even be combined with the simple majority system: A fixed number of seats being elected under each of the two systems.

While political scientists hold proportional representation as more appropriate to plural societies, it is also often argued that the system encourages proliferation of parties and is thus a grave threat to the survival of democracy. Ferdinand A.. Holmes believed that the system of proportional representation was responsible for the failure of Weimer Republic and the rise of Hitler. Arend Lijphard dismisses the proposition as without any general validity and points out to a number of countries with multiparty systems having long records of reasonably stable democracy.

The party system in a democratic regime is the natural product of the issue dimensions in the country. Two party system can support a democratic polity where only one issue dimension is significant. Multidimensional political conflict finds expression in a large number of parties. The strength of the multiparty system in accommodating a number of issue dimensions gives it democratic superiority over the two party system in a pluralistic society. The issue dimensions may relate to socioeconomic, religious, cultural, linguistic, ethnic, urban-rural and other cleavages and may determine not only the number but also the form and nature of political parties.

Arend Lijphat made a study of twenty-two democracies during 1945-1980. He found that party attitudes and policies towards religion and religious values wielded great importance along with socio-economic issues, in more than half of the twenty-two democracies. Since the late 1960's a host of issues concerning marriage, divorce, birth control, abortion etc., have acquired great prominence. Thus Continental Western Europe, Germany, Italy, Austria, Switzerland, Belgium, Netherlands, and the Scandinavian countries have major Christian Democratic Parties. The Norwegian Christian People's Party has found representation in several cabinets since its establishment in 1933. There are orthdox religious parties in Israel. The National Religious Party of Israel plays a significant role and secures crucial participation in Israel coalition cabinets. Japan has a vigorous Mahayana Buddhist Party. The Fair Play party of Japan represents the Soka *Gokkai* sect of the country. The Democratic Labour Party of Australia resembles the European type Christian Democratic Parties in its composition, policies and goals. India has the Bharatiya Janata Party (BJP), Shiv Sena, Muslim League, Akali Dal, etc.

The political process in any democratic country is characterised by the reflection of issue dimensions in the party system. In the field of religio-political issues, there are three major phenomenon involving religion and party politics: (i) The exploitation of the electoral process with the avowed object of 'establishing' a religion; (ii) controversial political issues loaded with religious overtones; and (iii) political parties, loosely called communal parties.

Secular democracy is seriously threatened and the unity of multiple society is at stake when the electoral process is exploited for 'establishing' a religion either through its imposition as the officail. doctrine of the State or through grant of any privileged position. In 1956 elections in Sri Lanka, the SLEP led by Bandernaika pledged itself to restore Buddhism in its rightful place in national life. Recently, the BJP and the Shiv Sena in India contested elections openly on the planks of Hinduism, *Hindutva, Hindu Rashtra* and *Ram Rajya.* As we have already seen earlier, there is a plethora of election petitions challenging the validity of the successful BJP/ Shiv Sena candidates.

A sharp distinction needs to be drawn between a phenomenon where the motivating factor is establishment of religion contrary to the basic concept of the constitution and the one where political issues affect religious values. Political issues which form the subject matter of controversies may have religious bearing for a community and a political party may legitimately have its views on the controversy. The relevant political controversies involving considerations of language and religion will have to be taken into consideration before pronouncing on the legitimacy of the reigion-political phenomenon. The Supreme Court has in *Kaltar Singh v Mukhtiar Singh,* at least conceded that political issues at election meetings might indirectly and incidently introduce considerations of language or religion.

In *Jagdev Singh Sidhanti v. Pratap Singh Daulat,* the Supreme Court held that where, for conservation of a language, appeals were made to the electorate and promises were given that steps would be taken for conserving it, there was no corrupt practice.

The question of abolition of the so-called 'communal' political parties has been engaging the attention of all since independence of the country. The communal parties sought to be banned were, however, supposed to be only those which restricted their race membership to the members of any particular race, religion or community or the names of which indicated the racial, religious or communal character of the body, irrespective of their ideology or programme. Then again, such organizations were not to be banned; they were only to be prevented from participating in elections.

The trauma of Gandhiji's assassination soon after the independence focussed attention on the dangers of organizations promoting communal hatred. The G.R. published in Gazetter Extraordinary said :

> There is no place in India for any organization preaching violence or communal hated............ No such organistion will therefore be tolerated.

The Congress Working Committee in its resolution passed on 7 February, 1948 after the said tragedy called upon all Congressmen to carry on an intensive drive against communalism by removing the cause of friction. On 3 April, 1948, the Constituent Assembly adopted a resolution Moved by the M. Ananthasayanam Ayyanger, The resolution runs as under :

> Whereas it is expedient for the proper functioning of democracy and the growth of national unity and solidarity that communalism should be eliminated from Indian life, this Assembly is of the opinion that no communal organization which by its constitution or by the exercise of discretionary power vested in any of its officers or organs, admits to or excludes from its membership persons on grounds of religion, race and caste or any of them, should be permitted to engage in any activities, other than those essential for the bonafide religious cultural, social and educational need of the community, and that all steps, legislative and administrative necessary to prevent such activities should be taken.

Clearly, the Constituent Assembly decision went off at a tangent. The spectacle of communalism seems to have been envisaged in a highly coloured form ignoring the magnitude of the problem. Political parties with communal nomenclature or membership became the seat of all the sin. While the G.R. and the Congress Working committee resolution noted earlier emphasized upon banning organizations preaching violence or communal hatred and the need to eliminate the cause of communal frictions, the Constituent Assembly resolution was obsessed by and restricted to eliminating from politics such parties as might have had communal titles or membership, irrespective of their policies, programme and action. Such political parties may exist for legitimate purposes and may in fact be dedicated to promotion of communal harmony. On the other hand, political parties rabidly communal in their thinking and approach or resorting to appeal to sectoral loyalties may masquerade themselves under secular pretensions. Then again there are organi-zations preaching communal hatred but not participating in elections directly.

It is not surprising that the founding fathers of the Constitutions were carried away by the idea of a ban on the political parties with communal nomenclature or membership. Indeed their political thought had developed in a direct way out of their pre-independence political experience or prejudice which had reached their climax in the trauma of the partitioning of the country with Muslim League generally being held as solely respsonsible for the partition.

However, the founding fathers of the Constititution having adopted the aforesaid resolution, did not give it any legal or constitutional shape or authority. Perhaps, they realised the prevarication implicit in the formula, and deliberately refrained themselves from impairing the functioning of democracy in the country. Consequently, the courts have also observed that the law has not prohibited the formation of such parties, and, in fact has recognised them for the purposes of election and parliamentary life. it is, here, significant to note that an attempt made in the Constituent Assembly to include in the Constitution a specific article to eliminate political parties on 'religious basis' was frustrated. On 7 December, 1948, Damodar Swarup Seth moved an amendment for addition of a new article 22 as follows :

> 22(a). The use of religious institution for political purposes and the existence of political organisations on religious basis is forbidden,

Dr.Ambedkar pointed out that it was covered by draft articles 19 (2) (a), which corresponds to article 25 (2) (a) H.V.Kamath clarified that while draft article 19(2)(a) merely regulated or restricted political and other activities associated with religion, Seth Damodar Swarup's amendment forbid them altogether. Pandit Thakurdas Bhargava commented that an amendment to draft article 19(2) which sought to prohibit the activities had not been accepted by the House.There upon the Vice-President who was presiding over the session, disallowed the motion moved by Seth Damodar Swarup. In fact, in order to eliminate communalism from Indian Life, the need is to focus attention on the organizations, irrespective of their nomenclature and membership and both political and non-political, which Promote ill-will, malice and hatred between different classes of citizens on grounds of religion, community, etc. and, as we have already seen, there is no dearth of laws in this respect.

An important step towards regulation of political parties was taken by the passage of the Representation of the People (Amendment) Act, 1988. The Act provided for registration of political parties with the Election Commission. Hitherto the field of registration of political parties had been covered by the Election Symbols (Reservation and Allotment) Order, 1968. A parliamentary law now occupies the field. Sub-section (5) of Section 29A of the Act makes it incumbent upon every party applying for registration that its memorandum or rules and regulations shall contain a specific provision that the party shall bear true faith and allegiance to the Constitution of India as by law established and to the principles of Socialism, Secularism and Democracy, and would uphold the sovereignty unity and integrity of India.

The Commission is empowered either to register the party or not. The full implications of registration of political parties and the extent of the authority and the jurisdiction of the Election Commission in regulating them are yet to be decided. A petition was filed before the Election Commission in October 1990 seeking deregistration of the Bhartiya Janata Party. The petitioner, Mr. Arjun Singh, contended that after the campaign undertaken by the BJP for the construction of a temple at the Ram Janmabhoomi which was really a religious issue, the party ceased to be secular in character and notwithstanding the amendment to its constitution it had to be de-registered as a political party. He also pleaded that the lotus symbol of the BJP be frozen.

In its interim reply filed with the Election Commission, the BJP has contented that there is no power under the Representation of the People's Act that once a registration is granted to a political party the same can at all be revoked. It has contented that the Election Commission does not have the authority to review and assess the ideology and programme of a political party in order to decide weather the party is actually implementing what the Election Commission feels is secularism, socialism and democracy. If such an authority is given it would mean authority to the Election Commission to decide on it's subjective satisfaction as to whether the programme of the party is actually secular and democratic or not. The subjective discretion of the Election Commission with regard to the assessment and review of the ideology and programme of a political party would be subversive of democracy and the rule of law. The petition is still pending before the Election Commission.

The religio-political interaction in India expresses itself in an amorphous complexity of patterns and thus defies every attempt at conceptualization of the relationship between religion and politics in terms of precise, concrete propositions. The Indian State is characterized as a secular state but the principles on which the Indian State operates do not fully conform to the common notion of the usage of 'secularism'. Our Constitution-makers steered clear of the normative abstractions concerning secularism and looked mainly to the functional concept to provide for the working of the state suited to the Indian ethos.

Gandhiji and Pandit Nehru differed in their approach to religion; nevertheless, both concurred in the same theory of the secular state. Gandhiji believed all religions to be true and supported a political dispensation based on respect for and equal treatment to all religions. Nehru, on the other hand, believed all religions to be mostly untrue but favoured a liberal model of democratic system that tolerated all religions and provided for their freedom to function. The two, thus, argued differently, but reached the same conclusion; a secular state adapted, to Indian conditions.

The two different approaches to religion may have found the secular polity to fit in with their belief. Nevertheless, the two approaches differ substantially in their qualitative content. A pattern of religio-political relationship in a country cannot be shaped in vaccum; it is designed by the native thought and woven in the total fabric of the life of the society *Sarvadharmasanwbhava* or respect for all religions is an attitude shaped by belief in the truth of all religions, for untruth does not inspire respect. The gates of the Parliament House in India have words embossed on them: *"ekam sadvipara bahudha vadanti meaning"* that the truth is one but is interpreted differently by the learned people. This leads to the concept of equal treatment. This concept does not presuppose the state distancing itself from religions. The state may help or aid religions provided all are treated equally and no religion receives a preferential treatment. This is an attitude of benevolent neutrality as distinct from that of the negative *dharmanirapekha* which means "having no need of, or no relation with, or standing over and above religion". Nehruvian tolerance of religion needs to be properly understood. Tolerance may be due to indifference, neglect, confusion, doubt, fear, deference, derision or a host of other feelings. As Miller points out:

> Each manifestation will produce a different scenario, form of accommodation, style of social relation and political conflict.'

The effort at separation of religion and politics manifests itself in a variety of secular creeds and ideologies. However, no creed has ever succeeded in freeing itself totally from the religious influence. Every secular model interacts with religion though in varying degrees of influence. Religion is a social force in its own right. It is an inescapable historical fact that religion, as a sociocultural dynamic, occupies a place in human affairs that cannot be expected to wither away. Society needs religion to enrich and ennoble its life. In the words of Christopher Dowson, religion is the guardian of tradition, the preserver of the moral law, the educator and the teacher of wisdom. Accordingly, an attitude.

> that mechanistically separates the religious from the secular (including even the social and the cultural) and is inclined to be cavalier or dismissive about issues of religion and religious identity, this will simply not do-however scientific or secular all this may appear to be.

The relationship between religion and politics gives us three broad theoretical models of secularism: the Marxian, the Western and the Indian. The classical Marxian model is based on counter-religiousness and involves a total abandonment of religion. Religion, it is believed, perpetuates injustice, hinders economic and social advance and retards human progress. The underlying idea is that material means alone can advance the growth of human being. Secularism, in the Marxian sense, is, therefore, a way of life and conduct guided by materialistic considera-tions bereft of religion. Marxist secularism is an all-pervading anti-religious influence which is not restricted merely to public life but encompasses the individual in his private life, too, including his private habits and motivations and thus from every sphere of human existence.' There is no room at all for religion. The Marxist victory is 'incomplete without the demise of religion'. The Marxist secularist takes sceptical, profane and contemptuous position with respect to religion. He considers it 'a wicked fraud'. At best, he concedes religion as an 'escape' from the indignities of capitalism. As Marx wrote:

> Religion is the sign of the oppressed creature, the heart of a heartless world, just as it is the spirit of a spiritless situation. It is the opium of the people.'

Marxian secularism of the extreme type is, however, an ideological label; even in socialist countries, such a secularism is found only at different levels on the spectrum of attaintment. The real level of secularism in any country is conditioned to a great extent by the historical traditions of the country. The historical absence of any strong religious tradition makes for a higher level of secularism. This factor in particular accounts for the Chinese society in being considered comparatively secular despite the distinct ethical tradition of Confucianism, Communism, even before its present process of dismantling in the Soviet Union, had to come to terms with religion.

This was essentially because of the basic deficiency of Marxism; its failure to appreciate the dual nature of man possessed of both body and soul, and the preoccupation of its historic materialism with only the secular destiny of man. Marxist secularism may choose not to deny people their faith or spiritual commitment and may concentrate on the economic, political and social levels; but these will only be a strategy in its campaign to bring about a decline of religion. As is pointed out:

> (Religion) must be attacked not at its strongest point the level of spiritual commitment and faith which must necessary have its ritual expression...
>
> Religion must be attacked at its weakest point its inability to address itself to, let alone resolve, the secular (the basic economic, political and social) problems of human existence. This is also the best way to bring about the ultimate disappearance of religious faith.'

A great deal of the leftist bias against religion springs from its misconception of the religion as an impediment in historical transformation. It is a historical fallacy to look upon religion as a retrograde or status quoist element in class struggle. Religion is a social force; its tenets and ideology structure the political situation. Religion has displayed a great potential and vitality to challenge the prevailing, systems, mobilise revolts by the exploited and the oppressed classes and usher in revolutionary changes.'

Interestingly, dissenting religious sects all over the world have generally received Marxist support in their struggle against the state for their rights. The Bolsheviks supported the struggle of the religious sects against Czarist persecution. The revolutionary Marxist did not hesitate to join with the Catholics of Northern Ireland struggling against the 'Protestant dominated British imperialism'. They lined up with Muslims, Hindus and Buddhists in their struggle against colonial masters. These seeming paradoxes, Marxists explain, are in actuality in conformity with the thoughts of Marx and Lenin. Both of them held that the concrete demands of class struggle need prevail over the ideological struggle against religion. The Communist Manifesto, too, declared that the Communists everywhere would support every revolutionary movement against the prevalent social and political order.

The tactical subordination of the ideological struggle against religion to the demands of class struggle recognises the power and sweep of the religion to structure the political situation and represents Marxist exploitation of religion for common political objectives. Thus, Lenin welcomed religious believers into the ranks of the Bolshevik Party on their acceptance of the political programme of the party. As at present, not more than 20% of Central Asian Muslims can be said to be atheist according to official figures." At the time of the October Revolution, an estimated 15% of the members of the Bolshevik Party were Muslims. Even Priests who agreed to work for the party programme were admitted irrespective of the obvious contradictions between the party programme and the philosphy of the priests.

Both Soviet Russia and China had a chequered history in Church-State relationship. The Russian decree of 1918 and the Chinese Soviet Republic Constitution of 1931 proclaimed separation of the Church and the State and disfavoured State financial assistance or grants to religious bodies. The Soviet Russia abolished the annual subsidy and other privileges granted by the Czarist government to the Russian Orthodox Church; churches were forbidden to have property; church buildings were taken over by the State though made available for congregational prayers free of rent; none was exempeted from civil service on religious grounds; and religious oaths and prayers at State functions were abolished. Later, however, there was a reversal to Czarist policy of dominating the church through concessions extended to the Church to enhance its authority especially in its confrontation with the dissenting religious sects. Similarly, the Chinese State granted concessions like property tax exemptions to religious bodies and centres engaged in religious activities. Thus, the experiment at separation of the church and the state with the ultimate objective of extinction of religion led only to the subjugation of the church to the state, rendering Russian Orthodox State and the Chinese Buddhist Association creatures of their respective governments

The Western model of secularism is accommodative of religion but implies separate operational spheres for the Church and the State. The word 'secularism' is claimed to have been coined by George Jacob Holyoake around 1850 and he advocated the concept without necessarily involving counter-religiousness. His contemporary Joseph Bradlaugh, however, advocated the system as a rejection of religion and a triumph of science. U.S.A. is generally hailed as the model of Western secularism. U.K. has an established Church, namely, the Anglican Church, and hence is not regarded strictly a secular state according to the book. The Crown of England and the Lord Chancellor of England must necessarily be Protestants and cannot be Roman Catholics. The application of the Common Law of blasphemy is restricted to Christianity, perhaps because truth is suppossed to be on the side of the established religion.

In the United States, secularism is interpreted to imply that the State and the Church co-exist in the same society but have nothing to do with each other. This is the American ideal embodied in the First Amendment:

> Congress shall make no law respecting an establishment of religion or prohibiting the free exercise thereof.

This doctrine of the separation of the Church and the State finds an eloquent expression in Everson v. Board of Education.

> Neither the state nor the Federal Government can set up a church. Neither can pass laws which aid one religion, aid all religions, or prefer one religion over another. Neither can force nor influence a person to go to or to remain away from church against his will or force him to profess a belief or disbelief in any religion. No person can be punished for entertaining or professing religious beliefs or disbeliefs, for church attendance or non-attendance. No tax in any amount, large or small, can be levied to support any religious activities or institutions, whatever they may be called or whatever form they may adopt to teach or practice religion. Neither a state nor a Federal Government can, openly or secretly, participate in the affairs of any religious organisations or groups and *vice-versa.*

The constitutional theory of the United States erects, to use the famous expression of President Jefferson, 'a wall of separation between the Church and the State'. Nevertheless, it will be erroneous to believe that the American political life is free from the influence of religion. The recognition of Sunday and Christmas Day as public holidays, the opening of both the Houses of the U.S. Congress daily by the Chaplains invoking Divine blessing, the daily commencement of the Supreme Court with prayer, the inscription of the motto 'In God We Trust' on all U.S. currency, public documents and public buildings, the words 'Under God' in the Pledge of

Allegiance, all reflect the positive aspects of religio-political interaction in the United States, Justice Douglas declared in *Zorach v. Clauson*:

> We (Americans) are a religious people whose institutions presuppose a Supreme Being.

President-elect Eisenhower, however, jumped the fence when he proclaimed:

> Our form of government has no sense unless it is founded in a deeply felt religious faith and I dont't care what it is. With us of course, it is the Judeo-Christian concept...

A searching analysis of the U.S. political developments will reveal varied forms of the mutual entanglement of religion and politics namely : the political articulation of religious issues at stake, exploitation of religion for political power, and religious involvement in politics. Controversies surrounding issues like abortion, school prayer, tax-exemption for religious organizations, etc. have witnessed, amidst loud protests, sharp political articulation in response to state action offending religious susceptibilities. The 1980 and 1984 presidential campaigns witnessed entwining of religion and politics to an un-precented extent. Ronald Regan's sweep to power owed much to the solid support by the evangelical and fundamentalist Christians. During the 1940's, the Judeo-Christian tradition promoted united democratic action against Hitler's fascism and later against Communism. The American judiciary, too, has gradually moved away from the strict concept of a formidable wall of separation between the Church and the State. Secularism is not meant to imply an exclusion of religion from American polity.

From the recognition of friendly gestures', the Court travelled to the position of the State protecting and promoting religious freedom for all with impartiality and neutrality which is not callous indifference to religion.

We sponsor an attitude on the part of government that shows no partiality to any one group and that lets each flourish according to the zeal of its adherents and the appeal of its dogma. When the State encourages religious instruction or cooperates with religious authorities by adjusting the schedule of public events to sectarian needs, it follows the best of our traditions. For it then respects the religious nature of our people and accommodates the public service to their spiritual needs. To hold that it may not, would be to find in the constitution a requirement that the Government show a callous indifference to religious groups. That would be preferring those who believe in no religion over those who do believe. We find no constitutional requirement which makes it necessary for the Government to be hostile to religion and to throw its weight against efforts to widen the effective scope of religious influence.

The Indian concept of secularism, too, is not one of hostility towards religion. It is not thought of as antithesis to religion. It is neither non-religious nor anti-religious. The Indian Constitution does not seek to create the famous Jeffersonian wall of separation between the Church and the State. In fact, neither Hinduism nor Islam has a Church in the Western sense. The expression 'Secular State' has only been used for the sake of convenience in describing the nature of the Indian State. As early as 1954, Pandit Nehru himself stated that the use of the expression was perhaps not a very happy one and that it was being used for want of a better word. Dr. Radhakrishnan pointed out that the religious impartiality of the Indian State was not to be confused with secularism or atheism." It is not surprising that attempts to introduce the word secular in the Constitution failed twice in the Constituent Assembly. It was the

Constitution (Fortysecond Amendment) Act, 1976 that inserted the word 'secular' in the preamble to the Constitution to describe India as 'Sovereign, Socialist, Secular, Democratic Republic'. Nevertheless, the discussions in the Constituent Assembly had made the State's attitude to religion unmistakably clear.

The ideal of a Secular State, in the context of the Indian Constitution, implies that the State (i) does not establish or uphold any particular religion and (ii) protects or treats all religions equally. These implications of Indian secularism have led to an interesting thesis with Dr. Radhakrishnan declaring that secularism so defined was in accordance with the ancient religious tradition of India. Nineteenth century had witnessed pronounced articulation of doctrines of transcendental unity of all religions and the belief that all paths led to the same ultimate reality. Thus, Ramakrishna 'saw in all forms of worship the adoration of one Supreme Being and in all religious quests the search for the same God towards whom all are directing their steps, though along different paths. The Western educated Vivekananda found in the teachings of the 'god-intoxicated mystic', Ramakrishna, the message of religious pluralism that could quench the thirst of his soul as also the cravings of the educated elite. If all 'paths' reach the same destination, then the logical political implication is a formula of secularism that respects all religions. To be secular is to be pluralistic. This Hindu ideology of religious pluralism, expressed by Vivekananda, Radhakrishna and Gandhiji is claimed to be an important landmark in the development of the theory of India as a secular state. Thus concieved, this religio-political interaction, while based on Hindu idea, provides a political framework which is nevertheless open to all. An Ex-Chief Justice of India underscored that Indian secularism subscribes to the Hindu philosphical tenet that all religions have elements of truth and no religion can claim the monopoly of truth, From ancient times, Hindu phiosophers have consistently proclaimed that all religions lead to God and unlike some other religions, Hinduism has never put forth the claim that it alone is the true religion. The spirit of toleration is the, foundation of the theory of secularism.

It is a political irony that while secularism is generally understood in terms of separation of religion and politics, there is no dearth of those who find the roots of secularism in India in ancient Hindu religion. They look upon the very concept of secularism as religious in character. From the concept of Indian secularism as a Hindu concept to it being an euphemism for appeasement of minorities is the wide range of conflicting views in the Indian context.

Attitudinal positions

Some attitudes towards religion and politics may be noted. Gandhiji said that those who talked of separation of religion and politics did not know what religion was. He Maintained that religion had to guide politics lest politics should turn immoral. Maulana Azad asserted that religion and politics were inseparable.

Islam views life as 'an indivisible unity in which the spiritual and the mundane are not sundered'. There is no separation between God and Caesar, for Islam recognises no Caesar. Sovereignty rests with Allah and none else. Man is only the vicegerent of Allah on earth. Sovereignty of God is absolute, indivisible, permanent and comprehensive. The two revolutionary concepts in Islam, namely those of the unity of God and the unity of the human origin, shape its political structure, too. The essence of *Tawhid* (Unity of God) lies in acknowledging that there is no god but God. His sovereignty is indivisible and He is the Sovereign in moral, social, cultural, political and every sphere of life. His will is the Supreme Law. All the fundamental principles of life flow from the strong concept of monotheism in Islam: all human beings are equal, racial prejudices and social disabilities are abolished, equality before law is recognised. God alone is the Supreme Lawgiver; this law being received through revelations on the Prophet, (peace be upon him) is immutable. The *Quran* and the *Sunnah* (precepts of the Prophet, peace be upon him) are the basis of law. If the *Quran* and the *Sunnah* do not contain any instructions on a particular matter, recourse could be had to *Ijma* as the consensus of juristic opinion not being inconsistent with *Quran* and *Sunnah. Iima,* the third source is an important legal notion in Islam and derives its authority as a source of law from both the Quran and the Sunnah. The noted Muslim jurist Abdul Rahim, defines *Ijma* as 'an agreement of the jurists among the followers of the Prophet Mohammed (peace be upon him) in a particular age on a question of law'.

The other source of law is *ljtehad* (exposition) which includes Qiyas (analogical deduction), etc. The object of *Ijtehad,* as explained by Shah Wali Allah, is to exert to find out that in case a particular problem had occured before the Prophet (peace be upon him) what would have been his judgement.

In fact, what are generally described as 'sources' of law are, strictly speaking, methods of discovering the law from the Islamic system. The Prophet (peace be upon him) led in both spiritual and temporal matters. He was succeeded by the Caliphs who conducted the affairs of the State in accordance with the dictates of the *Quran* and *Sunnah.* The period of the four *Khulfa-e-Rashideen* (Classical Caliphate) lasted from 632 A.D. to 660 A.D. Thereafter, in course of time, new situations developed. In the first place, the Umayyids changed the system of caliphate to hereditary kingship. Secondly, there came about a division of religious and political functions (as distinct from separation of religion and politics as such) which were initially combined in the institution of *Khilafat.* The Ottomon empire, in particular, formulated extensive sets of administrative rules and decisions under the title *'Qanun'*. Thirdly, the phenomenon of Muslims under non-Muslim rule got accentuated. The close of the twelfth century witnessed substantial Muslim population under non-Muslim rulers consequent upon the invasion of Central Asia, Iran and Iraq by the Mongols in the East and of Sicily by the Normans in the West. Juristic validity under the *Sharia* of the cooperative role of the Muslims under non-Muslim rulers was traced to two major precedents, namely: (i) the Quranic mention of Hazrat Yusuf (Prophet Joseph) consenting to serve as a minister to the polytheistic king of Egypt and (ii) the migration of the eighty companions of the Prophet (peace be upon him) to Abyssinia and their cooperation with the Christians King who received them well. These comapanions also offered their services for defence of the country against foreign invasion.' The test is, as we shall see later, whether the Muslims are permitted to be governed by the *Sharia* in their personal lives and to conserve their religious identity.

As S.G. Mohiuddin puts it succinctly, it is the juristic validity under the Sharia that can alone make any new concept acceptable to the Muslims and hence the stipulation that it should not involve any injury to the religious identity or any interference in their religious affairs. Maulana Azad felt no contradiction between his duty towards Islam and his duty towards the nation.

Sikhism views life as indivisible into arbitrary compartments of religion and politics. There can be no separation between an individual and society; the religious, spiritual and political activity covers the totality of life of both the individual land the society. Sikhism, therefore, devotes itself to changing the inequality and injustice in all the spheres of life-social, religious and political.

Guru Nanak was the first of the line of ten Sikh Gurus. He was the founding father of the Sikh faith. The Sikh gurus from Nanak to Arjun were held in great reverence by the Mughal emperors. Then came Jehangir's execution of the fifth Guru Arjun in 1606 A.D. with grave consequences. It is popularly believed that Guru Arjun's death was on religious gounds. Others say that it was for political reasons. Guru Arjun's death is regarded as a clear instance of religious intolerance and the Guru is hailed as a martyr in the cause of his religious conviction. Dr. Beni Prasad points to political reasons. He says:

> Without minimising the gravity of Jehangir's mistake, it is only fair to recognise that the whole affair amounts to a single execution, due primarily to political reasons. No other Sikhs were molested. No interdict was laid on the Sikh faith.

It is argued that the strong organisational strength of Sikhism, the position of the Guru as the undisputed head of a compact community and the Sikh belief of the Guru being the 'Sachcha Padshah', all bestowed Sikhism with the unique position of *imperium in imperio* (State within the State) and created prejudice against the Guru. The Guru was also accused of helping the rebel Khusrau against the King. Jehangir ordered the Guru to pay a fine of two or two and a half lakh of rupees. On the Guru's refusal to pay the fine, he was put into prison where he died of illtreatment. While Jehangir is said to have written in his *Jehangirnama* that he confiscated the property of the Guru and commanded that the Guru be put to death, there are conflicting accounts of the Guru's death which absolve Jehangir of the responsibility for the death of the Guru. One account attributes the Guru's execution to the conspiracies of Chandu Shah, the Diwan of Lahore. Jehangir is said to have even helped Guru Har Govind avenge himself against Chandu Shah for the death of his father.40 It is not here intended to comment upon the tragic event but only to indicate some controversies.

Guru Arjun's death is one of the few executions that have changed the entire course of history. It proved to be a turning point in the development of the Sikh movement. Politics and religion got more closely enmashed in Sikhism. Guru Har Govind, who succeeded Guru Arjun, emphasised the need for political power to defend the faith and turned into a soldier-saint. He girded two swords of *Peree* and *Meeree,* representing the spiritual and temporal power respectively; he was the master of both *tegh* (the sword or the swordlike qualities) and *degh* (the couldron or the spirit of hospitality and compassion). He combined in him spiritual grace and temporal power. He laid the foundation of the Akal Takhat at Amritsar in 1606 A.D. The fusion of politics and religion became complete. Manu Subhas writes :

> The existence of Harmandar (the temple of God) and the Akal Thakht (the throne of God) within the same precinets is the greatest proof of the symbiosis of religion and politics, like the combination of soul and body so that the political life of the Sikh may be directed by the moral truths of their religion.

The relation of Sikhs with Mughal rulers had a chequred history. It is a strange irony that the movement launched by Guru Nanak to reconcile Hinduism with Islam witnessed, with the passage of time, most bitter feuds between Sikhs and the Mughal rulers. With the execution of Guru Tegh Bahadur by Aurangzeb, the Sikhs hated the Mughal rule like a scorpion. It is generally believed that Aurangzeb's orders for destruction of Sikh temples and expulsion of Sikh masands (agents) made Tegh Bahadur defy Aurangazeb and face martyrdom.

There are, however, wide differences among historians. Some point out to the *firman* of Aurangzeb addressed to the Hakim of Benares, mentioned in a book written by a Brahmin, forbidding forcible conversions and destruction of temples and describing them as great sins punishable in the Hereafter. Others point to several reasons for the royal displeasure.

The last of the ten Gurus, Guru Gobind Singh, completed the religio-political transformation of Sikhism, giving it a democratic form and a clearly distinct identity. He established an effective order, the *Khalsa* brotherhood. Five distinct signs were enjoined (unshorn hair and beard, a comb, steel *Kada* on the right wrist, undershorts and a sword worn at all times) and the name 'Singh' (lion) for the men and 'Kaur' (lioness) for women was to be used by all of the *Khalsa* (the pure) brotherhood. The hair *(Kes)* and the turban were also supposed to give added protection to men from sword cuts and lathi-blows. Guru Gobind Singh gave his people a common salutation: *Wah Gurji Ka Khalsa, Wah Guruji Ki Fathe (Khalsa is* thine, O Lord; victory belongs to you, O Lord). He is also said to have given the slogans: *Raj Bina Nahin Dharam bache Hai* (religion is not safe without political power)and *Raj karenga Khalsa* (the Khalsa shall rule)' These slogans shape the ideals of Sikh political activity. Manju Subash contends that these were not the utterances of the Tenth Guru and are the slogans coined by the Sikhs in the eighteenth century under special circumstances. It is to the credit of Guru Gobind Singh that he established a theocratic democracy. He declared that the line of Gurus would come to an end with his death and that thereafter both the religious that the temporal decisions shall be made by the elected representatives of the *Khalsa.* Thus, Guru Gobind Singh, despite having four sons, provided Sikh theocracy with a democratic form at the end of the line of ten Gurus.

The Sikh movement gained political power towards the end of the eighteenth century. Maharaja Ranjit Singh established a powerful state. His Khalsa Kingdom of Lahore extended over a vast territory, including Peshawar beyond the Indus, Multan, Kashmir, Kangra, the neighbouring hill states and the tribal areas on the frontier. Religio-political interaction was reinforced through increased allocations of land revenue for religious purposes. While religious grants in the Mughal province of Lahore under Akbar accounted for two per cent of the total revenue these increased to nearly seven per cent towards the end of Maharaja Ranjit Singh's rule. These grants were, however, extended to all types of religious institutions. Secondly, the State drew freely on the services of the Priests, *Sants, Fakirs, Ragis, Purohits, Shaikhs, Sayyeds* and other religious personalities. Thirdly, the civil services and the army included Hindus, Muslims and Sikhs both in the rank and among the officers; nevertheless, there was a considerable increase in the share of Sikhs among the ruling elite.

From the beginning, Sikhism faced the perrenial question of conservation and assertion of its distinct identity. In the first place, Sikhism incorporated a number of Hindu beliefs, practices and religious rituals. Some of the priests, because of their close affinity to Hinduism, introduced Hindu images in the gurdwara worship. As D.E. Smith puts it:

> Sikh's own priests thus increased the danger of absorption by Hinduism.

Secondly, Sikh's and Hindus shared a number of common social customs. They practised common personal laws. Thirdly, intermarriages and the custom of many Hindus giving their firstborn sons to Sikhism promoted mixed families comprising of both Hindus and Sikhs. While these were positive forces of cohesion, they increased the apprehensions of Sikhism relapsing into Hinduism. Declining number of Sikhs further threatened the preservation and assertion of Sikh identity. Some Sikh sects like *Ram Rai* disappeared altogether. However, the census of 1911 recorded a phenomenal rise of 37.1% in Sikh population in a decade in which the total population of Punjab recorded a decline of 2.2% consequent to famines and plagues. This phenomenal increase is ascribed to the British Policy of reserving jobs in the army and later in civil services for *Keshadharis* (Sikhs with long hair). Khushwant Singh says that as many Hindu jats had the same surname 'Singh' they had only to stop shaving and start growing hair to qualify as *Keshdharis.*

There is a strong tendency to regard Sikhism as an offshoot and a branch of Hinduism and the Sikh community to be an integral part of the Hindu social order. It is asserted that the British, pursuant to their policy of 'divide and rule' tried deliberately to create and promote a separate Sikh identiy; otherwise, the distinction between the Hindus and the Sikhs was more functional than fundamental. Accordingly, it is argued that a Sikh was a Hindu in a "particular role and if this role could not be performed, he reverted to his original status." The British, it is argued, encouraged and put scholars to the task of proving that Sikhism was different from Hinduism and that the latter was even hostile to the former. A German Indologist, Dr. E. Trump, a notable British administrator, M.A. Macauliffe, another, Lepel Henry Griffen, an Englishman, W. Owen Cole, and several others were said to have taken up the cause of Sikh identity. Max Arthur Macauliffe pleaded for 'state support to save Sikhism from its ultimate destruction.' Thus it.is argued:

For 400 years, Sikh and Hindu identities remained inter-linked and overlapping, and yet the British succeeded in driving a wedge between the two. That was the policy they envisaged after the annexation of the Punjab in 1849, to build them up as a counterpoise to the Hindus, as in the case of the Muslims, so as not to face a combined opposition of Hindus and Sikh. The question of a separate Sikh identity, arising from the growing apprehension that Sikhism might be absorbed into the Hindu social and religious system, is the underlying question in the entire Sikh movement. The *Gurumukhi* script is one of the early assertions of this distinct identity. *'Gurumukhi'* means one who obeys the commands of the Guru. Thus, Punjabi in Gurumukhi script became the language of the sacred Sikh scriptures. A chain of developments accentuated the identity crisis. A demonstrative reconversion of more than two hundred outscaste Sikhs called *Rahtias* by the Arya Samajists precipitated matters. The Gurdwara Reform Movement (1920-25) further supported the identity process. The Gurdwaras were in the hands of *mahants* and Hindu priests. The natural desire to reform the Gurdwaras necessited their being brought under the control of the community. The legal process was both expensive and uncertain as in a number of cases the priests had titles registered in their names. The movement culminated in the formation of the Shiromani Akali Dal in 1921. The volunteers of this Akali Dal resorted to forcible takeover of the gurdwaras from the hereditary mahants. This brought them in increasing conflict with the British authorities. Thirty thousand Sikhs were arrested, two thousand were wounded and four hundred lost their lives during the movement. The government enacted the Sikh Gurdwaras and Shrines Act of 1925. The Act abolished the hereditary tenure of the priests and placed the control of gurdwaras in the hands of Shirornani Gurudwara Prabandhak Committee (SGPQ) elected for a term of five years by every adult Sikh. Thus evolved an interesting framework for relgio-political interaction: the

SGPC appointed hot only hundreds of priests who recited the sacred scriptures and propagated Sikh religious views, but it also appointed the head of the Akal Takht which is the supreme temporal authority among the Sikhs. The head priest of the Akal Thakht has also the power to excommunicate anyone violating the tenets of Sikhism. The SGPC emerged as a unique institution with characteristic blending of religion and politics.

The religious revivalism of the Sikhs came in no way in conflict with the national movement for independence. Pandit Nehru has remarked:

> One, of the best test of its (communalism's) true nature is what relation it bears to the national struggle.

Not even a fanatic can accuse the Sikhs of loyalist political position in relation to the British. The British may have responded positively to the call of Max Athur Macauliffe for "State support to save Sikhism from its ultimate destruction and they may have promoted Sikh solidarity pursuant to their policy of 'divide and rule', but the Sikh remained in the vanguard of the national movement to end the foreign domination. The Akali Dal remained an ally of the Congress and it strongly opposed partition. As the partition of the country became clear, the Akali leadership found itself compelled in the then prevailing conditions, to think in terms of safeguards for the community in the future political set up of the country. An official resolution incorporating the demand for a Sikh State was adopted by the Akali Dal in March 1946.

The Executive Committe of the Akali Dal clarified:

> Whereas the Sikhs, being attached to the Punjab by intimate bonds of holy shrines, property, languages, traditions, and history, claim it as their homeland

> and holy land and which the British took as a "trust" from the last Sikh ruler during his minority rule, and
>
> Whereas the identity of the Sikhs is being threatened on account of persistent demand for Pakistan for the Muslims on the one hand and of danger of absorption by the Hindus on the other hand:
>
> The Executive Committee of the Shiromani Akali Dal demands for the preservation and protection of the religious, cultural, and economic rights of the Sikh nation, the creation of a Sikh State.

After the independence, the Akali Dal chose to opt for 'Punjabi Suba' claimed to be consistent with the principle of linguistic provinces propounded by the Congress since 1928. The demand was formally adopted by the Akali Dal in April 1949. It was not a demand for secession and the 1951 election manifesto of the party explicity stated that the Dal believed "in a Punjabi speaking province as an autonomous unit of India". The demand was dubbed as an untouchable communal demand, for the proposed state would have a Sikh majority.

The subsequent events, like the open campaign during the census exorting the Hindus to repudiate Punjabi and declare Hindi to be their mothertongue, the States Reorganization Commission's rejection in 1955 of the demand for a Punjabi speaking state (which had later to be conceded in 1966), the question of Chandigarh as the sole capital of Punjab, the agitation for several demands including centre-state relations and those concerning the Sikh identity such as granting of the 'holy city' status to Amritsar and permission to wear kirpans (sword) during air-travel, the demand for amendment of article 25 of the Constitution which clubbed Sikhs with Hindus, growing extremism, indiscriminate humiliation of all Sikhs going to Delhi for 1982 Asian games, the 'Operation Blue Star', the assassination of the Prime

Minister Indira Gandhi and the subsequent large-scale massacre of Sikhs particularly in Delhi, all have contributed to aggravating the situation.

The Sikh history has not only raised the issue of the relation of religion and politics in India in bold relief but it also points to the dismal failure to comprehend the legitimate dimensions of the issue and to devise a sound and acceptable political strategy to deal with them. Another attitudinal position may be briefly examined. Equation of nationalism with the dominant religion represents the extreme form on the spectrum of religion-politics relationship. In fact, it is totally destructive of secularism in any sense. Rashtriya Swaymsevak Sangh, Bharatye Janata Party, Hindu Mahasabha, Shiv Sena, all equate nationalism with Hinduism. Golwalkar drew up the charter of Hindu militancy when he wrote in 1939 :

The non-Hindu peoples in Hindustan must either adopt the Hindu culture and language, must learn to respect and hold in reverence Hindu religion, must entertain no idea but those of glorification of the Hindu race and culture, that is, they must not only give up their attitude of intolerance and ungratefulness towards this land and its age long tradition but must also cultivate the positive attitude of love and devotion instead-in one word, they must cease to be foreigners, or may stay in the country, wholly subordinated to the Hindu nation, claiming nothing, deserving no privileges, far less any preferential treatment-not even citizen's rights. V.D. Savarkar and M.S. Golwalkar both defined nationhood in a manner that excluded Muslims, Christians, Parsis, Jewsin fact, all non-Hindus. The politics of *Hindutva* and the *Hindu Rashtra* have recently acquired an increasing militancy; but we may have to look back to the two fateful decades, 1890-1910 to discern the development of Hindu thought in this respect. The nationalism of Bankirn Chandra Chatterjee, Sri Aurobindo, Bipin

Chandra Pal and Dayananda was essentially religious and Hindu in orientation. To stimulate such nationalism, they appealed to religious and cultural mores. Though Amales Tripathi tries to 'dispel the cobwebs of misunderstanding that hang around Bankim's thought, Sri Aurobindo proclaims:

> Of the new spirit which is leading the nation to resurgence and independence, he (Rishi Bankimchandra) is the inspirer and political guru.

This new spirit' is well clarified by Sri Aurobindo Ghosh. He said in 1909:

> I say no longer that nationalism is a creed, a religion, a faith; I say that it is the Sanatan Dharma which for us is nationalism. This Hindu nation was born with the Santan Dharma; with it, it moves and with it, it grows.'

In the same vein, Bipin Chandra Pal acclaimed in 1910 that the old *Vedantism* of the Hindus stood behind the new nationalism in India. It is not the purpose here to analyse the factors and the ideological environment that led to the 'new spirit' but only to indicate the attitudinal dimensions in Religio-political relationship and to focus attention on the complexities consequent to the wide range of the spectrum of the relationship between religion and politics.

The political parties are indispensable for the working of democratic government. They play an important role in interest, articulation and interest aggregation and thus enable the people to take part in the government decision-making. In an era of mass suffrage they establish a direct and intimate contact with their supporters and sympathisers and contest elections with a view to capture power and implement their programmes of social reconstruction and economic development. The different political parties compete with each other to win the support of largest number and of voters and to capture governmental power. Before exam programme and role of the political parties in the Indian system, it shall be desirable to understand the meaning of political parties.

A political party according to Burke is "a body of men united for promoting by their join endeavours, upon some particular principles in which they are all agreed." MacIver defines political party as "an association organised in support of some principles or policy which by constitutional means it endeavours to make the determinant of government." Prof. Gilchrist says "Political Party is an organised group of citizens who profess to share the same political views and who by acting as a political unit try to control the government. The chief aim of the party is to make its own opinions and policy prevail." Yet another definition of political parties is provided by Prof. Leacock. He defines it as "a more or less organised group of citizens who act together *as a* political unit. They share or profess to share the same opinions on public questions and by exercising their voting power towards a common end, seek to obtain control of the government".

On analysis of the definitions of political parties enumerated above we can deduce the following features of a political party.

(i) It is voluntary association.

(ii) It is formed by persons holding common views on certain basic political, economic and other matters.

(iii) It must be organised and possess well laid-down rules and regulations.

(iv) Its members believe in peaceful and constitutional methods.

(v) It aims at capturing political Power with a view to promote public rather than narrow interests of the members.

In view of the introduction of parliamentary system of government and promulgation of the principle of universal adult franchise the political parties have come to occupy an important position in the Indian political system. The history of the origin of the political parties is generally traced back to the year 1885 when the Indian National Congress was founded. Though numerous political groups existed prior to that date which served as a forum for discussion and debate on various political and public issues, but they were largely sectional in character. The first national forum which concentrated on the various political and public issues at national level was the Indian National Congress. Though during the initial years the Indian National Congress did not possess the objectives of a political party, viz., to capture power, it provided important training to the Indian elite to apply collective thinking country's problems. With the turn of the century the Indian Congress came to be divided into two groups—the moderates and the extremists. The moderate group held full faith in the British and tried to get its objectives through peaceful and constitutional methods like speeches and resolutions. The other group known as extremists did not approve these methods and believed in building up necessary pressure on the government to compel it to concede their demands. Though the members of Indian National Congress held opposite view they continued to operate under the umbrella of the same party.

Almost around the same time the Muslims under Sir Sayyed Ahmad Khan evolved their independent political party under the name Muslim League. This party was open only to the Muslims and was founded with a view to infuse a sense of loyalty in the heart of the Indian

Muslims towards the British community and to safeguard the political rights and interests through their representatives. As a reaction to the founding of the Muslim League, a rival organisation of the Hindus was formed under the name Hindu Maha Sabha. In addition to these a large number of sectional and local organisations of' land owners, Anglo-Indians, Merchant Europeans etc. also emerged., However of all these organisations only three could be Put in the category of political parties, viz., Indian National Congress the Muslim League and the Hindu Maha Sabha. Actually if these parties were subjected to the rigid test and requirements of a political party none of them could claim to be a political party in the true sense. During the subsequent years more parties like the Schedule Caste Party, the Justice Party, the Krishak Praja Party of Bengal, the National Agriculturist Party of UP, the Unionists Party of Punjab, the Democratic Swaraj Party of Bombay, and the Community Party etc. appeared, but they also lacked the genuine features of a political party.

It is only in the post independence period that the political parties in true sense made their appearance in India. Most of these political parties were formed by the splinter groups from the main political party, viz., Indian National Congress. In addition a large number of state or local political parties were also formed. At present there are more political parties in India than the number of states. While some of these parties are national parties, he other are merely state parties. A national party is one which has the support of four per cent of the electorate in any four states of India. At present there are seven National parties. These are

1. Bhartiya Janata Party
2. Communist Party of India
3. Communist Party of India (Marxists)

4. Indian National Congress (1)
5. Janata Party
6. Lok Dal
7. Indian National Congress (Socialist)

In addition there are over forty state and other parties. A party acquires the status of a state party if it gets at least four per cent of the total votes in any one state. Some of the prominent State Parties existing in India at present are:

1. All India Anna Dravida Munnetra Kazhagam in Tamil Nadu
2. All India Forward Bloc in West Bengal
3. All India Muslim League in Kerala
4. All Party Hill Leaders Conference in Meghalaya
5. Dravida Munnetra Kazhagam in Tamil Nadu
6. Jammu and Kashmir National Conference in Kashmir
7. Jammu and Kashmir People's Conference in Jammu and Kashmir
8. Kerala Congress (J) in Kerala
9. Kranti Ranga in Karnataka
10. Kuki National Assembly in Manipur
11. Maharashtrawadi Gomantak in Goa
12. Manipur People's Party in Manipur
13. Muslim League in Kerala
14. Naga National Democratic Party in Nagaland
15. Peasants and Workers Party in Maharashtra
16. People's Conference in Mizoram

17. People's Party of Arunachal in Arunachal Pradesh
18. Plains Tribals Council of Assam in Assam
19. Public Demands Implementation Convention in Meghalaya
20. Revolutionary Socialist Party in West Bengal
21. Shiromani Akali Dal in Punjab
22. Sikkim Congress (R) in Sikkim
23. Sikkim Prajatantra Congress in Sikkim
24. Sikkim Janata Prishad in Sikkim
25. Telugu Desham in Andhra Pradesh
26. Tripura Upajati Juba Samiti Tripura
27. Vishal Haryana Party in Haryana

Apart from the National and State Parties there are number of other unrecognised parties which can acquire the status of a registered party if they secure at least one per cent of the votes in a state. As it is not possible to examine the policy and programme of all these political parties, we shall confine the study to some of the important political parties only.

After having an insight into the working of some of the major political parties in India, it shall be desirable to have a brief idea about the main features of the party system as it operates in India.

1. *Multi-Party System.* In the first place, India has developed a multi-party system and the number of political parties is certainly Much more than found in other democratic countries of the world. It has been estimated that over 200 political parties have existed in India since independence. This multiplicity of the political parties, was due to a number of factors Soon after independence a large

number of groups which had worked with the Congress during the freedom struggle, disaligned themselves with the Congress they could not reach an agreement with it and decided to set up independent parties. Certain individuals set up political parties to increase their personal importance. Due to the introduction of universal adult franchise some of the numerically strong communities were encouraged to establish their own parties to fight for a share in the political power. The reservation of seats for the members of scheduled castes and scheduled tribes also encouraged the members to form independent parties. The creation of separate parties by Khasis and Mizos in Assam is an example of this. The disgruntled landlords, dispossessed Zamindars and the deposed Maharajas also formed a number of political parties. The increasing feeling of dominance by the north over the south led to the formation of Parties like DMK, Nam Tamil Party, Cochin Party etc. Linguistic, caste and religious consideration also encouraged the formation of a number of parties in different parts of the country. Finally, a number of new parties emerged due to factional fights within the larger parties.

2. *Single party dominance.* Another important feature of the party system in India has been that the country has for the most of the time been under the dominance of a single party, the Indian National Congress. The Party enjoyed absolute majority at the Centre and most of the states up to 1967. This popularity of the Indian National Congress was partly due to the significant role it had played during the freedom struggle and partly due to the skilful handling of the problems which confronted the country in the wake of partition. The unsolicited

support which the Congress party could muster up to 1967 led to the description of India as one-party state. Though the election of 1967 gave a serious setback to the Party because its majority was considerably reduced at the Centre and in some of the states non-Congress coalition governments were formed, yet by and large the party maintained its dominant position, In the midterm elections of 1971 the party won back the predominant position and re-emerged as a monolithic and monopolistic party. During the national emergency of 1975-77, there was virtually no opposition because most of the opposition leaders were either underground or behind the bars.

In the general elections of March, 1977 which followed the lifting of the national emergency, the return of the Janata Party (a newly formed party of the groups consisting of Jan Sangh, Bhartiya Lok Dal, Congress(I) and the Socialists and subsequently joined by Congress for Democracy with an overwhelming majority gave the impression that the dominance of the Congress party had ended. The Congress was for the first time called upon to sit in the opposition. It appeared that this would mark the beginning of the process emergence of two powerful parties in the country. However, these hopes were belied and the Janata Party broke down due to, internal bickerings and frictions. When the elections were called in early 1980 the Congress Party once again re-emerged with a thumping majority in the Parliament. After some time when the elections to the state assemblies were held it repeated its performance there. Thus once again the country came under the domination of a single party—the Indian National Congress(I).

3. *Presence of Large Number of Parties based on Language, Religion, Caste, etc.* Another peculiar feature of the party system in India is that unlike other

democracies where the political parties are formed on the basis of social, economic and political programme, a large number of political parties in India have been formed on the basis of religion, language caste etc. Some of the important parties which had been formed on the basis of these principle include the Hindu Mahasabha, Ram Rajya Parishad, Muslim League on the basis of religion, S.M.S. and M.J.P., Akali Dal etc. on the basis of language, Commonwealth Party and Tamil Nadu Toilers, etc. on the basis of caste loyalties etc. Some of these parties do not possess any social or economic ideology and cannot be considered as political parties in the strict sense, Again, a number of parties have been formed by disgruntled landlords, dispossessed zamindars and deposed Maharajas, which have chalked out their programmes primarily with a view to protect their interests rather than promote the general interests of the people or the country.

4. *Very Limited Membership.* Another feature of the party system in India is that as compared to advanced democracies, the membership of the political parties is rather very low. This is largely due to the fact that the people of India have not been able to develop sufficient sense of political participation. In the urban areas, no doubt, with the spread of education the people are becoming politically conscious and the membership of the political parties is fast increasing, but the rural people still lag far behind. Even in urban as most of the people prefer to support the various parties with funds from behind the scene rather than come out in public in support of a particular party. The number of persons openly committed to various political parties is certainly very limited.

5. *Laxity of discipline.* Again, the political parties in India are characterised by laxity of discipline. The presence of such a large number of parties with resembling ideologies and programmes has encouraged the members of the various parties to flout the rigid party discipline. The member quite often flout the party directives knowing it fully well that no disciplinary action will be taken by the party leaders. Even if any disciplinary action is contemplated against them they can always get away with it by threatening to join some other party or actually crossing over to the other party. This laxity of discipline among the members has been reflected in the ever-growing practice of defections, which has greatly contributed to instability of governments in the states.

6. *Importance of Leadership.* It is a peculiar feature of the party system in India that the parties are quite often organised around an eminent leader. The importance and the popularity of the party is not judged on the basis of the programme offered by it, but by the leadership which leads it. It is a well known fact that the popularity of the Congress up to 1967 was largely due to the leadership of Pandit Jawaharlal Nehru. The Party suffered a set back under Shastri and Indira Gandhi for a short while because they could not provide the leadership of the stature of Jawaharlal Nehru. However after 1969 once again Mrs. Gandhi provided an effective leadership to the Congress Party and the party was returned, to power with an overwhelming majority on. the wave of Mrs. Gandhi's popularity. In the elections of 1977, it was the appeal from the national leader Jaya Prakash Narain, which returned the Janata Party to power. The presence of number of outstanding national leaders among the ranks of the

Janata party also made its contribution. After the fall of the Janata Government when elections were held in early 1980 the personal popularity and appeal of Mrs. Gandhi returned her badly organised and battered party in to power with an overwhelming majority. Even at present the Congress(I) Party is surviving chiefly due to Mrs. Indira Gandhi.

7. *Closely Resembling Policies of Parties.* In view of the multiple party system in India, we find a close resemblance in the policies and programmes of the various political parties. With the exception of the ideologically based Communist Parties the exception of the ideologically based Communist Parties the programmes of other political parties look alike. Almost all the parties lay emphasis on the need of raising the standard of the people, reducing disparity between the rich and the poor, pursuing a policy of non-alignment, improving relations with neighbouring countries, conde-mnation of racialism, colonialism etc. In fact, a casual look at the manifestoes of the various political parties is likely to give the impression that there is only minor variation in the programme of the different parties and that too in the matter of emphasis on certain aspects. The closeness of the policies of the various political parties is further confirmed by the fact that quite often the members of one party cross in to another party knowing it fully well that there is not much of difference in the policies and programmes of the two parties.

8. *Promotion of Party Interests.* The political parties in India have shown the tendency to foster narrow party interests, quite often at the cost of national interest. Though the American practice of spoils system which leads to replacement of all important

officials by the party which returns to power, does not fully operate in India a bad trend has been noticed for the past few years. Generally the political parties, on assumption of power, at the Centre as well as the States have tended to offer all important positions to their loyal party members unmindful of their merit Even in the civil services the more reliable civil servants are posted on key and important positions so that they may be able to give a proper projection to the image of the party in power. This trend has posed a serious threat to the well accepted British principle of neutrality of civil services. It is time that the political parties should try to rise above their narrow party considerations and permit the civil servants to give their best without involving themselves in politics.

9. *Defections*. Defections has been an important feature of party system in India. Though this practice has been in vogue right from the time India gained independence, it gained greater currency after the fourth general election of 1967. With the loss of majority by Congress in some of the states the various political groups started openly trading for power and members started shifting their loyalty from one party to another party to get into power. In some states like Haryana the members shifted their loyalty so frequently that no stable government could be possible. Though the political parties felt greatly concerned over this development and expressed their desire to check the evil of defection at the earliest, they could not arrive at any consensus. It was only in 1985 that Rajiv Gandhi Government imposed a ban on defection through 52nd amendment. It provided for the disqualification of a legislator who left the party on the symbol of which he or she was elected. The

Government described this bill as the first step in the direction of cleansing the public life.

10. *Presence of Large Number of Regional Parties.* The presence of a large number of regional parties is another outstanding feature of the Indian party system. Over the past two decades not only the number of the regional parties has shown a tremendous increase, but the regional parties have also succeeded informing governments a number of states, viz., Telugu Desam in Andhra Pradesh, A.I.D.M.K. in Tamil Nadu, Akali Dal in Punjab, Assam Gona Parishad in Assam, National People's Conference in Jammu and Kashmir, Janata Party in Karnataka. The growing importance of regional parties in Indian political system is further evident from the fact that at present one of the regional political parties (Telugu Desam) has emerged as the largest opposition party in Lok Sabha.

The Indian National Congress-

The Indian National Congress is the oldest political party of the country. It was formed in 1885 with a view to mobilize the public opinion in India on various problems confronting the country. Though initially it served primarily as a national forum for the discussion of socio-economic problems of the country but subsequently it emerged as a strong leader of the nationalist movement. The country was ultimately led to independence under this party. The party witnessed a number of cleavages both in the pre-independence and post-independence period, but succeeded in maintaining the political leadership in its hands.

The party has an elaborate organisation. The basic unit of organisation of the party has not been specified in the Constitution and is left to be determined by the District Congress Committees. Accordingly this unit is known by different names in different areas, viz., Block or Constituency, or Subordinate Congress or Taluka Congress Committee. Above the basic units stand the District Congress Committee. The District Congress Committee consists of four indirectly elected members, some co-opted members and the party leaders of the district. The Pradesh Congress Committee which is the next higher organisation in the hierarchy is also constituted in the similar manner. Above the Pradesh Congress Committee stands the All India Congress Committee (AICC). Each Pradesh Congress Committee sends one-eighth of its members to the AICC. These members are indirectly elected. But the most powerful organisation of the Party and twenty members. Ten of these members are elected by the AICC and the rest are nominated by the President of the Party. Thus the Working Committee consists of the top party leaders. Though the Working Committee of the Party is accountable to AICC, it is vested with extensive powers. It supervises the working of the Pradesh Congress Committee and receives annual-reports about their working. It can form new Pradesh Committees or abolish the existing one. It can also suspend the Pradesh Committee for violation of party constitution or failure to carry out its directives. The Party finances are also under the control of the Working Committee.

The All India Congress Committee also sets up two other committees, viz., Parliamentary Board and Central Election Committee. The members of these committees are prominent party leaders. Some of these members are also members of the Congress Working Committee.

The Congress enjoys a fairly wide social base and draws its support from various sections of society. In the main the party draws its support from religious minorities. The Muslims, the Christians, and the Sikhs have consistently supported the Party and the party in return has always tried to champion their cause. The backward classes, labourers and women are also staunch supporters of the party which has projected itself as their benefactor and supporter. The rich and the capitalists classes also support the party because they feel this party alone can provide political stability which is so vital for the economic prosperity of the country. On its part the Congress party has also tried to promote the interests of the capitalists despite its profession of faith in socialist society. In short it can be said that the Congress has a fairly wide social base. According to D.L. Sheth, who made a survey of Indian electorate in 1967, the supporters of Congress consist of middle-aged and old voters and less of young voters; higher proportion of illiterate voters support the Congress than educated voters; more rural people support Congress than the urban people. It receives less support from higher income groups than poor and middle income groups.

As regards the ideology of Congress(I) Party, it has affirmed its faith in socialism, secularism and democracy. It seeks to establish socialistic pattern of society through democratic methods. The party also holds faith in liberal and Gandhian principles.

The policy and programme of the party, has undergone consistent changes according to the requirements of the time. Initially the chief objective of the Congress was to attain independence. After independence it extended its objective to work for social and economic freedom of the people. In its Avadi Session, the Congress party declared its goal as establishment of 'socialistic pattern of society'. On other issues also the Party made different pronouncements and adopted different resolutions. From the perusal of all these we can glean the following programme of the Party:

1. In the first place the party stands for a 'socialistic pattern of society' to be attained through establishment of a social and economic order based on equality of opportunity and on social, economic and political justice; removal of distinctions based on caste, creed, sex or social or economic status; right of work and living to all able-bodied persons; effective control of the means of production and material resources of the community; organisation of the economic system in a manner as to prevent the concentration of wealth and means of production in the hands of few persons: speeding up the production of country's wealth; decentralisation of economic and political power. It may be observed that party wants to attain all this through peaceful and constitutional methods.

2. Secondly, in the industrial sphere the party stands for maximum production, full employment, social and economic justice and building up of key industries like iron and steel, machinery and *tools* electric power, transport communication etc. It stands for the development of public as well as private sector but would like the basic industries to be located in the public sector. It stands for discouraging imports and stands for meeting the demands of the country through indigenous resources and efforts. However, it is not against import of goods which are absolutely essential for internal consumption.

3. Thirdly, in the foreign sphere the party has advocated the policy of non-alignment. It has kept away the power blocs which emerged in the Post World War II period and tried to steer an independent foreign policy. It has opposed colonialism and imperialism and extend full support

to the national liberal movements in various Asian and African countries.

The party remained in saddle at the centre and most of the states up to 1967, but in the subsequent years its fortunes fluctuated a great deal. In 1969 the party faced the major split because certain members of the party wanted it to adopt more radical policies. After the split of 1969 it was expected that the party under the leadership of Mrs. Indira Gandhi would adopt radical programme, but these expectations were belied. A new vigour was imparted to the policies of the party in the wake of its sweeping victory in the mid-term elections of 1971, which were sought by Mrs. Gandhi following Supreme Court's judgements in the case of bank nationalization and privy purses of the princes. However, soon the party was confronted with internal bickerings. In the face of growing agitations in different parts of the country the Congress Government of Mrs. Indira Gandhi imposed national emergency and introduced a number of progressive laws. It launched a twenty-five point programme for improving the lot of oppressed classes. During this period the liberties of the citizens were jeopardised and there was great resentment against the government.

In view of the mounting pressure when elections were held in 1977 the party miserably failed at the polls. The defeat was attributed to the excesses of Indira Gandhi government during the emergency and resulted in second split, with a number of Congress stalwarts like Brahmanand Reddy, S.B. Chavan, Karan Singh, Swaran Singh etc. disassociating themselves with the party in the first week of 1978. The two wings of the Congress drifted farther after differences cropped up between Mrs. Gandhi and Dev Raj Urs, and the breakaway group jointed hands with Urs. In the elections of 1980 the Congress Party under the leadership of Mrs. Gandhi returned to power with an overwhelming majority, while the other wing of the Congress could not give a good account of itself. the elections of 1984-85 the Congress gave a good account of itself. At the centre it secured an unprecedented majority. It captured 401 seats and managed a three-fourth recapture power in the states where it was earlier ruling, even though its strength was considerably reduced. Thus the Congress(I) is in power at the Centre and a large number of states.

The Janata party

The Janata Party was formed in January 1977, by four parties viz., Congress, Jana Singh, Socialist Party, and Bhartiya Lok Dal, though the formal merger of these parties took place on 1 May 1977. These four parties decided to merge themselves to form a new party, which could provide an alternative to the Congress party, at the instance of Jaya Prakash Narain. Even Congress for Democracy under Jagjivan Ram voted to join this party.

The party gave a good account of itself in the Parliamentary as well as state elections of 1977. It not only replaced the Congress Party at the Centre but also secured control of the government most of the north Indian states. However, the Party could not remain in office for long. Soon due to internal bickerings of the components of Janata Party, the Party disintegrated. The objectives of the new party were described as "Restoration of civil liberties freedom of Press, independence and dignity of the judiciary, establishment of genuine egalitarian social order, and the formation and implementation of an economic policy designed to eliminate unemployment and maximise production, agricultural and industrial, while safeguarding the just and fair claims in particular of small and marginal farmers, agricultural labourers industrial workers and of the weaker sections generally".

The party possess quite wide base and its supporters hail from different sections of society. This wide base of the party is largely due to the presence of leaders of different shades of opinion in the party. The party has been able to get support of workers due to presence of certain socialist members. Similarly the Muslims and the Christians have extended support to the party on account of their loyalty to the respective leaders who are now members of the party. The weaker sections of society have also extended support to the party.

As regards the ideology of the party, it stands for liberal principles and is a firm supporter of democracy, individual rights, secularism, decentralisation of authority, etc. It is a staunch supporter of funda-mental liberties of people and opposed to all encroachments which seek to restrict these liberties. It stands for equal treatment to people belonging to various regligions and holds firm faith in secularism. It is in favour of decentalisation of administration and stands for maximum autonomy even for the lowest units of administration. The party is opposed to all types of despotism and strongly opposed to dynastic rule. The party also holds faith in socialism and stands for betterment of the condition of weaker sections of society.

We get an idea about the programme of the party from its election manifesto and the various pronouncements made by the party leaders. The party expressed its faith in the ideals of freedom and democracy and promised to restore fundamental freedoms to the citizens and a rightful place to the judiciary. It indicated its determination to rescind the forty-second amendment and to make necessary amendments in the constitution to ensure that President rule in the state was not misused to benefit the ruling party. It promised to abolish censorship and to restore to the Press the immunity which it enjoyed with regard to reporting of legislative proceedings before the emergency.

In the economic sphere the party emphasised the Gandhian principles of *antyodaya* and austerity. It affirmed its determination to delete property right from the list of fundamental rights, grant of right to work and full employment; end of destitution in ten years; reduction of disparities between the rural-urban nexus, primacy to agriculture, agrarian reforms etc. in planning, wage goods production for mass consumption, formation of national water policy and national emergency policy, improvement of environ-ments etc.

In the social sphere the party promised middle schooling for all within twelve years, eradication of illiteracy, provision of safe drinking water for all, group health insurance, low cost building and mass public housing, family planning as a part of large population policy without coercion, new deal for scheduled castes and scheduled tribes, legal aid and inexpensive justice etc. In the foreign sphere the Janata Party laid stress on ten traditional principles of foreign policy followed so far. However, it promised to follow a more *genuine* non-aligned policy. It also laid more stress on improvement of relations with immediate neighbours.

In view of the hetrogeneous character of the party, doubts were expressed in certain quarters that the party shall not be able to work as a team and fall before ending its full term. These doubts arose chiefly due to growing bickering and in-flight amongst the various components of the party soon after the assumption of power. These predictions proved quite true. The Party got disintegrated after the various groups headed by Raj Narain, Charan Singh, Jagjiwan Ram and the Jana Sangh members decided to quit it. Thus the Janata Party which exists at present consists mainly of Congress some socialist members.

In the Lok Sabha elections of 1980 the party managed to capture only 31 seats, as against 298 seats captured in the 1977 elections. In the Assembly elections of 1980 also it failed to give good account of itself and managed to capture only 69 seats in nine states where elections were held. In the Lok Sabha elections of December 1984 the party was virtually wiped out from northern states and retained only some influence in the states of Bihar Orissa, Maharashtra, Gujarat and Rajasthan. It captured 10 seats in Lok Sabha. In the elections held in 1985 Janata Party managed to capture 113 seats in 12 states/union territories. However, it managed to retain power in Karnataka. Thus now Janata Party has virtually been reduced to the position of a regional political party and has lost its all India character.

The communist party

The Communist Party is the second oldest party of India. It was founded in 1924. However, soon after its formation it was banned. It continued its activities underground till the ban was lifted in 1954. The party supported the English during the Second World War following Russia's entry into the war. After the independence of country the Communist Party consolidated its position and captured 29 seats in the first election to Lok Sabha. In the States it captured 193 seats. In the 1957 elections the Party captured 29 seats in Parliament and 162 seats in state Legislatures. It emerged as the largest single party in Kerala and thus gained the distinction of being the first non-Congress Party to form the government.

The Communist Party was also confronted with a cleavage among the members. Certain members like P.C. Joshi, Ajoy Ghosh and Dange favoured closer links with Soviet Union. The other group led by Namboodiripad, Jyoti Basu etc. believed in violent and revolutionary activities. The cleavage between the two groups came to force in 1959 following border dispute between India and China. While the former group supported the Government of India's stand aspire to acquire other country's territory. This division became more sharp at the Eighth Congress of Communist Parties held at Moscow in 1960 when the two groups supported Soviet Union and China respectively. For some time efforts were made to bridge the gulf between the two groups of the Communist Party, and some sort of compromise was arrived at. But this unity proved short-lived and in the wake of Chinese aggression of October, 1962 the two groups again took opposite stands. While the moderate group supported the Government of India and condemned Chinese aggression, the extremist leaders like Jyoti Basu, Sundarayya, Surjeet Singh etc. refused to do so on the plea that a socialist country could not commit aggression. In 1964 the two groups of the party held separate conventions. In September 1964 the Communist members under A.K. Gopalan formed a separate party and named it as Communist Party (Marxist-Leninists). The two Parties issued separate manifestoes during the fourth general election and put up separate candidates. Thereafter they continued to operate as independent Parties. Occasionally efforts have been made to bring the two parties together but so far no success has been achieved in this direction.

The Communist parties in the main draw support from the labourers and peasants. The other Supporters of the party include educated unemployed in the urban areas and the low caste groups in the rural areas. In certain states like Kerala, Andhra Pradesh and Tamil Nadu even the Muslims and other religious minorities have extended support to the two communist parties. A notable point about the base of the Communist Parties is that their supporters are not evenly distributed in all the regions. They are mainly concentrated in West Bengal,

Kerala, Andhra Pradesh, etc. The party firmly believes in the ideology of Marxism and Lenin and wishes to replace the present social and economic order by a new system which shall be free from inequalities, caste system, exploitation and social evils and shall assure social and economic security to the weaker sections of society.

The organisation of the Communist Part is based on the principle of democratic centralism. This means that the central leadership is based on intra-party democracy and the intra-party democracy is based on centralised leadership. In simple language this means that the members of the party enjoy complete freedom of debate within the party. They can criticise the action of the leaders and make suitable suggestions for party programme. However, once the programme has been decided the members are expected to strictly follow the direction and guidelines of the party leaders.

The primary unit of the organisation of the party is know as Branch. These branches are present in the village, panchayat, municipal ward, street, industry etc. They work as the basic units for collection of membership fees and sale of party literature. Above the Branch exist the Local Council, the District Council, the State the Council and the National Council. The National Council, the most powerful organ of the party, is responsible for convening the party Congresses and enforcing party constitution. Being an unwieldy Executive Committee can also set up such other bodies as it deems necessary to handle the party work. Then there are Chairman and General Secretary of Party. In addition there is a Central Secretariat which works like an inner cabinet of the party and directs the party administration.

Though there is not much of difference in the policy and programme of the two communist parties, it is desirable to study their programme separately. The

Communist Party of India wants to establish people's democracy led by the working people and realise the ultimate goal of socialism and communist. It stands for confiscation of foreign capital, abolition of Zamindari without payment of compensation, abolition reorganisation of state, full social security and employment for all development of industries in public sector. The Party is opposed to communalism, untouchability and caste system.

In the foreign sphere it stands for cooperation among various countries. It stands for closer relations with the Communist countries and favours full support to the anti-imperialist struggle of the colonial and dependent peoples. At its meeting held at Varanasi from 22 to 29 march 1982, the CPI expressed opposition to Mrs Gandhi's reactionary and authoritarian internal policies and the Soviet Union. The Party condemned Maxism and Euro Communism and described the Soviet Communist Party as 'vanguard' of the world Communist movement.

Policy and Programme of the Communist Party of India (Marxists). The Party believes in establishing social democracy with the help of leftist and democratic parties. It favours take over of foreign capital and a ban on investment of private foreign capital, a moratorium on foreign debt payment, nationalisation of monopoly houses and adequate financial assistance to small and medium industries, take over of foreign trade, eradication of corruption and bureaucratism in public sector undertakings, abolition of land lordism, take over of the entire land of the landlords and their distribution gratis among the landless labourers and poor peasants, cancellation of debt of peasants, landless labourer and rural poor, supply of inputs and essential articles at cheap rates to them, remunerative prices for the produce, firm measures against oppression of Harijans, making of right to work a fundamental constitutional right etc. In the foreign sphere it stands for a foreign policy based on co-operation with the socialist countries and condemnation of anti-imperialist activities all over the world.

In its Conference held from 3-12 July 1982 the CPI(M) defined its policy as "one of support for both the Soviet Union and China without siding with either, and criticized the Soviet Party for its enemity to China, the Chinese party for its alliance with the United States against the Soviet Union, and the CPI for its 'right reformism' and the CPI(ML) for its left adventurism". Though the programme and policy of the two Communist parties seems to be identical, there are differences between the two parties. In the first place while the CPM holds that revolution can be brought about by the working class leaders alone, the CPI holds that socialist transformation can be achieved by close alliance with other democratic forces. Secondly, the CPM believes in dislodging the existing states and replacing it with a People's Democracy led by the working classes. CPI is not in favour of dislodging the existing government and favours formation of a national democratic front for the elimination of the reactionary forces. Thirdly, CPI holds faith in peaceful and constitutional means. It wants to transform Parliament into a genuine instrument of people's will. The CPM, however, holds that the ruling classes would never give up power voluntarily and therefore asserts the imperative need of use of force. Fourthly, CPI is in favour of extending full support to the Government of India for resolving the border dispute with China, CPM stands for peaceful settlement of the border dispute without describing China as an aggressor.

The Communist Party took part in the first general elections held in 1952 and captured 26 seats in Lok Sabha and 193 seats in the various state legislatures. In 1953 the

Party was recognised as an All Indian Party by the Election Commission. In the second general elections held in 1957 the party increased its strength in Lok Sabha to 29, while in the states its strength dropped to 162. However, in Kerala it emerged as the largest single party and formed government. In the elections of 1962 once again the party captured 29 seats in Lok Sabha and secured 197 seats in state Assemblies. In the elections of 1967 the two groups of Communist Parties viz. CPI and CPM contested elections separately and managed to capture 23 and 19 seats respectively in the Lok Sabha elections. In the Assembly elections these parties secured 123 and 126 seat respectively. In the mid-term elections to five state Assemblies in 1969 the two parties captured 25 and 3 seats respectively. In tile Lok Sabha elections of 1971 CPI captured 24 seats while CPM got 19 seats. In the Assembly elections of 1972 CPI captured 107 seats and CPM captured 34 seats. In the Lok Sabha elections of the CPI could capture only 7 seats, while CPM managed to get 21 seats. In the Assembly elections of 1977 CPI and CPM secured 47 and 205 seats respectively and CPM government was formed in West Bengal. In the Lok Sabha elections of 1980 the CPI captured 10 seats as against 35 claimed by the CPM. In the State Assembly elections in nine states held in 1980 CPI captured 58 seats as against 29 captured by CPM. In the Lok Sabha elections of 1984, the strength of the two Communist parties considerably declined with CPI claiming 6 seats and CPM claiming 22 seat. In the Assembly elections held in states, union territories in 1985 CPI captured 34 seats and CPM got 20 seats. Thus we find that Communist Party has not been able to capture any substantial number of seats in Lok Sabha, although it managed to give good account of itself in Kerala and West Bengal, where it even succeeded in forming the governments.

National conference

The Party came into existence during the pre-independence period and maintained close links with the Indian National Congress. It ruled over the 1947 to 1965. The working committee of the Jammu and Kashmir National Congress decided to merge itself with the Congress. However, a section of the party did not agree with the decision and contested the elections in 1967 as a separate group. It managed to capture 8 seats in the Assembly. In the elections to Assembly held in 1972 this group could not capture any seat.

The Party was revived in 1975 under the leadership of Sheikh Mohammed Abdullah. In 1977 the Jammu and Kashmir National Conference contested the elections to ten state Assembly and captured 47 of the 76 seats. It also captured two Lok Sabha seats. In 1978 the Party faced a split following dismissal of Afzal Beg, its Vice-President. Afzal Beg along with his supporters left the party and formed the *Inqalabi* (Revolutionary) National Conference. In 1980 the National Conference contested the elections in alliance with the Congress.

Something marvellous is happening to our planet but only a tiny fraction of the world population are aware of it. From ancient times and in every known human civilization, people have longed to experience it, some actually have experienced it, albeit to a limited extent. Prophets and seers have foretold its inevitable fulfillment; poets and bards have been singing of it throughout the ages. What is it? The dawning of a new era in human history, India including. This new age will witness the establishment of a just society and the emergence of a united and peaceful world community! In other words, Vasudhaiva kutumbakam, or "the Kingdom of God on earth" truly the Ram Raj, World history, in its core and in its essence, is the story of spiritual evolution of human society. From this all other activities of human beings proceed and around it all other activities revolve. The spiritual view of evolution is the constant theme of religion or dharma (justice and righteousness). Each outpouring of divine guidance refers to the past, looks forward to the future and concentrates upon the immediate need for spiritual regeneration and enlightenment. The crisis India and the world are experiencing is that instead of turning to divine guidance we have been aping the popular culture of rampant materialism that is rapidly penetrating even the remotest corners of our planet. Any attempt to resolve the acute crisis in India must squarely address the issue of religion which is an integral element in the life of all its peoples. Arnold Toynbee, an eminent historian, described religion as a "faculty of human nature". That the perversion of this faculty in man has contributed to much of the confusion in our society and the resultant conflict in and between individuals and communities is the root cause of world crisis. In whichever direction we turn our gaze, no matter how cursory our observation of the doings and sayings of the present generation, we cannot fail to be struck by the evidences of moral decadence which, in their individual lives no less than in their collective capacity, men and women around us exhibit.

Most people see only darkness in both current affairs and recent history; many parts of the world Somalia, Bosnia, Northern Ireland, Afghanistan, parts of northern India, parts of Iraq, Pakistan and, most recently Rwanda are plagued by racial, ethnic and religious conflicts; defenceless peoples, like those of Tibet and East Timor, are oppressed by stronger powers while the United Nations, the single representative of sociopolitical unity, seems powerless.

A broader consideration of history is needed to understand a deeper truth : the human race, like an individual human being, is subject to change, development and evolution, In the history of human relationships, the most primitive stage is that of individual self-interest. This loyalty extends to the family unit, then to the tribe. After the constitutional city states, there is nationhood, whose culmination has been marked by the achievement, in the case of the majority of the world's nations, of independence from the former colonial powers. Now we face the challenge of the last and crowning stage in our collective social development : that of world unity. It is clear, however, that genuine unity must be inspired by more than just political necessity, inasmuch as treaties and resolutions cannot bring about lasting peace. As a UNESCO statement puts it: "Since wars begin in the minds of men, it is in the minds of men that the defence of peace must be constructed."

What is this greater force than politics that can reach our hearts and minds and unite humanity? To many, if not most people, religion is irrelevant. It has become preoccupied with vacant rituals, impoverished by superstitious traditions and thoroughly corrupted by self-serving individuals and groups. Yet these obvious failings lie not in the original, divine teachings of religion, but in the accretions of centuries of human influence. True religion requires personal, independent investigation on the part of each individual. Science, which can produce more tangible progress, may seem more valuable than religion, though the two cannot be opposed: They must operate in harmony, for as Albert Einstein observed : "Religion without science is blind; science without religion is lame."

Religion often denies opportunity and equal rights to women. Until very recently, it was men who tightly held the reins of power in virtually every sphere of human endeavour. This inequality of men and women remains one of the root causes of war, since peace can be built and maintained only upon the foundation of justice. Again, judging from today's world, religion seems the least plausible answer to humanity's manifold and increasingly urgent problems. Inter-religious conflict lies at the heart of almost every war; fundamentalism impels bloodthirsty terrorist groups and spawns dangerous cults.

The greatest obstacle to religion as a source of unity appears to be the differences found among the world's great Faiths. Surely the animosity that has long divided Christian from Jew and Muslim from Hindu can be overcome? For, a closer study of these Faiths shows that the essential message of each is the same.

The foremost challenge to the followers of every religion today, then, is the claim to be the sole possessors of truth, clinging rigidly to their own narrow interpretation of the teachings of their religion. This stubborn refusal to appreciate and accept other Faiths can lead only to bitter antagonism and futile division, as it has in the past. The interfaith declaration entitled "Towards a Global Ethic", which was produced by an assembly of religious and spiritual leaders from virtually every major world religion and spiritual movement at the 1993 centenary of the Parliament of World's Religions in Chicago, suggests that it is indeed possible for the world's religions to find much common ground in this regard. The declaration states: "We affirm that a common set of core values is found in the teachings of the religions, and that these form the basis of a global ethic... There already exist ancient guidelines for human behaviour which are found in the teachings of the religions of the world and which are the condition for a sustainable world order." The Golden Rule, a universal ethic, is part of the spiritual heritage of humankind. It is taught in one form or another in all the world religions and systems of belief and can be found among the traditions of the world's most ancient societies:

Buddhism: "Hurt not others in ways that you yourself would find hurtful."

Zoroastrianism: "That nature only is good when it shall not do unto another whatever is riot good for its own self."

Judaism: "What is hateful to you, do not to your fellow men, That is the entire Law, all the rest is the commentary."

Hinduism: "This is the sum of all true righteousness : deal with others as thou wouldst thyself be dealt by. Do nothing to thy neighbour which thou wouldst not have him do to thee after."

Christianity: "As ye would that men should do to you, do ye also to them likewise."

Islam: "No one of you is a believer until he desires for his brother that which he desires for himself."

Taoism: The good man "ought to pity the malignant tendencies of others; to regard their gains as if they were his own, and their losses in the same way."

Confucianism: "Surely it is the maxim of loving-kindness : Do not unto others that you would not have them do unto you."

Jainism: "In happiness and suffering, in joy and grief, we should regard all creatures as we regard our own self,..."

Sikhism: "Be thou not estranged from another. For, in every heart, Bervades the Lord."

Baha'i Faith : "He should not wish for others that which he doth not wish for himself, nor promise that which he doth not fulfill."

Let us, therefore, collectively endeavour to foster an all-embracing approach towards the world's religions; to identify their common denominators, and to map out the shared terrain between them, From the resulting codification of the truths common to all religions, we can begin to work towards evolving a foundation of true justice upon which the lasting and permanent peace on earth would be established. Ultimately we must develop a unified and integrated vision of the nature of the human being and of the world society. Such a vision was supremely achieved by Gandhiji, who sacrificed his all for the salvation of our country and whose favourite bhajan was: Ishwar Allah tero naam, Sub ko sanmati dey Bhagwan. The people of India would do well to remember the gospel he preached and practised and live up to his ideals, were too late.

Disunity is a danger that the nations and peoples of the earth can no longer endure; the consequences are too terrible to contemplate, too obvious to require a demonstration. In many other societies too, the understanding of justice stems from religious Law. An interface of these ideas would call for acceptance of the individual spiritual development in realising justice, and at the same time the need for establishment of a universal administrative order. Without such an order universal peace, unity and love will be like a beautiful flower which will eventually wilt. Our survival and happiness now depend on our recognition of the oneness and the wholeness of the entire human family and of the essential oneness of religion and the fundamental unity of its founders.

7

Untouchability and the Government

Traditional Hindu law, as expressed in the various *Dharmashastras*, systematically graded punishments and privileges according to *varna*. Thus Brahmans' crimes were punished less severely than were those of kshatriyas, whose crimes were punished less than those of vaishays, and so on. During the British period, that tradition was displaced by a principle of equality of all before the law. However, this principle was accompanied by a British policy of non-interference in caste affairs and little attempt at reform. The courts did not punish a caste for boycotting another, or for ordering a servant caste to boycott others. A caste could outcast its members without overrule by the court. Courts even upheld caste by issuing injunctions prohibiting lower castes from entering temples, and awarding damages for purificatory ceremonies after lower caste persons had "polluted" a sanctuary. Even reformers working against the abuses of the caste system received no protection from the courts. As the legal scholar, Marc Galanter, observed:

> the criminal law was interpreted to give a broad immunity to the efforts of higher castes to keep lower castes in their place.

Reformers and politicians did not become concerned about untouchability until the early twentieth century. Indeed, the term "Untouchable" was first used by the Maharaja of Baroda before the Depressed Classes Mission of Bombay in 1909.

Two leaders who fought for betterment of untouchables

Two leaders fought for the betterment of Untouchables. The first, M.K. Gandhi, emerged as a leader of the nationalist movement; and he linked the eradication of Untouchability, as well as unity between Hindus and Muslims, with the goal of independence from Britain. The other, himself a Mahar Untouchable, educated at Columbia University, was Bhimrao Ramji Ambedkar.

The goals of the two men differed. Gandhi's aim was to absorb the Untouchables into the Shudra varna and for all "caste Hindus" to treat them with respect; in his ideal world of the future, he would have maintained the four varnas, but all would be of equal rank and worth in society. Ambedkar, on the other hand, wanted education, political power, and high position in the modern sector for Untouchables; he was against the entire caste system.

The two men also disagreed about the role of the Untouchables in the modern Indian democratic society about to be established. Ambedkar wanted separate electorates so that Untouchables could elect their own representatives from among themselves. The Muslims had made such a demand, and Ambedkar could see its advantage as a device for attaining political power. Gandhi argued that separate electorates would perpetuate the category of Untouchables instead of encouraging them to merge with the Shudra population; he feared conflict between "caste Hindus" and Untouchables.

In 1932, Gandhi began a fast to protest the award of separate electorates to Untouchables. Ambedkar bowed to its pressure, giving up his demand for separate electorates in return for a much higher number of seats in parliament *reserved* for Untouchables. The number of reserved seats was made proportionate to the number of

Untouchables in the total population (12.5%). The occupants of such reserved seats were elected by the total voting population, not by an electorates of Untouchables alone. This arrangement continues today One in seven seats in central and state legislatures is occupied by an Untouchable representative.

In the 1920s, both Gandhi and Ambedkar worked for the opening of Hindu temples to low-caste worshippers. Their efforts were rewarded by a large number of bills passes in central and state legislatures and, in princely states, by the opening of temples to all and the protection of low castes from various disabilities More such acts were passed after the Second World War.

"Protective discrimination"

The term "Scheduled Castes", by which Untouchables are also called, refers to a list of castes prepared in 1935 by the British government in India. Such a list is kept today, supplemented by lists of Scheduled Tribes and Backward Classes. All of these groups are beneficiaries of "protective discrimination", a term applied to the laws reserving seats in legislatures, government employment, places in schools and universities, as well as provisions for certain financial assistance for scheduled Castes. Dushkin concludes from her assessment of these programs that, in spite of them, Untouchables still lag behind the rest of the population in literacy. Thus, in 1961, only 10.3 percent of Untouchables were counted as literate as compared to 24 percent in the total population. The proportion of Scheduled Caste persons in government white-collar positions, also, is far below the reserved percentages.

The constitution of India of 1950 abolishes Untouchability and prohibits discrimination in "access to shops, public restaurants, hotels and places of entertainment," or in "use of wells, tanks, bathing ghats, roads, and places of public resort," or in admission to educational institutions. Article, 23 forbids forced labour, commonly part of the dominant caste rule or feudal regime. Article 25 allows for entrance to Hindu religious institutions. In addition to these protections in the Constitution, in 1955 the parliament passed the Untouchability (Offences) Act.

Galanter found that very few cases have ever brought under the Untouchability (offences) Act, and of those, few have been decided in favour of the Untouchables. Of the 476 taken by the *Harijan Sevak Sangh* (The Services Society for the Children of God—i.e., Untouchables) between 1961 and 1966, only 90 cases (19 percent) resulted in convictions; and the median fine in such cases was ten rupees (a little over one dollar). As Galanter concludes: "It is, simply, very hard to win one of these cases" He believes that legislation protecting Untouchables could be improved and that other kinds of initiatives could be taken by the government to seek out "patterns of discrimination". However, he says: "There is no interest in the intellectual community in the mechanics of programs for attacking Untouchability, no debate about alternatives, no assessment of protests"

However, because such legislation exist, other Hindus often assume that Untouchables are doing very well, and indeed are getting ahead at the expense of caste Hindus.

In her assessment of Untouchable political power through the "reserved seats" in parliament, Dushkin found that control of the Untouchables' one -seventh of the electorate is often important to a candidate. In 1967, when Indira Gandhi's return as Prime Minister was accomplished by a very narrow margin of votes, there were enough Congressmen holding reserved seats to have "brought down the government". Their support of

Mrs. Gandhi was rewarded by Various legislation favouring Untouchables.

Religious conversion and defection from Hinduism

A major threat which Untouchables used from time to time is defection from Hinduism, for it implies independence from, defiance of the control by upper-caste Hindus. For example, the temple entry proclamation of 1936 in the religiously conservative princely state of Travancore was the culmination of a movement begun in 1921 when the sizeable Irava Untouchable caste threatened to convert to Christianity. In the past, Untouchables have converted to Islam, Christianity, and Sikhism. Usually, however, they have continued to be considered Untouchables by Hindus. The latest, most dramatic movement has been the conversion of millions of Central and North Indian Untouchables to Buddhism.

Ambedkar and Buddhism. Ambedkar had worked for temple-entry for Untouchables in the 1920s. He had made other efforts also to Sanskritize Mahar caste life but in 1935, he declared, "I was born in the Hindu religion: but I will not die in the Hindu religion". There was speculation over the years that Ambedkar might convert either to Sikhism or to Islam. In fact, in Nagpur, on October 14, 1956, he converted to Buddhism. The occurred in the presence of hundreds of thousands of Mahar Untouchables, most of whom also underwent conversion.

Ambedkar wrote *The Buddha and his Dharma* as a guide for the Mahar, "a secular rational social interpretation of Buddhism". He rejected some of the basic tenets of Buddhism such as the four Noble Truths concerning suffering and the requirement of Renunciation. He was not attracted by philosophical or mystical Buddhism, but Ambedkar liked Buddha's insistence that he was not divine, that his teachings were not revelations but discoveries by man. Patwardhan says, " It was the moral bases of equality, justice, and wide humanitarianism that attracted him (Ambedkar) to Buddhism". Ambedkar also preferred Buddhism to Islam or Christianity, because it was a religion of Indian origin; yet, like Islam and Christianity, Buddhism is against the caste system.

Ambedkar saw Buddhism as an excellent alternative to communism for Untouchables. He pointed out that "Buddhism contained all of communism's violent methods". He also thought that Buddhism was a religion to which all of India could eventually turn. The fact that Ambedkar rejected communism in favour of Buddhism had perhaps had immense effect on Indian politics.

In converting to Buddhism, the Untouchable rejected all Hindu gods and ritual. Most threw their idols of Hindu deities and many gave up their lowly ritual duties in the *baluta* system of Maharashtra state, the Maharashtrian equivalent of the North Indian jajmani system. Since there is a dearth of leaders trained in Buddhism, however, most new Buddhists of continue to celebrate Hindu festivals and to perform life cycle rites according to Hindu liturgy.

In converting to Buddhism, the individual makes five moral affirmations which refraining from harm to living beings and abstention from theft, sexual misconduct, wrong speech, and intoxicants.

In his study of the Untouchable Jatav Shoemakers of the city of Agra in Uttar Pradesh where there were many few Buddhists, Owen Lynch noted that their worship centered more upon Ambedkar than upon Buddha. Thus, important holidays celebrated included Ambedkar's birthday and the anniversary of his death. Ambedkar's birthday was the most important holiday.

Ambedkar already headed a political party called, first, the Independent Labour Party, and then renamed the Scheduled Castes Federation. After his death in 1957, it became the Republican Party, composed again almost entirely of Mahars. Some of the leaders of the Buddhist order were also leaders in the Republican party, but there were Buddhist religious leaders who were not so involved. Where a high proportion of the population is Mahar, as in some localities in Maharashtra, the Republican Party has been successful in gaining office. However, its success otherwise has depended upon its uniting with other parties in coalitions.

The new Buddhists

It is estimated that 75 percent of the Mahars of Maharashtra have states as well—Madhya Pradesh, Punjab, Uttar Pradesh, Andhra Pradesh, Gujarat, Kerala, Assam, Bihar, And Madras. In all of India, the number of Buddhists increased from 180, 823 in 1951 to 3,250, 227, in 1961; and most of the growth is due to the conversion of Untouchables.

One of the problems for the new Buddhists is whether to claim and to accept the special benefits legally reserved for Hindu Untouchables. In Maharashtra, but not elsewhere, they have succeeded in insuring these benefits. The Republican Party has agitated for such benefits for Buddhists; it has also demanded land for Untouchables, slum clearance, and implementation of the Minimum Wage Act. Zelliot reports that many of the Mahars themselves say they experienced a new psychological freedom upon conversion. As might be expected, members of the higher castes of Hindus still consider the new Buddhists to be Untouchables. Patwardhan records a number of newspaper reports of atrocities committed against new Buddhists—in part "punishment" for the Buddhists' refusing to fulfill traditional Mahar ritual duties such as sanitation work, carrying lanterns during high caste jajmans' wedding and so on.

Educated Buddhists have no problem getting employment since proportions of Places in government are reserved for Untouchable. This drainage of potential leadership talent into government has weakened religious and political efforts in behalf of Untouchables.

There is no question that Untouchables are not advancing as rapidly as the legislated quotas originally forecasted. Possibly, discrimination against Untou-chables will persist long after the rules of pollution between pother castes and caste segments have disappeared. The Untouchables in India might, then, take a place in society similar to Untouchable groups in Japan and Korea, where small communities of Untouchables, once connected with occupations considered by Buddhists to be violent—cobblers, leatherworkers, fishermen—still persist as groups with whom the rest of the population refuses to intermarry.

Dalits in Indian Politics

The President of India was given powers under article 341, Para XVI of the Constitution of India to specify the castes, races or tribes or parts thereof as 'Scheduled Castes/Tribes' in relation to each State or the Union Territory. Dalit loyalties towards the Congress remained unflinching since independence till late 1980s, barring their brief honeymoon with Janata Party in 1977 after the emergency. Though the Republican Party started by Dr. Ambedkar, also surfaced in U.P. after its success in Maharashtra, it failed. Neither could it expand its roots all over the State nor could it make any major electoral gains. Instead its leaders travelled from one party to another in desperation for recognition with the dalits by and large refusing to toe the line. Even this Republican

Party of India was eaten away by the late *Jat* leader Charan Singh in his endeavour lo build a vote bank of dalits-minorities-OBCs. In the late 1960s dalits whose social and economic interests were diagonally opposed to those of the backwards remained glued to the Congress as they saw their messiah in the late Prime Minister, Indira Gandhi. The Congress suffered its first setback when a section of the Scheduled Castes, specially a prominent caste, deserted it during the emergency and travelled to the Janata Party along with its leader, Jagjivan Ram. But again in 1980 and 1985 elections, which were fought during the Indira and Rajiv waves respectively, dalits returned to their original home-the Congress. After Indira Gandhi's death, when the dalits had started; feeling orphaned," Kanshi Ram emerged on the scene and floated the All India Backwards (SC, ST, OBC) and Minorities Communities Employees Federation. The Congress too tried to fill the vacuum by drafting. Mrs. Meira Kumar, daughter of Jagjivan Ram, in politics. However she failed to emerge as a dalit leader to consolidate them.

Despite the steady decline of the Congress since the 1989 elections, a section of dalits continued supporting the party even till the 1993 elections. In fact the dalits constitute a sizeable chunk of the 14.5 per cent of the votes polled in favour of the Congress in the 1993 Assembly elections when the minorities had completely deserted it for Mulayam Singh Yadav and Vishwanath Pratap Singh and the upper-caste had switched loyalties towards the Bharatiya Janata Party. Thereafter the Congress's desperate efforts to win back dalit support by projecting various dalit leaders as UPCC president or in the central cabinet failed to make any impact for the influence of Kanshi Ram had started growing, slowly but steadily. And eventually he filled the vacuum of a dalit leader created by the demise of Jagjivan Ram.

After BAMSEF, Kanshi Ram floated another party whose prime objective was to build up a cadre devoted to educating the dalits about their rights. Later came the Bahujan Samaj Party, which was the political arm of the BAMSEF, The Bahujan Samaj Party tasted elections for the first time in Bijnore in 1985 where its candidate Ms. Mayawati fought against Meira Kumar of Congress and Ram Vilas Paswan of the Lok Dal. In fact the enmity of Ram Vilas Paswan and Mayawati started from Bijnore where they had fought for the dalit votes. Ms. Mayawati lost the elections by getting a mere 61,504 votes against 1.28 lakh going to Meira Kumar and 1.22 lakhs to Ram Vilas Paswan.

Again in 1987 in the Hardwar by election Mayawati jumped in the fray and secured 1.25 lakh votes against 1.49 lakh that went to Ram Singh of the Congress. The BSP mustered a mere four per cent votes in the 1985 Assembly elections which shot up to 9.33 votes in the 1989 elections in which it won 13 of the 373 seats fought. Then in the 1991 elections, the BSP won 12 seats with its percentage of votes going upto eleven per cent. In the 1993 elections, in which Kanshi Ram had forged an alliance with Samajvadi Party of Mulayam Singh Yadav to keep the BJP at bay, the party won 67 seats by poling 11. 11 per cent votes. Even in the 1993 elections, Kanshi Ram got the support of the *Jatavs, Dohre* and *Chammars* which constitute 50 per cent of the 21 per cent vote bank of dalits. The remaining subcastes of dalits were split between the Congress and BJP. Since then Kanshi Ram has been carrying on a campaign to win over *pasi, balmikis* and *sonkars* from the BJP and some of the other smaller castes from the Congress. After the catapulation of Ms. Mayawati to Chief Ministership, dalits' confidence has]increased and the prospects of their unity among themselves have brightened. It is the possibility of the 21 per cent dalit electorate voting *enbloc* for the first time in the coming elections that has perturbed the leadership of various political parties, forcing them to modify their strategies, whether Kanshi Ram would eventually succeed in his mission of revolutionising the country's politics will be known in coming days but there is no denying the fact that he has awakened dalits by giving them a new voice of assertiveness.

Index